DEVON & CORNWALL RECORD SOCIETY

New Series, vol. II.

Issued to members of the society
for the year 1955

Two Elizabethan houses in Fore Street, Exeter (formerly nos. 78 and 79), destroyed in the air raid of May 1942. These houses were originally built as one, and formed the *Fountain Tavern*—one of the most important inns of the city—during the greater part of the seventeenth and eighteenth centuries.

Frontispiece

DEVON & CORNWALL RECORD SOCIETY

NEW SERIES VOL. 2.

EXETER IN THE SEVENTEENTH CENTURY: TAX AND RATE ASSESSMENTS 1602–1699

Edited with an Introduction by

W. G. HOSKINS

Reader in Economic History in the
University of Oxford

Printed for the Society by
THE DEVONSHIRE PRESS LTD.
TORQUAY

1957

New Series

1. Devon Monastic Lands: Calendar of Particulars for Grants 1536-1558, edited by Joyce Youings (1955). 30s. or $4.75 post free.
2. Exeter in the Seventeenth Century: Tax and Rate Assessments 1602-1699, edited by W. G. Hoskins (1957). 30s. or $4.75 post free.

In Preparation

William Carey, Bishop of Exeter: Replies to Queries before Visitation, 1821, vol. I Cornwall, vol. II Devon, edited by Michael Cook.

Caption of Seisin for the Duchy of Cornwall, 1337, edited by D. L. Farmer.

The Earliest Act Book of the Exeter Cathedral Chapter (c. 1380-1420), edited by Audrey M. Erskine.

Reprinted 1973

TO
MY FATHER
1873-1955

a citizen of Exeter

CONTENTS

KEY TO PARISHES

INTRODUCTION

EXETER was one of the principal cities of England throughout the sixteenth and seventeenth centuries. Like Norwich and Bristol in the same period, she was the capital of a large province: a cathedral city, a centre of county administration and for county society, and a wealthy commercial town. Like those cities, too, Exeter showed a remarkable degree of economic stability. Other towns rose and fell in importance as the generations passed: Exeter remained consistently fourth or fifth in wealth and population among provincial cities, as Norwich always remained first and Bristol second. In the 1520's Exeter ranked after Norwich, Bristol, Newcastle, and Coventry. In the 1540's, with the decline of Coventry as an industrial centre, she ranked fourth for a time.[1] In the hearth tax assessment of 1662 she was still fifth in size among the provincial towns (judging by the total number of hearths) and she probably remained so at least until the end of the seventeenth century, when some of the rising midland and northern towns were beginning to overtake her in size and wealth[2].

The taxation and rating assessments which comprise this volume, running in date from 1602 to 1699, give us therefore some sort of picture of an important English town during the seventeenth century. The later lists, especially, give us much information about the comparative wealth and population of the nineteen parishes, and (in the hearth tax assessment of 1671) about the size of houses in the different parts of the town. The latest list, that for the poor rate of 1699, also gives us a certain amount of topographical information, besides telling us about the numbers of the poor in the different parishes and the relief they received week by week. The economic and social historian will be able to extract a good deal of information about the city from these records.

The value of the volume to genealogists will be obvious. The poll tax assessment of 1660 embraced 6,845 persons, and since the tax fell on all persons above the age of sixteen it is in fact a more complete directory than any in modern times. The poor rate of 1699 serves much the same purpose nearly

[1] W. G. Hoskins, "English Provincial Towns in the Sixteenth Century", *Trans. Royal Hist. Society*, vol 6 (Fifth Series) (1956), p. 4. The ranking for the 1540's can be ascertained from the account of the subsidy of 34 Henry VIII (P.R.O. Exchequer Accounts, E. 359/42). The leading towns at this date were Norwich and Bristol. Newcastle was untaxed (as in 1523-27) but ranked a little below Bristol in size. York and Salisbury followed closely behind Exeter in taxable wealth.

[2] The hearth tax figures are usefully gathered together by C. A. F. Meekings, *Dorset Hearth Tax Assessments* 1662-64 (1951), Appendix III, pp. 107-110. The largest towns in 1662 were Norwich (7,302 hearths), York (7,294 hearths), Bristol (6,925 hearths), Newcastle (5,967 hearths), and Exeter (5,294 hearths), followed by Ipswich with 5,020 hearths. Only six towns in the provinces had more than 5,000 hearths, excluding Oxford and Cambridge where the colleges greatly swelled the totals. Birmingham had 15,032 people in 1700 (Hutton, *History of Birmingham*, 1795 edn. p. 57), and so had probably just overtaken Exeter at that date.

forty years later; while the hearth tax assessment of 1671, coming between the two, contains nearly 2,400 names. In the latter case, the names are those of householders only—hence the great discrepancy between the total for 1660 and that for 1671.

The two subsidy assessments for the early part of the century (1602 and 1629) cover only the more well-to-do of the population. As they contain 400 names and 399 names respectively, it will be seen that on an average only one Exeter family in every five or six was liable for the subsidy. The proportion liable to pay the subsidy varied considerably of course from parish to parish. Thus in St. Petrock the 41 payers in 1602 represent every household in the parish; in St. Kerrian about two in every three paid. But in St. Edmund only about one in every ten or eleven families are in the subsidy assessments, and in Allhallows-on-the-Walls about one in every twelve. The genealogist will do well to bear these facts in mind when he makes use of these assessments for his own purposes.

General description of the city and suburbs

By the beginning of the seventeenth century the city of Exeter comprised nineteen parishes. Of these, thirteen lay entirely within the walls, three entirely outside (St. David, St. Sidwell, and St. Edmund), and three partly inside and partly outside (St. Mary Steps, Holy Trinity, and Allhallows-on-the-Wall). The boundaries of the city and suburban parishes had been fixed in the year 1222 under bishop Simon of Apulia,[1] but until the middle of the sixteenth century the parish of St. Sidwell was regarded as a separate fee, outside the city for purposes of local government and central taxation, and similarly with the parish of St. Edmund outside the west gate.

The parish of St. David, however, though wholly outside the walled area, was regarded from time immemorial as within the city for all purposes. In all probability it was so because it represented, together with the considerable extra-mural area of Holy Trinity parish to the south-east, " the land for twelve ploughs " which the burgesses already had by 1086 and which rendered no custom except to the city itself. The parish of St. David seems also to have been identical in area with the manor of Duryard which already belonged to the city when the records begin in the twelfth century; and there cannot be much doubt that the origin of this manorial property lies back in pre-Conquest times.

It is significant, too, that the parishes of St. David and Holy Trinity actually meet (in what is now Southernhay), by means of a long and curious extension of the St. David's boundary around the eastern walls of the city, so that they form together a continuous tract of territory. Moreover, the 1149 acres of St. David, with the 45 acres of Holy Trinity outside the city walls,[2] together make up an area of 1194 acres of land, or twelve ploughlands if we reckon, as we reasonably may, a hundred acres to the ploughland.

[1] John Hooker, *The Description of the Citie of Excester* (ed. by Harte, Schopp, and Tapley-Soper, 1919), vol. 2, p. 35.

[2] The total area of Holy Trinity was 49.565 acres (see Appendix I), of which about 4½ acres lay within the walls.

The greater part of the parish of St. Mary Steps also lay outside the walled area, together with a small part of Allhallows-on-the-Walls. These two extra-mural areas gave the citizens of Exeter access to the river from ancient times, though much of the land must originally have been marsh, as it was originally on the other bank also (*cf.* Marsh Barton in St. Thomas). The extension of Holy Trinity for about a quarter of a mile beyond the walls, besides taking in what must have been part of the open fields of the Domesday burgesses, also served another purpose. It gave the city access along a stretch of some six or seven hundred yards to a stream which served as an open sewer, into which the human refuse of the city must have been periodically deposited. This stream, which bore the name of Shitbrook,[1] flowed into the Exe well below the city and therefore did not contaminate its water for human use. It had a rapid fall of about a hundred feet in the course of one mile and in a heavy downpour of rain (such as is not unknown in Devon) it must have acted as an effective method of disposal for the city. It is worth noting that the leper hospital of St. Mary Magdalen, founded early in the twelfth century, if not sooner, was carefully placed on the farther side of this noxious stream, well away from the city.

The parish of St. Edmund lay wholly outside the walls and was regarded as part of Wonford hundred until the middle of the sixteenth century, although a populous suburb had grown over it since the construction of a stone bridge over the river in the late twelfth century. It lay mostly if not entirely within the manor of Exe Island, which belonged to the earls of Devon until the downfall of the Courtenays in 1538. In 1550 this manor, which had reverted to the Crown upon the attainder of Henry Courtenay, Marquis of Exeter, was granted by the king to the city in recognition of its faithful defence against the Prayer-Book rebels of the previous year. Until that date, then, the parish of St. Edmund, though a purely suburban area immediately outside the west gate and an integral part of the commercial life of the city, was taxed separately and will not be found in the Exeter assessments.

The large parish of St. Sidwell also lay originally outside the jurisdiction of the city authorities, and was taxed as a part of Wonford hundred until the act of 1549 which fixed the city boundaries. It had been part of bishop Osbern's lands in 1086 and had been granted to the dean and chapter by a subsequent bishop some time in the twelfth century. Here, too, a suburb had grown up at an early date, outside the east gate of the city, and difficulties had arisen between the civic authorities and the dean and chapter over their respective rights therein.[2]

The existence of considerable suburbs outside the west and east gates, and of the different jurisdictions of the bishop, the dean and chapter, and the county, within the built-up area, gave rise to so many difficulties for the city authorities that a clarifying act became urgently necessary to fix the boundaries of the city and to determine its liberties. The text of this act of 2 Edward VI,

[1] The name is recorded from the twelfth century onwards and its meaning is perfectly clear. Genteel writers of later times have tried to turn this into Shutebrook and even into Southbrook. Even the editors of *The Place-Names of Devon* struggle to find a polite meaning for the name, but in vain.

[2] See, for example, the preamble to the Act of Parliament fixing the boundaries and liberties of St. Sidwell in 1436 (Hooker, op. cit. II, pages 174-181), and also Curtis, *Some Disputes between the City and the Cathedral Authorities of Exeter* (History of Exeter Research Group, monograph No. 5, 1932), *passim.*

as confirmed on 17 March 1549, is given by Hooker in his *Description of Excester* (vol. II, pages 438-447). The bounds henceforth included the parishes of St. Sidwell and St. Edmund, but excluded the cathedral precinct and the castle precinct. The parishes of St. Leonard and St. Thomas were still left outside the city boundaries, and the taxation assessments for these will be found included with the hundred of Wonford. Neither parish will be found in this volume for that reason.

The tax and rate assessments in this volume are based upon the parishes of the city. It is therefore essential for their fullest use that there should be a large-scale map of the inner parishes at least, showing the details of their boundaries, which are extremely complicated in places. This map has been specially prepared for this volume in order to help students interested in the topography of the streets and of the city generally to find their way about. A careful student might well be able to locate every house in a particular parish for the year 1671 or 1699. For this purpose, I have tried, in my footnotes, to locate such landmarks as the principal inns, as a starting point in the reconstruction of a late-seventeenth century street. For different reasons I have also given in Appendix I a table showing the size of the historic parishes and precincts of the city. I hope that this table and the map will prove useful to future students of local history. One may search in vain, as I have done in the past, for a long time for exact information about the boundaries and extent of the old Exeter parishes. I feel, too, that this information is all the more worth putting into print in view of the drastic rearrangement of the ecclesiastical parishes of the city which has recently (1956) taken place.

The taxation and rating assessments are mainly concerned with the built-up areas of the city. There were still considerable open spaces within the walled area, the largest being the cathedral precinct or Close, the castle precinct, and the Bedford precinct. These were not of course entirely unbuilt-on —there were obviously large and important buildings within each of them—but they consisted mostly of open spaces. Between them they covered just under twenty-six acres, or well over a quarter of the walled area (92.6 acres). There were also smaller open spaces within the walls, of which the Friars' Hay (Friernhay) was the largest, as well as numerous large gardens and orchards like those behind St. John's Hospital. Altogether about one-third of the walled area consisted of substantially open spaces, most of which were not available for building on.[1] On the other hand, some of the city parishes were closely built-up. At the end of the seventeenth century (1695) St. Mary Major had twenty houses and 140 persons to the acre. As a contrast the rich parish of St. Stephen (with Bedford Precinct) had under eleven houses to the acre, and 68 people.[2]

In a city with a rapidly growing population, such as Exeter in the seventeenth century, the greater part of the new housing developed outside the walls, in the parish of St. Sidwell above all, and to a marked extent also in St. David and St. Edmund. This growth is, I think, noticeable in the extra-mural

[1] Mr. Mainwaring built a row of nine good-class houses in the castle ditch early in the seventeenth century, the beginning of Bradninch Place, but this was exceptional. They are shown on John Norden's Survey of the Castle of Exeter, made in 1617 (B.M. Add. MSS. 6027, fo. 81).

[2] These figures are based upon a return of 1695 (following the act of the previous year) and only survive for two Exeter parishes. There is also a figure for St. Thomas (see Glass, article in *Eugenics Review* (1946), p. 178, and in *Population Studies* for March 1950).

parishes even between the hearth tax of 1671 and the poor rate of 1699. The filling-up of the open spaces inside the walls—or of such of them as were available—did not develop much until the late eighteenth century and the early nineteenth, and a discussion of this must await a volume for that period.

The opening up of brickfields in St. Sidwell's parish by 1690[1] probably reflects what must have been a building boom in the closing year of the century. Bricks were first used in Exeter for the building of the Custom House in 1681. Unfortunately the building accounts among the city records (which are incomplete) do not record where they came from, though they were undoubtedly of local origin. There was a brickfield in Holy Trinity by 1706,[2] but it does not appear to have been in operation at the time of the 1699 poor rate.

The subsidy of 1602

In 1601 Parliament passed an act (43 Eliz. *c.* 18) granting the Queen four subsidies and eight fifteenths and tenths.[3] The fifteenths and tenths do not concern us here. As regards the subsidies, they were to be levied on all subjects with personal estate worth £3 and over, and on all subjects with landed property worth twenty shillings a year and upwards. The first subsidy on personal estate (' goods '), which was to be paid by 31 December 1601, was at the rate of 2s 8d in the pound. The second subsidy was to be paid in two instalments: the first instalment, at 1s 8d in the pound, was to be paid by 31 March 1602, and the second instalment, at 1s in the pound, was to be paid into the Exchequer by 31 October 1602. It is this particular assessment, the second payment of the second subsidy, which is transcribed in the following pages.

The third subsidy was also payable in two instalments of 1s 8d and 1s respectively, and the fourth likewise. The last payment was due in the Exchequer by 31 October 1604. On lands the rate was fixed at 4s in the pound. The first subsidy was payable in one instalment and the other three in two instalments each of 2s 8d and 1s 4d. The dates for payment into the Exchequer were the same as for the subsidy on personal estate, and the same assessment includes both types of payment. Aliens were to pay at double the rates for natives, whether on goods or on lands. There was, further, a poll tax on aliens not liable to be taxed on goods or lands. They were to pay 8d to the first subsidy, and 4d in each instalment of the remaining three subsidies, and all aliens of seven years of age and upwards were liable to this poll tax. The master (if the alien was an apprentice) or the head of the household in which he or she lived (if not an apprentice) were liable to pay in default. It will be noticed in the assessment that only two aliens are recorded for the entire city, a fact which it seems difficult to credit and yet is possibly true in view of the liability of masters and heads of households to pay in default.

The rate of tax, especially on landed property, sounds high even to modern ears, but it was greatly softened by the fact that the assessments were notoriously unreal. The subsidies had ceased to approximate to a true valuation

[1] E.C.M. Misc. Book 159a (An assessment or rate made . . . March 1690) refers to two brickfields in St. Sidwell, one of them belonging to Edward Cheeke, the other to Mr. Berrill (who is called John Burell in a poor rate of 1691).

[2] The reference to a brickfield in Holy Trinity parish (near Larkbeare) occurs in a marriage settlement relating to the Larkbeare estate and is taken from the abstract of title to 28, St. Leonard's Road, Exeter, by the kindness of Sir Cyril Fox.

[3] The text of the act is given in full in *Statutes of the Realm*, vol. IV, Part II, pp. 991 *et seq.*

of a man's lands or goods as far back as the accession of Edward VI, and it was openly said in the 1590's that no one was assessed at above a tenth of his true wealth and some at a thirtieth or less. This was certainly true in the town of Leicester in this period[1] and was probably equally true at Exeter. The 1602 assessment is therefore of no value as an exact indication of a man's wealth, though it serves to show who were the richest men and which were the richest parishes in relation to each other at that date.

It has already been said that the great majority of the population escaped this subsidy by reason of the exemption limit. Very few persons possessed landed property, and comparatively few reached the £3 exemption limit for goods (which must be regarded in effect as an exemption limit in the region of £100 in the light of the Leicester figures). In the city as a whole between two-thirds and four-fifths of the population escape notice in this subsidy, rising to about 90 per cent. in the poorest parishes.

The subsidy of 1629

In June 1628 Parliament voted Charles I five whole subsidies, payable within two years. The record transcribed in the following pages is the fifth of these subsidies. Once again, the exemption limit was £3 for goods and £1 for lands. The rate of tax was 2s 8d in the pound on goods and 4s in the pound on lands. Aliens and Popish recusants were to pay double rates, but only one of each is recorded in the whole city. The same remarks about the incidence of the tax in 1629 apply as in 1602. Yet though there were 399 taxpayers in 1629, as against 400 in 1602, there are some changes as between the parishes which it is difficult to explain without a minute enquiry that would be beyond our present purpose. Thus in St. Petrock, the richest of the Exeter parishes, the number of taxpayers fell from 41 to 30, and in St. Mary Arches from 28 to 22, while St. Martin rose from 39 to 45 payers and St. Paul from 13 to 21. Otherwise the differences between the two years are no more than one might expect in the course of nearly thirty years.

The poll tax of 1660

In 1660 Parliament voted a sweeping tax, one partly on social rank, partly on wealth, and partly a poll tax, which covered all persons (male or female) above the age of sixteen years. This was " An Act for the speedy provision of money for disbanding and paying off the forces of this Kingdome both by Land and Sea ".[2] A similar sweeping tax had been levied in the summer of 1641 " for the speedye provision of monie for disbanding the Armies and setling the peace of the Two Kingdomes of England and Scotland ", and

[1] W. G. Hoskins, " An Elizabethan Provincial Town: Leicester ", in *Studies in Social History* (ed. J. H. Plumb, 1955), p. 44.

[2] *Statutes of the Realm*, vol. V, pp. 207 *et seq.* (12 Charles II, c. 9). The text of the amending act (c. 10) will be found in the same volume, pp. 225 *et seq.*

the lengthy assessments for this tax will also be found among the Exeter muniments. It was decided to transcribe the 1660 assessment rather than that for 1641 as it was considerably longer and the record was in better condition; but the attention of genealogists and others should be drawn to this earlier assessment, which is so much more comprehensive than the subsidy assessments of the first part of the century.[1]

The commissioners appointed under the act of 1660 for the raising of the tax were the Mayor; Sir Thomas Mallet, Justice of the King's Bench; Christopher Clarke, Simon Snow, Robert Walker, James Marshal, Nicholas Brooking and Ralph Herman, esquires; Alderman Martin, Alderman Crossing, Richard Evans, Henry Gandy, John Mane (*sic*), Thomas Westlacke, John Ackland, Walter Holditch, and Edmond Star.

Dukes were to pay £100 towards this tax, Marquesses £80, and so down the social scale to baronets at £30. A Knight Bachelor was assessed at £20, an Esquire ' or soe reputed ' at £10. Widows were rated at one-third, according to the rank of their husbands. Every man who was, or had been, an alderman of any city in the kingdom was to pay £5. The Lord Mayor of London, the Aldermen, and many others in the city of London, were specially assessed, but they do not concern us here.

Apart from taxing persons according to their social rank, the tax fell on the well-to-do who had no particular rank according to their incomes. " Every person that can dispend in Lands, Leases, Money, Stocke, or otherwise, of his or her owne proper estate one hundred pounds per annum [shall pay] the summe of forty shillings and soe proportionably for a greater or a lesser estate provided it extend not to persons under five pounds yearely ". The under-£5 class were subjected to a poll tax. Every single person above the age of sixteen years was to pay 12d, and all other persons not otherwise rated and not receiving alms 6d.

An amending act (c. 10) enacted that within two days after a demand by any assessor the householder (master or mistress) should deliver a list to the assessor of all persons above sixteen years of age residing within the family. Failure to deliver the list incurred the heavy penalty of £5. An incomplete or evasive list incurred a penalty of ten shillings for every person omitted. Half the penalties went to the informer, and the other half to the purposes of the act. The penalties were to be met by the distraint and sale of the offender's goods.

With penalties such as this we may be certain that the parish assessments contain the names of every person liable to pay the tax. Only those under sixteen years of age, or those in receipt of alms, were omitted. The result is the most comprehensive catalogue of the city population to be made before the census of 1801.[2] The totals of population and of tax yields for each parish are set out in the following table:

[1] E.C.M., Box of assessments for subsidies &c., nos. 2 and 3. The tax of 1641 fell savagely on the clergy. The bishop of Exeter paid £100, the dean £40, the canons £20 each, and the prebendaries £10 each. Altogether the Close yielded in tax £613 11s 6d as against £917 19s 6d for the rest of the city. In 1660 the clergy was not taxed as such.

[2] The census schedule for 1801 does not survive. There is no complete schedule before 1841, nearly two hundred years after this poll tax.

Parish	*Gross tax yield*	*Net tax yield*	*Tax population*
St. Martin }	£166 9s 0d	}£111 0s 0d	226
The Close }			226
St. Petrock	£68 14s 6d	£65 14s 6d	222
St. Stephen	£41 17s 6d	£40 8s 4d	220
Holy Trinity	£36 14s 6d	£29 4s 4d	494
St. Sidwell	£45 1s 0d	£38 14s 2d	738
St. Mary Arches	£90 11s 2d	£87 12s 6d	240
St. Olave	£48 12s 8d	£44 1s 4d	319
Allhallows-on-the Wall	£9 1s 0d	£8 9s 2d	161
St. Edmund	£35 4s 9d	£33 6s 8d	412
St. Kerrian	£55 3s 2d	£54 11s 0d	126
Allhallows (Goldsmith St.)	£49 6s 2d	£46 19s 4d	159
St. Pancras	£22 13s 8d	£19 1s 0d	83
St. Lawrence	£31 18s 0d	£28 4s 4d	310
St. Paul	£54 2s 10d	£53 0s 6d	371
St. David	£32 1s 0d	£27 19s 7d	431
St. Mary Major	£139 5s 0d	£132 1s 6d	1266
St. George	£23 13s 0d	£23 4s 2d	246
St. Mary Steps	£21 18s 6d	£21 10s 0d	302
St. John's Bow	£29 16s 6d	£28 7s 10d	293
Totals	£1002 2s 6d	£893 10s 3d	6845[1]

Gregory King estimated at this period that forty per cent of the population of England and Wales were under the age of sixteen years. Applying this estimate to Exeter we get a total population for the city in 1660 of 11,410, excluding those in receipt of alms. The grand total (including the paupers) would probably have been in the region of 12,000 people.[2] St. Thomas, the suburb across the river, was an integral part of Exeter economically and topographically (though not included in its jurisdiction). In 1695 this suburb contained 1,705 people,[3] and we might reasonably put the corresponding figure for 1660 at about fifteen hundred. ' Metropolitan Exeter ' in 1660 therefore contained about 13,500 people. Norwich, the leading provincial city at this date, was just about twice as populous as Exeter.[4]

The hearth tax of 1671

I discussed the main conclusions to be drawn from this assessment some twenty years ago in *Industry, Trade, and People in Exeter*, 1688-1800[5] (pp. 111-122), and there is no need to traverse the same ground beyond making a few small corrections. The roll is undated and I formerly suggested that it was the

[1] This figure includes the 376 who were subsequently written off as too poor to pay the tax, though they were not in receipt of alms.

[2] The so-called Compton Return of 1676, in the William Salt Library at Stafford, gives a total of 7,798 inhabitants aged sixteen years and over in Exeter. This gives a grand total (including children) of 13,000 for the city in that year. The ' Compton ' figure would include those in receipt of alms. As a total it agrees well with my estimate for 1660, allowing for some growth in the intervening sixteen years.

[3] Glass, loc. cit. St. Thomas in 1695 had 309 houses, 1705 people, and an average of 5.52 persons per house.

[4] Norwich had 28,546 people in 1695, Bristol 19,403.

[5] Published by the Manchester University Press for the History of Exeter Research Group, monograph no. 6 (1935).

assessment of Lady Day 1672. In fact it is the assessment of Michaelmas 1671, of which a copy exists in the Public Record Office. With the Exeter copy are two other hearth-tax assessments—one for Michaelmas 1672 and Lady Day 1673, and the other for 1674 (no exact date given).[1]

My earlier discussion overlooked the importance of the large inns in the city. I referred to 62 households in houses of ten hearths and more, but I should have perceived that a considerable proportion of these large dwellings were inns. Thus in St. Stephen's parish (see p. 84) the three largest dwellings (with 22, 13 and 11 hearths respectively) can all be identified as inns, and the same would apply to the other parishes on what were then the principal streets. The largest dwellings in St. Mary Major (see pp. 80—81) almost certainly represent the inns for which the parish was noted—the Dolphin, Bear, Mitre, Mermaid, White Hart, Globe, and Black Lion, to name only the more famous of them. I therefore unwittingly exaggerated the number of private households living in houses of 6-9 hearths and 10 hearths and over. Nevertheless, there still remained a considerable class of the well-to-do in Exeter who occupied large houses with 10 or more hearths.

The hearth tax assessment is clearly based on the household and not the house. In the richer parishes the two are synonymous, but in the poorer parishes two, three, or more families might share a large decaying house. Thus there were 60 assessments to the hearth tax in St. Stephen in 1671, and the return of 1695 shows that the parish (with Bedford Precinct) contained 69 houses. We may assume that in this parish every assessment in the hearth tax represents a separate house. But in St. Mary Major, the only other parish for which we know the total number of houses, there were 341 assessments to the 1671 hearth tax, and only 255 houses in 1695. A considerable number of families in St. Mary Major were therefore " doubling up " in the 1670's, and the same is true of the large and poor parish of St. Sidwell where the hearth tax assessment refers to " Thomas Bicknell and Tenements ", to " Evill Foxwell and Tenants ", and to other houses occupied by a number of poor households (see p. 67).

If a student interested in the minutiae of topography could identify all the inns concealed in the hearth tax assessment (with the aid of clues from the 1699 poor rate and other sources) he could probably determine the route taken by the assessor and therefore the whereabouts of some of the larger and more important houses. In this search the great collection of city deeds, wills, rate-books and so on, as well as the reports of the Charity Commissioners (a neglected source for urban topography), would give him a good start; and he should be able with much patience to elucidate the detailed topography of the seventeenth-century city in a way not possible in this volume.

The poor rate of 1699

A number of paper books, hitherto unlisted, came to light among the Exeter muniments a few years ago. These were five books of Poor Rates for the whole city, arranged by parishes, for the years 1691, 1692-3, 1696-7, 1697-8 and 1699.[2] It is the latest of these which has been transcribed here. Owing to the way in which it is set out the record is valueless for estimating the

[1] E.C.M. Misc. Rolls, No. 74.
[2] E.C.M. Misc. Books, 159b, 2—6.

population of the city at that date, but the reader will find, on the other hand, a mass of topographical information, information about the owners and occupiers of houses, and details about the incidence of poverty in the various parishes.

Ratepayers paid both on personal estate and on their property. The figures given in the books represent the weekly rate. The richer parishes coped comfortably with their own poor, but the large parishes with many paupers (such as St. Sidwell and St. Mary Major) were hopelessly placed. It was impossible for them to raise enough money within their own boundaries to meet the needs of their own poor. Some parishes were spending every week between two and three times as much as they could raise. The richer parishes contributed something towards the needs of the poorer. For example, St. Stephen, St. Olave, and St. Petrock all contributed to St. Mary Major; and the Close and St. Pancras contributed to St. Sidwell; but there was still a big deficit in the receiving parishes.

It is not clear upon what principle the contributions were made, and it must be left to a student of the poor law to work out the administrative and financial questions involved.[1] By the 1690's it was obvious, not only in Exeter, that the relief of poverty could not be carried out on a parochial basis, least of all in the larger towns where the poor congregated in large numbers in certain districts. A Corporation of the Poor was set up at Exeter in 1698, following the Bristol model, to deal with the poor of the city as a whole. A new and larger workhouse was built " in a commanding and airy situation on the old London Road " to the design of one Ralph Mitchell.[2]

The new system had the advantage of equalising the poor rate throughout the city, and of avoiding much of the complexity of the law relating to settlement. It is not certain when it came into operation at Exeter, but possibly it was in the year 1700 (when the new building seems to have been completed for use) and the rate book for 1699 transcribed here may be the last in that form.

One does not gather anything of the true annual value of house-property, or of the level of rents paid by the different classes of occupier, from this rate-book, but this can be ascertained to some degree from another assessment among the city muniments made in March 1689-90.[3] This gives " the Yearely Rent " of house-property in a number of parishes, and the figures for five parishes (four well-to-do, and one poor) are given below:

Parish	Annual Value of Houses								Total Houses
	£1-£4	£5-£9	£10-£19	£20-£29	£30-£39	£40-£49	£50-£74	£75 & over	
St. Petrock	4	5	16	6	8	7	4	1	51
St. Kerrian	0	5	8	7	8	1	0	0	29
St. Stephen (with Bedford)	3	12	13	15	12	5	2	4	66
St. Martin	0	4	11	15	10	3	4	0	47
St. Sidwell	124	37	19	4	0	0	0	0	184

[1] There is a brief discussion of the subject in my *Industry, Trade, and People in Exeter*, pp. 141-5, but the whole subject deserves separate treatment in a monograph.

[2] Oliver, *History of Exeter* (1861 ed.), pp. 151-2. Nothing is known about Ralph Mitchell, whose design was approved by the Committee on 7 February 1699. Much of his building was destroyed in May 1942 and what is left is now known as the City Hospital on Heavitree Hill.

[3] E.C.M. Misc. Book 159a. Unfortunately it is not complete for all parishes.

The poor-class housing of St. Sidwell is very striking. Two houses in every three were valued at only £1 to £4 a year, a great number at only £1 to £2.[1] There were only four houses of any substance in the entire parish, and two of these were owned and occupied by the Cheeke family, who formed a sort of dynasty of brewers in the city from the late sixteenth century down to the eighteenth. The range of annual values in this parish is only from £1 to £24, whereas in St. Martin it is from £5 to £65. The most valuable properties in St. Stephen were the inns. The New Inn, with an annual value of £196, was the most valuable single property in the city. The solid middle-class comfort of St. Kerrian comes out clearly: 24 of the 29 houses fell into the £10 to £40 class. The general picture that emerges of these five parishes agrees well with that presented by the hearth tax assessment, as we might expect.

Conclusion

Exeter possesses one of the finest collections of civic records in England, probably in Europe outside a few capital cities. Certainly I think it may be the most comprehensive archive collection of any city in England outside London. It is regrettable that the archives have never been systematically published, as the records of Nottingham and Leicester have been. Exeter has not even published its fine collection of charters. This modest volume is, I believe, the first to be drawn from the Exeter archives but I hope that others will now follow. I hope myself to follow this volume on Seventeenth-Century Exeter with similar ones on the sixteenth and eighteenth centuries, and possibly, in the course of time, with one on Medieval Exeter, so that in the end we have in print a body of material about the families and topography of the city from about 1300 to 1800.

Method of Transcription

The records which follow have, with certain modifications mentioned below, been transcribed as they stand. Christian names have, however, been translated throughout, wherever there is a modern equivalent. Thus 'Maria' becomes Mary, 'Joanna' Joan, and so on, but names such as Dionisia or Richord have been left unchanged. Surnames are everywhere printed as in the original record.

All editorial insertions are placed within square brackets. A complete blank indicates that the record is either so defective or illegible at that point that no reading is possible. Occasionally it is possible to fill in deficiencies in the subsidy assessments of 1602 and 1629 by calculation. Gaps in the Exeter copy of the poll tax of 1660 have been largely filled from the copy in the Public Record Office (E. 179. 102/482) but a few blanks nevertheless remain where neither copy can produce a reading.

[1] The total of 184 houses for St. Sidwell is not complete. It does not include 45 entries of "houses" which make an exact analysis difficult, but this omission does not in any way affect the general picture of the parish as a mass of poor cottages. The large-scale owner of poor property appears in the person of one 'Mr. Long', probably the forerunner of a new social type.

In the case of the subsidy assessments of 1602 and 1629 the headings to the rolls (in Latin) have been translated and given as abstracts, all essential information being included. Headings to the other records have been given in full.

Designations of rank, occupation, etc., where used, have been translated and italicised. References to particular buildings and other topographical features have also been italicised for ease of reference. Roman figures have everywhere been translated into Arabic for the comfort of the modern reader.

To conserve space, the single columns of the original records have been printed as far as possible in double columns, and any marginal matter has been placed in the text at the point to which it refers.

The abbreviations used in the footnotes are:

B.M. Add. MSS.	British Museum (Additional Manuscripts)
E.C.M.	Exeter City Muniments
P.R.O.	Public Record Office.

Acknowledgments

I have to thank the Town Clerk (Mr. C. J. Newman) for permission to transcribe and publish these records in the Exeter muniment room, and also the Exeter City Council for a generous grant towards the cost of publishing them. The greater part of the cost of publication is borne of course by the Devon and Cornwall Record Society, but the grant by the City Council has made it possible to produce a bigger and more varied volume of records than would otherwise have been the case. I am grateful also to the City Librarian (Mr. N. S. E. Pugsley) and his staff for considerable assistance in transcribing and checking the material presented here. Without his help and active interest the volume would have been delayed by many months. The frontispiece was also supplied by the City Librarian, from an unpublished collection of drawings made in 1827.

The City Librarian has placed me further in his debt by preparing the considerable index of surnames to this volume at a time when I was particularly hard pressed with public business and unable to do it myself. Half the value of a book such as this lies in the index: Mr. Pugsley has spared no effort to make it accurate and completely comprehensive.

EXETER
July 1956

W. G. HOSKINS

1. THE SUBSIDY OF 1602.[1]

Abstract of Heading

Indenture made 20 October 44 Elizabeth [1602] between Richard Bevys mayor of the city of Exeter, George Smythe, Richard Prouze, and Christopher [? Manneringe], Commissioners of the Queen in the matter of the second payment of the second of Four Subsidies granted by Parliament at Westminster 20 September 43 Elizabeth [1601], of the one part, and Edward Herte of the city of Exeter and William Tickell of the same city of the other part, witnessing that the said commissioners appoint the said Edward Herte and William Tickell to be chief collectors of the said subsidy.

Signed Richard Bevis mayor
Richard Prouze

m.1

PARISH OF ST. STEPHEN

George Smythe *esq.* in lands	[assessed at] £30	[to pay] 40s
Hugh Vaughan *esq.* in goods	£8	8s
Jasper Bridgman in lands	£6	8s
John Trosse in goods	£5	5s
John Pill in lands	£3	4s
John Halstaffe in goods	£4	4s
Robert Staplehill in goods	£4	4s
Joan Clevelande in goods	£4	4s
John Vigurs in goods	£5	5s
Clement Owleborowe in goods	£3	3s
Nicholas Hatche in goods	£3	3s
Katherine Peryman widow in lands	20s	16d
Valentine Tooker in lands	20s	16d
John Savidge in lands	20s	16d

Total £4 12s

PARISH OF ST. PETROCK

William Martyn *esq.* in goods	£13	13s
John Levermore in goods	£10	10s
John Howell in goods	£10	10s
William Spycer in goods	£12	12s
John Ellacott in goods	£10	10s
John Lante in goods	£9	9s
John Lambell in goods	£5	5s
John Sheere in goods	£5	5s
John Eddes in goods	£5	5s
John Martyn in goods	£5	5s
Nicholas Martyn in goods	£3	3s
Thomas Cooke in goods	£5	5s
Elizabeth Martyn widow in goods	£4	4s
John Hayne in goods	£5	5s
Crispian Birdley widow in goods	£4	4s
Elliot Kenycott in goods	£5	5s
Gilbert Lambell in goods	£3	3s
Richard Bryndley in goods	£5	5s
Lawrence Collibeere in goods		
John Jurden in goods		
Edward Bidgood in goods		
Roger Phippes in goods		
Thomas Martyn in goods	£5	5s
William Parr in goods	£3	3s
Easter (*Paschasia*) Galley widow in goods		
John Gupwell in goods		
Thomas Richardson in goods		
Jane Wilmington widow in goods		
William Slade in goods		

[1] E.C.M., Assessments of Subsidies and other grants, Box 3. The heading to the record is somewhat obliterated but all the essential information is given above.

Nicholas Spycer in goods		
William Macey in goods		
Nicholas Ricrofte in goods	£3	3s
Robert Bennett in lands	20s	[16d]
Lewis Hatche *gent.* in lands	£8	[10s 8d]
Thomas Blackaller in lands	£8	[10s 8d]
Hugh Woode in lands	20s	16d
Hugh Redwood in lands	20s	16d
Stephen Tooker in lands	20s	16d
Joan Oliver widow in lands	20s	16d
Charles Hole in lands	20s	16d
Henry Willett in lands	20s	16d

Total £10 4s 8d

m.1d.

PARISH OF ST. SIDWELL

George Rowe in lands	20s	16d
John Gilbert in lands	20s	16d
John Mortymer in lands	20s	16d
Thomas Meade in lands	40s	2s 8d
Walter Peryam in lands	20s	16d
Thomas Bicknell in lands	20s	16d
John Packer in lands	20s	16d
Robert Doderidge in lands	20s	16d
Nicholas Stockman in lands	20s	16d
Edward Langdon in goods	£4	4s
John Galley in goods	£3	3s
William Whitley in goods	£3	3s
Thomas Tirrell in goods	£4	4s
Martin Bowerman in goods	£3	3s
Grace Grice widow in goods	£3	3s
Agnes Huishe widow in goods	£3	3s
William Morris in goods	£3	3s
John Podger in goods	£3	3s
Englishe Chicke widow in goods	£4	4s
Roger Morrell in goods	£3	3s
Martin Garrett in goods	£3	3s
Philip Pyne in goods	£5	5s
John Isacke in goods	£4	4s
John Tye in goods	£6	6s
Roger Fishmore in lands	20s	16d

Total £3 8s 8d

PARISH OF ST. PANCRAS

Richard Prouze *esq.* in lands	£6	8s
John Prouze in goods	£6	6s
William Tickell in goods	£4	4s
William Grigge in goods	£4	4s
Nicholas Downe in goods	£4	4s
John Gandye in goods	£3	3s
William Brayley in goods	£3	3s
John Challis in lands	20s	16d
Edith Hunt widow in lands	20s	16d

Total 34s 8d

PARISH OF ST. PAUL

Christopher Manneringe *gent.* in lands	£10	13s 4d
Oliver Cooke *gent.* in lands	£4	5s 4d
[blank] Argenton widow in goods	£4	4s
Valentine Todburie in goods	£5	5s
George Leache in goods	£5	5s
Henry Gandye in lands	20s	16d
John Chapple in goods	£4	4s
Robert Downe in lands	20s	16d
Humphrey Cade in lands	20s	16d
Thomas Bennett in lands	20s	16d
John Vowells in goods	£3	3s
Thomas Pope in goods	£3	3s
Thomas Mathewes in lands	20s	16d

Total 49s 4d

PARISH OF ST. GEORGE

William Lewes in lands	20s	16d
Alexander Mayne in goods	£6	6s
Jeremiah Helliard in goods	£5	5s
Lawrence Underhill in goods	£5	5s
Daniel Baker in goods	£3	3s
John Baker in goods	£3	3s
William Takell Sen. in goods	£3	3s
William Hellyns in goods	£3	3s
Matthew German in goods	£3	3s
Richard Bowyer in goods	£3	3s
William Goldinge in goods	£3	3s
John Harrys in lands	20s	16d
John Vucles in lands	20s	16d
Tristram Roo in lands	20s	16d
John Pole in lands	20s	16d
Henry Takell in lands	20s	16d
Anthony Hill in lands	20s	16d
Richard Geale in lands	20s	16d
[blank] Castell widow in goods	£3	3s
William Payne in goods	£6	6s

Total 56s 8d

PARISH OF ST. MARY STEPS

Richard Martyn in goods	£5	5s
John Waye in goods	£5	5s
Henry Dabbynott in goods	£3	3s
Thomas Hearde in goods	£4	4s
James Taylor in goods	£4	4s
Richard Halstaffe in goods	£4	4s
John Rewe in goods	£3	3s
Ellis (*Elizeus*) Fleye in goods	£3	3s
Philip Geans in lands	20s	16d

John Gresham in lands	20s	16d
William Nickes in lands	20s	16d
John Hethman in lands	20s	16d
Nicholas Evans in lands	20s	16d
William Reade in lands	20s	16d
Henry Jynkyns in lands	20s	16d
Norman (*Normannus*) Morhedd *alien*		4d
John Bartlett in lands	20s	16d

Total 42s

m.2

PARISH OF HOLY TRINITY

Peter Wolcott *gent.* in lands	£4	5s 4d
John Norrys *gent.* in lands	£4	5s 4d
Edward Wolcott *gent.* in lands	40s	2s 8d
Michael Thomas in lands	40s	2s 8d
John Moore in goods	£6	6s
Roger Selbye in goods	£6	6s
Nicholas Bolte in goods	£5	5s
George Serle in goods	£5	5s
John Barons in goods	£5	5s
John Streat in goods	£5	5s
John Blackmore in goods	£3	3s
Thomas Nicolls in goods	£3	3s
Roger Ford in goods	£3	3s
William Mathewe in goods	£3	3s
William Hore in goods	£3	3s
Silvester Maunder in goods	£3	3s
Nicholas Wills in goods	£3	3s
John Convers in goods	£3	3s
John Saunders in goods	£3	3s
Richard Baker in goods	£3	3s
Joan Shorke widow in lands	20s	16d
William Palmer in lands	20s	16d
Thomas Philmor in lands	20s	16d
William Androwes in lands	20s	16d
Richard Deymond in lands	20s	16d
Nicholas Stretchley in lands	20s	16d

Total £4 6s

PARISH OF ST. MARTIN

Hugh Wyatt *esq.* in lands	£6	8s
Evan Morrice in lands	£7	9s 4d
Isaac Cotten in lands	40s	2s 8d
Jonathan Lewes in lands	20s	16d
Thomas Banckes in lands	20s	16d
William Masters sen. in lands	20s	16d
Henry Pethericke in lands	20s	16d
Richard Colliskott in lands	20s	16d
Alexander Osborne in lands	20s	16d
Christopher Hunt in lands	20s	16d
George Lidgingham in lands	20s	16d
Henry Pennye in lands	20s	16d
Michael Harte in lands	20s	16d
Joseph Hosgood in lands	20s	16d
Roger Juell in lands	20s	16d
David Hockley in lands	20s	16d
Edward Greene in lands	20s	16d
William Masters jun. in lands	20s	16d
Robert White in lands	20s	16d
David Hancocke in lands	20s	16d
Elizabeth Spicer widow in goods	£10	10s
Richard Dewe *gent.* in goods	£3	3s
Thomas Trosse in goods	£8	8s
John Bartlett in goods	£6	6s
Edward Peard in goods	£4	4s
John Mogridge in goods	£4	4s
John Blighe in goods	£4	4s
Christopher Eston in goods	£3	3s
Josiah Evlighe in goods	£3	3s
William Ryder in goods	£3	3s
Alan Hackwell in goods	£3	3s
John Penny in goods	£3	3s
Angel Maddocks in goods	£5	5s
Anthony Turpyn in goods	£3	3s
Christopher Spycer in goods	£3	3s
John Baker in lands	20s	16d
Robert Parr in goods	£8	8s
Thomas Wakman in goods	£6	6s
Robert Ellacott in goods	£6	6s

Total £7 3s 4d

PARISH OF ST. DAVIDS

William Bynford *gent.* in lands	£5	6s 8d
John Drewe in lands	20s	16d
Martin Dynham in lands	20s	16d
Stephen Tremlett in lands	20s	16d
Philip Hagley in lands	20s	16d
Elizabeth Denys widow in goods	£6	6s
John Aulsopp in goods	£6	6s
Nicholas Dyer in goods	£5	5s
John Skynner in goods	£4	4s
Thomas Jurden in goods	£4	4s
Humphrey Holmead in goods	£4	4s
William Maunder in goods	£4	4s
Edward Leman in goods	£3	3s
Thomas Saunder in goods	£3	3s
Roger Maye in lands	[20s]	[16d]

Total 52s 4d

PARISH OF ST. OLAVE

Nicholas Hurst *esq.* in lands	£13	[17s 4d]
John Peryam *esq.* in goods	£20	20s
John Chapple in goods	£14	14s
Thomasine Chapple widow in goods	£10	10s
Thomas Poyntington in goods	£6	6s
John Radford in goods	£3	3s
David Bagwell in goods	£6	6s
John Plea in goods	£3	3s
Morrice Downe in goods	£3	3s
Edward Clement in goods	£3	3s
William Horsham in goods	£3	3s
John Collyns in goods	£3	3s
John Titherley in goods	£3	3s
William Berdall in goods	£3	3s
John Gill in goods	£3	3s
John Vaughan in lands	20s	16d
Thomas Chapple in goods	£3	3s
Richard Dorchester in goods	£6	6s
Thomas Chaffe in goods	£6	6s
John Taylor in goods	£10	10s

Total £6 6s 8d

m. 2d.

PARISH OF ST. MARY ARCHES

Richard Bevys *Mayor* in goods	£9	9s
John Davye *esq.* in lands	£20	26s 8d
Thomas Walker in lands	£10	13s 4d
Richard Blackaller *gent.* in lands	£10	13s 4d
Nicholas Ducke in lands	£3	4s
Lewis Plumbley in lands	20s	16d
John Smythe in lands	20s	16d
Robert Sherwood in lands	20s	16d
John Watkyns in lands	20s	16d
Robert Prouz in lands	20s	16d
George Mawditt in lands	20s	16d
Nicholas Spicer *esq.* in goods	£14	14s
Alice Aplyn widow in goods	£3	3s
Geoffrey Waltham in goods	?[£13]	?[13s]
Samuel Alforde in goods	£7	7s
Paul Triggs in goods	£6	6s
John Muddiford in goods	£6	6s
John Hackwell in goods	£5	5s
Lewis Martyn in goods	£3	3s
Peter Colton in goods	£5	5s
Nicholas Bevys in goods	£4	4s
Peter Bolte in goods	?[£4]	?[4s]
Thomas Martyn in goods	£2	2s
Abraham Pawle in goods	£3	3s
Ignatius Jurden in goods	£7	7s
Thomas Snowe in goods	£7	7s
Richard Sweet in goods	£7	7s
John Marshall in goods	£6	6s

Total £8 5s 4d

PARISH OF ST. MARY MAJOR

Thomas Edwards in goods	£7	7s
Elizabeth Seldon widow in goods	£8	8s
Robert Maddocks in goods	£6	6s
Richard Boddye in goods	£5	5s
Nicholas Webb in goods	£5	5s
John Taylor *Innkeeper* in goods	£5	5s
Hugh Morrell in goods		
William Martyn in goods		
Robert Hyne in goods		
Henry Elliott in goods		
John Tirrye in goods		
William Angevyn in goods		
Agnes Thomas widow in goods		
Thomas Kirridge in goods		
John Garrett in goods		
Humphrey Gilbert in goods		
Gawen St. Cleere in goods		
Edward Mynterne in goods		
Thomas Newman in goods		
William Austyn in goods		
George Pile in goods		
Thomas Flea in goods		
Bernard Pearce in goods	£4	4s
William Moore in goods	£6	6s
Roger Bridgwater in goods	£3	3s
Thomas Hitchcocke in goods	£3	3s
Laurence Barcombe in goods	£3	3s
James Skinner in goods	£2	2s
Richard Langhorn in goods	£3	3s
George Cotten in goods	£3	3s
Gilbert Smythe in goods	£8	8s
John Payne in goods		
Hugh Crossinge in goods		
Laurence Serell in goods	£7	7s
William Cowde in goods	?[£3]	?[3s]
William Lake in goods		
John Wotten in lands	20s	[16d]
Edward Alford in lands	20s	[16d]
Michael Abott in lands	20s	[16d]
Mark Laurenc *alien* in lands	20s	[16d]
John Medland in lands	20s	[16d]
Edward Fludde in lands	20s	[16d]
Henry Collyns in lands	20s	[16d]
Nicholas Evans in lands	20s	[16d]
Robert Robyns in lands	20s	[16d]

John Serle in lands	20s	[16d]
Nicholas Yeo in lands	20s	[16d]
John Witche in goods	£3	[3s]
George Acton in lands	20s	16d

Total £9 4s 4d

PARISH OF ALLHALLOWS IN GOLDSMITH STREET

Edward Parker *esq.* in lands		
William Martyn *gent.* in goods		
Edward Herte *gent.* in goods		
Robert Mitchell in goods		
Anne Vilvayne widow in goods		
Nicholas Weare in goods		
Nicholas Langdon in goods		
John Elliott in lands	20s	[16d]
Anthony Salter in lands	20s	[16d]
John Harman in lands	20s	[16d]
William Griffyn in lands	20s	[16d]
John Relfe in lands	20s	16d
Alexander Germyn in goods	£9	9s
William Newcombe in goods	£8	8s
Symon Leache in goods	£8	8s

Total £6 9s 8d

m. 3.

PARISH OF ST. KERRIAN

Henry Hull in goods	£7	7s
Richarda Sweete widow in goods	£5	5s
Walter Borrowe in goods	£8	8s
Elizabeth Halstaffe widow in goods	£3	3s
Philip Warde in goods	£3	3s
Honor Jurden widow in lands	20s	16d
Henry Hayne in goods	£4	4s
Joan Taylor widow in goods	£3	3s
Thomas Crossinge in goods	£4	4s
John Clavell in goods	£4	4s
William Tottell in goods	£3	3s
William Gill in goods	£3	3s
Robert Brocke in goods	£3	3s
Mary Coocke widow in lands	20s	16d
Margery Martyn widow in goods	£3	3s
Nicholas Chapple in goods	£4	4s
Richard Hatche in goods	£3	3s
John Trigge in lands	20s	16d
Alexander Penny in lands	20s	16d
Edward Waye in lands	20s	16d
Oliver Tapper in goods	£4	4s
Henry Sweete in goods	£4	4s
Nicholas Harmon in lands	20s	16d

Total £3 16s

PARISH OF ST. JOHN'S BOW

Corporation of Weavers & Fullers in lands	£4	5s 8d
William Maye in lands	20s	16d
John Haydon in lands	20s	16d
John Combe in lands	20s	16d
William Hole in lands	20s	16d
Margaret Howell widow in lands	20s	16d
Henry Taylor in lands	20s	16d
William Lawrence in lands	20s	16d
George Masters in lands	20s	16d
Eleanor Marshall in goods	£6	6s
John Bande in goods	£3	3s
William Clement in goods	£3	3s
Edward Warde in goods	£3	3s
Richard Person in goods	£3	3s
William Webber in goods	£3	3s
William Pope in goods	£5	5s
Emanuell Taylor in lands	20s	16d

Total 43s 4d

PARISH OF ST. LAWRENCE

Edward German in goods	£5	5s
[*blank*] Buckford widow in goods	£4	4s
Jerome Alley *gent.* in goods	£3	3s
Walter Pole in goods	£3	3s
James Warde in goods	£3	3s
John Wotten *gent.* in goods	£3	3s
Edward Esworthye in goods	£3	3s
Richard Longe in goods	£4	4s
Elizabeth Dreyton widow in goods	£3	3s
John Denslowe in goods	£3	3s
Philip Biggleston *gent.* in goods	£10	10s
Alice Peter widow in lands	20s	16d
Philip Hayne in lands	20s	16d

Total 48s

m. 3d.

PARISH OF ST. EDMUND

Richard Mayne in goods	£5	5s
Zachary Wills in goods	£5	5s
Richard Addis in goods	£4	4s
William Holder in goods	£4	4s
John Bruton in goods	£3	3s
Robert Jynkyns in goods	£3	3s
John Mayne in goods	£3	3s
Robert Westerne in lands	20s	16d
Nicholas Parker in lands	20s	16d
Philip Frenche in lands	20s	16d
Thomas Rider in lands	20s	16d

Total 32s 4d

PARISH OF ALLHALLOWS ON THE WALLS

Michael Jacobb in lands	20s	[16d]
Richard Audrie in lands	20s	[16d]
Richard Macey in goods	£3	[3s]
Richard Meller in goods	£4	[4s]
John Wills in goods	£3	[3s]

Total 12s 8d

Sum total £82 16s

2. THE SUBSIDY OF 1629.[1]

Abstract of Heading

Indenture made 22 April 5 Charles I [1629] between John Lynne esquire Mayor of the city of Exeter, Walter Borough, Thomas Crossinge, John Tailler, and John Hakewill esquires, commissioners of the King for a tax levied and collected as a fifth subsidy of five whole subsidies granted to the King in a Parliament held at Westminster 17 March 3 Charles I [1628] of the one part, and John Vigures of the city of Exeter merchant and Richard Evans of the same city merchant on the other part, witnessing that the said Commissioners appoint and constitute the said John Vigures and Richard Evans to be chief collectors of the said subsidy within the city of Exeter.

Signed John Lynne mayor
Walter Borough
John Tailler
John Hakewill

m. 1

East Ward

PARISH OF ST. PETROCK

Thomas Crossinge *Alderman* in goods	[assessed at] £9	[to pay] 24s
Nicholas Spicer in goods	£7	18s 8d
Nicholas Martyn in goods	£7	18s 8d
John Crocker in goods	£5	13s 4d
John Hayne in goods	£5	13s 4d
Elizabeth Lant widow in goods	£5	13s 4d
Philip Crossinge in lands	£4	16s
John Tailler in goods	£5	13s 4d
George Jurdaine in goods	£5	13s 4d
Richard Yeo in goods	£5	13s 4d
Thomas Trobridge in goods	£5	13s 4d
Mary Ricrafte widow in goods	£4	10s 8d
William Blackall in goods	£4	10s 8d
Andrew Quash in goods	£4	10s 8d
Richard Sweete in goods	£3	8s
John Cogan in goods	£3	8s
Isaac Mawditt in goods	£3	8s
Jasper Ratcliffe in goods	£3	8s
Richard Mayne in goods	£3	8s
Nicholas Carwithie [sic] in goods	£3	8s
Christopher Leigh in goods	£3	8s
The feofees of the lands of the parish church aforesaid in lands	£2	8s
Margaret Baskervile widow in lands	£1	4s
John Pynney in lands	£1	4s
George Edmonds in lands	£1	4s
Humphrey Tucker in lands	£1	4s
Henry Prigge in lands	£1	4s
Thomas Coplestone in lands	£1	4s
George Macye in lands	£1	4s
John Troute in lands	£1	4s

Total £14 18s 8d

PARISH OF ST. MARTIN

Elizabeth Southcott widow in lands	£15	£3
George Parry *Doctor of Laws* in lands	£10	40s
William Brewton *esq.* in lands	£8	32s
Robert Michell *Doctor of Laws* in goods	£10	26s. 8d

[1] E.C.M., Assessments of Subsidies &c. Box 3.

Arthur Southcott *gent.* in lands	£5	20s
George Kendall *gent.* in lands	£5	20s
George Langworthie in goods	£9	24s
Elizabeth Spicer widow in goods	£6	16s
Susanna Southcott widow in lands	£4	16s
Christopher Osmond *gent.* in lands	£4	16s
Judith Wakeman widow in goods	£6	16s
William Symons *gent.* in goods	£6	16s
William Kifte *gent.* in goods	£6	16s
Antony Salter in goods	£6	16s
Tristram Michell in goods	£5	13s 4d
John Moungwell in goods	£5	13s 4d
William Southcott *gent.* in lands	£3	12s
James Calthroppe *gent.* in lands	£3	12s
Samuel Izacke *gent.* in goods	£4	10s 8d
John Pennye in goods	£4	10s 8d
James Collyns in goods	£4	10s 8d
John Parr in goods	£4	10s 8d
Richard Beavis in goods	£4	10s 8d
John Sparke in goods	£4	10s 8d
Richard Harbert in goods	£3	8s
Thomas Bowridge in goods	£3	8s
Richard Langherne *gent.* in goods	£3	8s
Thomas Payne *gent.* in goods	£3	8s
Joan Weekes widow in goods	£3	8s
Edward Anthonie in goods	£3	8s
Alan Pennye in goods	£3	8s
Clement Cheriton *gent.* in goods	£3	8s
Joseph Martyn *gent.* in goods	£3	8s
Henry Rowcliffe in goods	£3	8s
John Baldwyne *gent.* in lands	£1	4s
Christopher Babbe in lands	£1	4s
Jane Gunne widow in lands	£1	4s
Gertrude Comyns widow in lands	£1	4s
Nicholas Streete in lands	£1	4s
Richard Lidgingham in lands	£1	4s
John Butler in lands	£1	4s
Thomas Potbery in lands	£1	4s
Edward Michell in lands	£1	4s
Hugh Bragge in lands	£1	4s
Thomas Deeble in lands	£1	4s

Total £28 13s 4d

m. 1d.

PARISH OF ST. STEPHEN

Richard Waltham jun. *esq.* in lands	£2	8s
Roger Mallacke in goods	£7	18s 8d
John Vigures in goods	£7	18s 8d
Thomas Bridgman *gent.* in lands	£5	20s
Edward Jones *gent.* in goods	£4	10s 8d
Richard Staplehill *gent.* in goods	£4	10s 8d
Humphrey Bidgood in goods	£4	10s 8d
Elizabeth Trosse widow in goods	£3	8s
Peter Trosse *esq.* in lands	£2	8s
Germann [sic] Shapcott *gent.* in goods	£3	8s
William Holmes in lands	£1	4s
Thomas Chappell in lands	£1	4s
William Milles in lands	£1	4s
Nathaniell Salter in lands	£1	4s
Robert Mathewe in lands	£1	4s
Nicholas Trosse in lands	£1	4s
William Winter in lands	£1	4s
John Milles in lands	£1	4s

Total £7 13s 4d

PARISH OF ST. SIDWELL

George Moncke *gent.* in goods	£6	16s
Robert White *gent.* in goods	£4	10s 8d
Peter Clappe in goods	£4	10s 8d
Elizabeth Retoricke widow in goods	£4	10s 8d
Alice Kingdome widow in goods	£4	10s 8d
Peter Chapman in goods	£3	8s
Thomas Courtis in goods	£3	8s
Beatrix Cheeke widow in goods	£3	8s
Elizabeth Pyne widow in goods	£3	8s
Gregory Tucker in goods	£3	8s
John Smith in goods	£3	8s
Elizabeth Webber in goods	£3	8s
Richard Clappe in goods	£3	8s
William Carrowe *gent.* in lands	£2	8s

Name	Assessment	Tax
George Rowe in lands	£1	4s
John Fall in lands	£1	4s
Roger Weekes in lands	£1	4s
Thomas Harris in lands	£1	4s
Thomas Bicknall in lands	£1	4s
Humphrey Smith in lands	£1	4s
Nathaniell Humfrie in lands	£1	4s
John Granett in lands	£1	4s
Alice Fishmore widow in lands	£1	4s
John Hoppyn in lands	£1	4s
Nicholas Clarke in lands	£1	4s

Total £8 14s 8d

PARISH OF HOLY TRINITY

Name	Assessment	Tax
John Norleigh *gent.* in lands	£7	28s
John Haunce in goods	£6	16s
Stephen Mosier in goods	£5	13s 4d
James Peeke in goods	£5	13s 4d
William Mathewe sen. in goods	£4	10s 8d
Nicholas Hellier *recusant* in goods	£3	16s[1]
Roger Wild in goods	£3	8s
Elias Potter in goods	£3	8s
John Pridham in goods	£3	8s
Robert Siblie in goods	£3	8s
Thomas Flaye in goods	£3	8s
John Tucker *fuller* in goods	£3	8s
Charles Basse in goods	£3	8s
John Blackmore in goods	£3	8s
William Mannowrie *alien* in lands	£1	8s
Richard Jarman in lands	£1	4s
John Tucker *yeoman* in lands	£1	4s
Richard Frie in lands	£1	4s
William Sparke in lands	£1	4s
Henry Dashwoode in lands	£1	4s
Robert Turner in lands	£1	4s
Thomas Cole in lands	£1	4s
John Abbott in lands	£1	4s
Peter Morrishe in lands	£1	4s
John Flay in lands	£1	4s
Edward Woode in lands	£1	4s
George Pellyton in lands	£1	4s
Joan Dawkins widow in lands	£1	4s
William Mathewe jun. in lands	£1	4s
Ambrose Palmer in lands	£1	4s
Dorothy Thomas widow in lands	£1	4s

Total £11 13s 4d

West Ward

PARISH OF ST. OLAVE

Name	Assessment	Tax
John Acland *Alderman* in goods	£6	16s
John Tailler *Alderman* in goods	£10	26s 8d
Adam Bennett in lands	£5	20s
Robert Walker in goods	£8	21s 4d
Christopher Clarke in goods	£6	16s
Hugh Crocker in goods	£6	16s
George Harris in goods	£6	16s
Ann Amye widow in goods	£4	10s 8d
Ursula Collyton widow in goods	£4	10s 8d
John Cupper in goods	£4	10s 8d
John Anthonie in goods	£4	10s 8d
Nathaniel Duncan in goods	£4	10s 8d
Richard Madocke in goods	£4	10s 8d
Jonathan Hawkins in goods	£3	8s
Robert Bolte in lands	£1	4s
John North in lands	£1	4s
Richard Jacobbe in lands	£1	4s
Richard Beavis in lands	£1	4s

Total £11

PARISH OF ST. MARY ARCHES

Name	Assessment	Tax
Ignatius Jurdaine *Alderman* in goods	£4	10s 8d
m. 2.		
James Walker *esq.* in lands	£10	40s
Gilbert Sweete in goods	£7	18s 8d
John Hakewill in goods	£5	13s 4d
James Tucker in goods	£10	26s 8d
Richard Saunders in goods	£5	13s 4d
Alice Marshall widow in goods	£5	13s 4d
Joan Jurdaine widow in goods	£5	13s 4d
John Pearce in goods	£5	13s 4d
Nicholas Mercer in goods	£5	13s 4d
James Gould in goods	£5	13s 4d
George Blackall in goods	£5	13s 4d
Abraham Paule in goods	£4	10s 8d
Joseph Trobridge in goods	£4	10s 8d
Henry Walker *gent.* in goods	£4	10s 8d
Elizabeth Dowrich widow in goods	£4	10s 8d
Francis Mapowder in goods	£3	8s
Samuel Jurdaine in lands	£3	12s

[1] Recusants were taxed at double rates, i.e. 5s 4d in the £1 on goods. Aliens also paid at double rates.

Francis Lippingcott in goods	£3	8s
Margaret Snellinge widow in lands	£1	4s
John Trigges in lands	£1	4s
Robert Chaffe in lands	£1	4s

Total £14 5s 4d

PARISH OF ALLHALLOWS ON THE WALLS

Mary Hayne widow in lands	£1	4s
George Hoyte in lands	£1	4s
John Glanfill in lands	£1	4s
Nathaniel Seaman in lands	£1	4s
John Soper in lands	£1	4s
Thomas Payne in lands	£1	4s
John Betson in lands	£1	4s

Total 28s

PARISH OF ST. EDMUND

Richard Payne in goods	£5	13s 4d
George Stone in goods	£4	10s 8d
Thomas Mayne in goods	£3	8s
William Mathewe in goods	£3	8s
Thomas Lacye in goods	£3	8s
Richard Cove in goods	£3	8s
Matthew Axe in goods	£3	8s
Thomas Hagon in lands	£1	4s
Matthew Symons in lands	£1	4s
William Coombe in lands	£1	4s
Richard Holder in lands	£1	4s

Total £4

North Ward

PARISH OF ST. KERRIAN

Walter Borough *Alderman* in goods	£12	32s
Henry Trosse *esq.* in lands	£7	28s
Henry Battishill in goods	£5	13s 4d
Mary Modyford widow in goods	£8	21s 4d
Dorothy Mogridge widow in goods	£7	18s 8d
Grace Sheere widow in goods	£6	16s
Walter White in goods	£6	16s
Thomas Blackall in goods	£6	16s
John Cooze in goods	£5	13s 4d
Oliver Tapper sen. in goods	£4	10s 8d
James White in goods	£4	10s 8d
John Richards in goods	£4	10s 8d
Philip Borough in goods	£4	10s 8d
Mary Pope widow in goods	£4	10s 8d
John Gill in goods	£3	8s
Thomas Knott in goods	£3	8s
Mary Yeo widow in goods	£3	8s
Hannibal Ratcliffe in lands	£2	8s
Prudence Borough widow in lands	£1	4s
Oliver Tapper jun. in lands	£1	4s
John Davye in lands	£1	4s
Thomas Robynson in lands	£1	4s

Total £13 16s

PARISH OF ALLHALLOWS GOLDSMITH STREET

Grace Ducke widow in goods	£8	21s 4d
Peter Beavis *esq.* in lands	£5	20s
Robert Vilvaine *Doctor of Medicine* in goods	£7	18s 8d
Lewis Hele *esq.* in lands	£4	16s
Thomas Shapcott *gent.* in goods	£6	16s
Peter Tayler in goods	£6	16s
Jane Martyn widow in goods	£4	10s 8d
John Berrie in goods	£4	10s 8d
William Martyn in goods	£4	10s 8d
Simon Snowe in goods	£3	8s
Mary Poyntington widow in lands	£1	4s
Robert Glanfeild in lands	£1	4s
William Kinge in lands	£1	4s
William Bickton in lands	£1	4s
John Vinicombe in lands	£1	4s

Total £8 8s

PARISH OF ST. PANCRAS

Ralph Herman in goods	£4	10s 8d
Edward Paynter in goods	£3	8s
Peter Southwood in goods	£3	8s
Eleanor Braylie widow in lands	£1	4s
John Eastcott in lands	£1	4s
John Pennye jun. in lands	£1	4s
Nicholas Somer in lands	£1	4s
John Robyns in lands	£1	4s
Phillip Foxwill in lands	£1	4s
John Baker in lands	£1	4s
Henry Hayne in lands	£1	4s

Total £2 18s 8d

PARISH OF ST. PAUL

Edwards Gibbons *gent.* in lands	£6	24s
Christopher Mannaringe *esq.* in lands	£5	20s
Clement Westcombe *Doctor of Medicine* in goods	£6	16s
George Potter in goods	£6	16s
John Whitlocke in goods	£6	16s
m. 2d.		
Margaret Sparke widow in goods	£5	13s 4d
George Lidgingham in goods	£4	10s 8d
Henry Gandye in goods	£4	10s 8d
Simon Saffyn in goods	£3	8s
William Birdall in lands	£1	4s
Aaron Midwinter in lands	£1	4s
John Chappell in lands	£1	4s
Humphrey Cade in lands	£1	4s
William Webber in lands	£1	4s
Thomas Pennyngton in lands	£1	4s
Corporation of Tailors in lands	£1	4s
John Boomer in lands	£1	4s
Michael Trosse in lands	£1	4s
Henry Palmer in lands	£1	4s
Roger Harlewyne in lands	£1	4s
John Watts in lands	£1	4s

Total £9 2s 8d

PARISH OF ST. LAWRENCE

Thomas Isacke *gent.* in goods	£5	13s 4d
Thomas Drewe *gent.* in goods	£5	13s 4d
Richard Longe *gent.* in goods	£4	10s 8d
Alexander Rolles *gent.* in goods	£4	10s 8d
Stephen Robyns in goods	£3	8s
Malachi Monday in goods	£3	8s
James Looman *gent.* in goods	£3	8s
William White in goods	£3	8s
Gertrude Marks widow in goods	£3	8s
Robert Sprague in goods	£3	8s
Thomas Awton in lands	£1	4s
Alan Robyns in lands	£1	4s
William Saunders in lands	£1	4s
William Tucker in lands	£1	4s
George Ralphe in lands	£1	4s
Edward Greenwaye sen. in lands	£1	4s
Henry Bagtor in lands	£1	4s
William Bicklie in lands	£1	4s

Total £6 8s

PARISH OF ST. DAVID

John Levermore in goods	£4	10s 8d
Edward Blackmore in goods	£4	10s 8d
Julian Trosse widow in goods	£3	8s
Andrew Turner in goods	£3	8s
Henry Ley in goods	£3	8s
Henry Pincklie in goods	£3	8s
Dorothy Prouz widow in lands	£1	4s
Nicholas Jefferie in lands	£1	4s
Antony Kifte in lands	£1	4s
Robert Gillard in lands	£1	4s
Henry Hancocke in lands	£1	4s
Richard Jefford in lands	£1	4s
Alice Jesse widow in lands	£1	4s

Total £4 16d

South Ward

PARISH OF ST. MARY MAJOR

John Lynne *Mayor* in goods	£8	21s 4d
Lady Elizabeth Champernone widow in lands	£15	£3
Thomas Flaye in goods	£9	24s
Francis Crossinge *gent.* in goods	£9	24s
Thomas Tooker in goods	£9	24s
Joan Crossinge widow in goods	£7	18s 8d
John Garland in goods	£6	16s
John Webbe *gent.* in lands	£4	16s
Humphrey Curson in goods	£6	16s
Robert Ridler in goods	£6	16s
Elizabeth Cotton widow in goods	£5	13s 4d
John Barrett *gent.* in goods	£5	13s 4d
William Bartlett in goods	£4	10s 8d
John Barons *gent.* in goods	£4	10s 8d
Bernard Pearse in goods	£4	10s 8d
John Baker in goods	£4	10s 8d
Alexander Osborne in goods	£4	10s 8d
John Maddocke in goods	£4	10s 8d
Francis Dyett in goods	£4	10s 8d
Gilbert Budgill in lands	£2	8s
Elizabeth Seldon widow in goods	£3	8s
Robert Hyne in goods	£3	8s

William Tayler in goods	£3	8s
Thomas Newman in goods	£3	8s
William Austyn in goods	£3	8s
Gregory Soper in goods	£3	8s
Richard Cater in goods	£3	8s
Richard Hooper in goods	£3	8s
Henry Drake in goods	£3	8s
Marmaduke Bevercombe in goods	£3	8s
Susanna Upton widow in goods	£3	8s
John Whitrowe in lands	£1	4s
Edward Leminge in lands	£1	4s
James Kinge in lands	£1	4s
Edward Pratt in lands	£1	4s
Peter Comyns in lands	£1	4s
Thomas Aire in lands	£1	4s
Humphrey Gilbert in lands	£1	4s
Edward Searle in lands	£1	4s
Thomas Gandye in lands	£1	4s
John Hyne in lands	£1	4s
Robert Carter in lands	£1	4s
Elias Foxwill in lands	£1	4s
Humphrey Bawdon in lands	£1	4s
George Couch in lands	£1	4s
Henry Everie in lands	£1	4s

Total £24 13s 4d

PARISH OF ST. GEORGE

George White *gent.* in lands	£3	12s
Richard Tickell *gent.* in goods	£4	10s 8d
William Gowldinge in goods	£4	10s 8d

m. 3.

Edward Laurence in goods	£4	10s 8d
Clement Blackingstone in goods	£4	10s 8d
Peter Payne in goods	£3	8s
Richorda Beavis widow in goods	£3	8s
Nicholas Grigorie in goods	£3	8s
William Spiller in goods	£3	8s
William Heathcott in goods	£3	8s
Charles Hoppyn in lands	£1	4s
Jeremiah Hilliard in lands	£1	4s
Tristram Rowe in lands	£1	4s
Robert Clarke in lands	£1	4s
John Lavers in lands	£1	4s
Richard Shilston in lands	£1	4s
John Daniell in lands	£1	4s

Total £6 2s 8d

PARISH OF ST. MARY STEPS

Richard Evans in lands	£5	20s
William Reede in goods	£5	13s 4d
Augustine Drake in goods	£5	13s 4d
Henry Dabynett in goods	£3	8s
Isaac Parradice in goods	£3	8s
Nicholas Markes in goods	£3	8s
Robert Lewes in lands	£1	4s
Alice Giles widow in lands	£1	4s
John Turner in lands	£1	4s
Nicholas Rawlyn in lands	£1	4s
Samuel Clarke in lands	£1	4s
Thomas Basse in lands	£1	4s
Michael Jones in lands	£1	4s
Gilbert Wheaton in lands	£1	4s
Richard Peake in lands	£1	4s
Simon Tucker in lands	£1	4s

Total £5 10s 8d

PARISH OF ST. JOHN'S BOW

Corporation of Weavers and Fullers in lands	[£3]	12s
Thomas Pope in goods	[£4]	10s 8d
Robert Trescott in goods	£3	8s
Nicholas Dennys in goods	£3	8s
Stephen Olliphewe in goods	£3	8s
Richard Pearson in lands	£1	4s
Thomas Hoyte in lands	£1	4s
Agnes Templar widow in lands	£1	4s
Sybil Wade widow in lands	£1	4s
Nicholas Orcharde in lands	£1	4s
William Isacke in lands	[£1]	4s
Thomas Davye in lands	[£1]	4s
Robert Phippes in lands	[£1]	4s

Total [torn: but adds up to £3 18s 8d]

Sum Total [torn: but adds up to £187 6s 8d]

[Signatures: torn]

3. THE POLL TAX OF 1660.[1]

A DUPLICATE Indented of the rates & moneyes assessed on the Inhabitants and Land (*Terr*) tennants within the City & County of Exeter by virtue of an Act of Parliament lately made Intituled An Act for the speedy provission of mony for the disbanding & paying offe the Forces of this Kingdome both by Land and Sea IN WITNES whereof wee the Commissioners in the foresaid Act named our Seales to these presents have put, Dated at the City of Exon aforesaid the First Day of November in the xijth yere of the Raigne of our Soveraigne Lord Charles the second by the grace of God of England Scotland France & Ireland King, Defender of the Faith &c anno domini 1660.

East Ward

PARISH OF ST. MARTIN

John Yeo
Tristram Michell *Collectors*

x	Ralph Herman *esq.* & wife	£10 0s 6d[2]
x	Nicholas Tripe	12d
x	Robert Davye	12d
x	Joan Moresteed	12d
x	Mary Baylie	12d
x	Sarah Hutchins	12d
x	Jane Hutchins	12d
x	Jane Norrish	12d
x	Hannah Whiteburne widow	6s
x	Clemence Blackingstone	12d
x	Christian Rowcliffe	12d
x	George Saffyn	5s
x	William Upton	12d
x	Alan Penny, *merchant*, & wife	40s 6d
x	Ann Penny	12d
	Ann Sherwill	12d
x	Rebecca Salter widow	12d
x	Henry Prigg & wife	4s 6d
x	Elizabeth Prigg	12d
x	Mary Prigg	12d
x	Margery Prigg	12d
x	Elizabeth Ford	12d
x	Hannah Bowdon	12d
x	Malachi Peale	12d
x	John Michell & wife	20s 6d
x	Tristram Michell & wife	8s 6d
x	Elizabeth Palmer	12d
C[3]	Frances Huchenson widow	5s
x	John Dix	4s
x	Elizabeth Dix	12d
x	Thomas Michell	12d
x	Sibyl Parr widow	40s
x	John Parr & wife	30s 6d
x	Hugh Piper *gentleman* & wife	20s 6d
x	Lydia Kerswell	12d
x	Florence Hore	12d
x	Ann Dight widow	2s
x	Walter Dight	12d
x	John Dight	12d
x	Elizabeth Ford	12d
x	Elizabeth Leigh	3s
x	Nicholas Saverye & wife	15s 6d
x	Sarah Pentire	12d
x	Elizabeth Maye	12d
x	Nicholas Hooper & wife	5s 6d
x	George Tuck	12d
x	Rebecca Hanniford	12d
x	Richord Kerslake	12d
x	Abisha Brocas & wife	5s 6d
x	Ann Smith	12d
x	Elizabeth Hickman	12d
x	Margaret Commings widow	4s

[1] E.C.M., Assessments of Subsidies and other Grants, Box 4. The duplicate in the Public Record Office will be found in the Lay Subsidies, E.179/102/482.

[2] Ralph Herman owned and occupied what is now No. 62 High Street (now Chalks' Stores), the second property E. of Broadgate. See *Exeter Charities* (1825), pp. 470-1. He left, in his will dated 25 July 1661, a rent-charge of 52s per annum on the property for the poor of St. Sidwell's parish.

[3] In the original ' Cert ' [for ' Certificate '] is written in the margin. Here, and wherever else it occurs, I have inset it as ' C ' in order to save printing costs.

x	Henry Foster	2s
x	Robert Shoulder	12d
x	Mary Medland	12d
x	Ann Commyns	12d
x	Thomas Smith & wife	5s 6d
x	Elizabeth Ley	12d
x	Humphrey Lee	3s
x	William Elston & wife	2s 6d
x	Henry Elston	12d
x	Juliana Bevercombe widow	2s
x	John Butler *merchant* & wife	40s 6d
x	Thomas Butler	12d
x	Edward Butler	12d
x	Judith Butler	12d
x	Elizabeth Butler	12d
x	Grace Rogers	12d
x	John Barons & wife	12d
x	Francis Stoakes	12d
x	Francis Moore	12d
x	Nicholas Ellerye	12d
x	Antony Salter, *Doctor of Medicine*, and wife	£10 0s 6d
x	Antony Salter junior	12d
x	John Salter	12d
x	Gertrude Salter	12d
x	William Flavell	12d
x	Thomas Avery	12d
x	Robert Parker	12d
m. 1d.		
x	Joan Potter	12d
x	[Frances] Tucker	12d
C	William Durston, *Doctor of Medicine*, & wife	£10 0s 6d
x	Mary Newberye	12d
x	Joan Acland widow	3s
x	Joan Putt	12d
x	Katherine Morrish	12d
x	James Acland	12d
x	Peter Humphry	12d
x	Matthew Allyn	12d
x	Frances Fetton	12d
x	Richard Addams	4s
x	Edward Painter and wife	12s 6d
x	Margaret Gird	12d
x	Elizabeth Jagoe	12d
x	Edward Portbury & wife	7s 6d
x	Joan Weekes	12d
x	Charles Johns	12d
x	Mary Portbury widow	2s
x	William Portbury	12d
x	George Portbury	12d
x	Elizabeth Barwicke	12d
x	William Moore & wife	5s 6d
x	Rachell Holmes widow	4s
x	Anne Wager	12d
x	John Markes	12d
x	Philip Hooper & wife	6s 6d
x	Henry Atherton	12d
x	Mary Weekes	12d
x	Robert Rous *gentleman, Attorney*	£3
x	John Ledgingham & wife	2s 6d
x	Sarah Michell	12d
x	Thomas Hayman & wife	2s 6d
x	William Hall	12d
x	Helen Mountioye	12d
x	John Yeo *cardwiner* & wife	2s 6d
x	Edward Banbury	12d
x	Ann Baker	12d
x	Benjamin Portbury	12d
x	Moses Tabb	12d
x	Richard Lemett & wife	12d
x	Humphrey Coplestone	12d
x	Francis Rolle *gentleman* & wife	20s 6d
x	Susanna Mallett	12d
	Elizabeth Norrington	12d
x	John Blackmore *esq.* & wife	£10 0s 6d
	Joseph Knowling	12d
x	Edward Rownsevall	12d
	Thomas Murry	12d
x	Elizabeth Upright	12d
x	Abigal Upright	12d
x	Joan Davye	12d
x	Elizabeth Fenamore	12d
x	John Warren & wife	20s 6d
x	Jane Fountayne	4s
x	Elizabeth Gale	12d
x	Abigal Gill	12d
x	Thomas Lane & wife	3s 6d
x	Robert Hooper & wife	3s 6d
x	James Averye	12d
x	Francis Beere	12d
x	Susanna Cooke	2s
x	Ann Cooke	12d
x	William Peterson	20s
x	Thomas Wright *gentleman*	12d
x	Lewis Stewklye	12d
x	Ann Arthur	12d
x	Edward Michell *gentleman*	40s
x	Agnes Remmett	12d
x	Samuel Isacke *gentleman* & wife	40s 6d
x	Elizabeth Izacke widow	10s
x	Ann Izacke	12d
x	Ann Macomber	12d
x	John Force	12d
x	Susanna [blank]	12d
x	Mary Tackell	12d
x	Thomas Crossing & wife	2s 6d
x	Christopher Brodridge *merchant* & wife	£3 0s 6d
x	John Addams	12d
x	Mary James	12d
x	John Edwards & wife	3s 6d
x	James Shapley	12d
x	Richard Canter	12d
	Charles Reeder	12d
	Samuel Vise	12d
x	Honor Hill	12d
x	Edward Searle & wife	2s 6d
x	John Williams	12d
x	Ann Jewell	12d
x	Elizabeth Hunt widow	12d
x	Henry Humfry & wife	12d
x	Ann Humfry	12d
x	Henry Humfry	12d

	Jane Looman	12d
x	John Somers & wife	6s 6d
m. 2.		
x	Samuel Strowde	12d
x	Elizabeth Fursdon	12d
	John Bidgood *Doctor of Medicine*	£10 0s 0d
x	John Bartlett & wife	15s 6d
x	Joan Michell	12d
x	William Mallett	12d
x	Alexander Bartlett	12d
x	Dorothy Babb	12d
x	Robert Warren & wife	15s 6d
x	William Cornish	12d
x	Richard Ewens	12d
x	Francis Cooke & wife	2s 6d
x	Elizabeth Dotyn	12d

Within the Close of the Cathedral Church of St. Peter Exon

x	John Cogan	3s
x	John Clarke & wife	12d
x	William Moone & wife	12d
x	Joseph Sams	12d
x	Thomas Parsons	2s
x	Robert Cuningham	12d
x	William Shapcott	12d
x	Thomas Sheeres & wife	12d
x	James Bolt	12d
x	William Kelland & wife	2s 6d
x	Katherine Kelland	12d
x	Joan Milles widow	4s
x	Joan Keene	12d
x	Thomas Magent *gentleman* & wife	14s 6d
x	John Slade & wife	3s 6d
x	Phoebe Snelling	12d
x	William Libbett	12d
	Francis Cudbell [altered from Cutbell]	12d
	John Tiderleigh	12d
	Arthur Southcott *gentleman*	40s
x	John Yeo, *merchant*, & wife	10s 6d
x	Katherine Goffe	12d
x	John Rowcliffe *gentleman*	20s
x	Henry Rowcliffe *gentleman*	12s
x	Nicholas Rowe & wife	12d
x	Robert Baller	12d
s	Elizabeth Manson	12d
x	John Jenkins & wife	12d
x	William Follett & wife	12d
	John Bury	40s
x	William Joice & wife	2s 6d
	William Joice junior	12d
x	John Clarke	12d
x	Joan Browne	12d
	Andrew Harford	12d
x	Edward Salter & wife	12d
x	William Awdrye & wife	12d
x	Judith Pinckley widow	15s
x	Jane Drewe	12d
x	Mary Squire	12d
x	John Bond & wife	12d
x	Thomas Babb & wife	12d
x	Robert Watercombe & wife	12d
x	Richard Greedy & wife	12d
x	Honor Pennye	3s
x	George Score & wife	12d
x	Andrew Holman & wife	12d
x	Edward Thomas & wife	4s 6d
x	Isaac Beere	12d
x	Nicholas Cooke & wife	2s 6d
x	George Conybeere	12d
x	Nicholas Cooke junior	12d
x	Thomas Greene & wife	12d
x	[blank] Dennys widow	12d
x	James Mountstephen & wife	12d
x	John Haydon & wife	12d
x	Paul Draper, *merchant*, & wife	£4 0s 6d
x	Roger Prowse	12d
x	Elizabeth Warrington	12d
x	John Browne & wife	12d
x	John Hoore & wife	12d
x	Henry Harris & wife	12d
x	William Harvy & wife	12d
C	John Davy *esq.* & wife	£10 0s 6d
x	Ann Smith	12d
x	Letitia Smyth	20s
x	Ebott Hatherlye	12d
[x]	William Pope	12d
m. 2d.		
[x	Margaret] Arnold	12d
[x	Mar]garet Barnard	12d
[?]	Margaret Crosse	12d
x	Katherine Davye	12d
x	Samuel Slade & wife	20s 6d
x	Mary Slade	12d
x	Beaten Slade	12d
x	Ann Geyllard	12d
x	Thomas Shapcott *gentleman, Attorney* & wife	£3 0s 6d
	Philip Shapcott *esq.* & wife	£10 0s 6d
x	Dorothy Shapcott	2s
x	Henry Hutchens	12d
x	Edward Penny	12d
x	Judith Bennett	12d
x	Elizabeth Candye	12d
C	Lady [blank] Martyn widow	£6 14s 4d
	Philippa Rolles	12d
	Alice Reeve	12d
x	William Bruton *esq.*	£10
x	Dorothy Bruton	12d
x	Elizabeth Bruton	12d
x	Margaret Bruton	12d
x	Rebecca Bruton	12d
x	Elizabeth Martyn	12d
x	Sarah Worthy	12d
x	Thomas North & wife	3s 6d
x	Elizabeth Lippingcott	12d
x	Nicholas Isacke, *merchant*, & wife	£8 0s 6d
	Margaret Rich	12d

x	Margaret Styling	12d
x	Ann Southcott	12d
x	Philippa Thomas	12d
x	Israel Franck & wife	2s 6d
x	Nicholas Bucknall	12d
x	Anthony Delton & wife	3s 6d
x	Joan Delton	12d
x	Francis Delton	12d
x	Margaret Dowlyn	12d
x	Christopher Sampford & wife	12s 6d
x	Dorothy Harcourte	12d
x	John Ellis	3s
x	Joan Colwill widow	12d
x	Jane Colwill	12d
x	John Dyer	12d
x	James Hoskins	12d
	John Tuckett & wife	12d
	Moses Tresley & wife	12d
	Thomas Taylor & wife	12d
	Richard Twiggs & wife	12d
	Samuel Kerswell & wife	12d
	Richord Loder widow	12d
	Joan Loder	12d
	Benjamin Mader & wife	12d
	William Trehane	12d
	John Skynner & wife	12d
	Grace Vanstone widow	12d
x	William Loder & wife	12d
	Agnes Strang	12d
	John Pope & wife	12d
x	William Bryant & wife	12d
x	Thomazine Bryant	12d
x	Juliana Bryant	12d
	Thomas Parker	12d
x	William Atherton	12d
x	Nathaniel Triggs & wife	12d
x	John Langham & wife	12d
x	John Langham the son	12d
	Susanna Langham	12d
x	Ann Langham	12d
x	Peter Ellis & wife	12d
x	Jonathan Buckepitt & wife	12d
x	Zachary Buckpit	12d
	David Rice & wife	12d
	William Triggs & wife	12d
	Ann Triggs	12d
x	John Gibbs & wife	12d
x	Richard Davy & wife	12d
	Henry Davye	12d
	Joan Clash	12d
	Richard Comyns	12d
	Mary Comyns	12d
x	William Saunders	12d
x	Robert Davy & wife	12d
	Margery Gardner	12d
x	Francis Fryer and wife	6s 6d
x	Joan Hernaman	2s
x	Mary Cord	12d
x	Thomas Ford, *clerk*, & wife	12d
x	Thomas Ford the son	12d
x	Sarah [blank]	12d
x	Thomazine [blank]	12d
x	John Bartlett, *clerk*	12d
x	Mary Bartlett	12d
x	Elizabeth Bartlett	12d
x	Wilmot Willes	12d
x	Elizabeth [blank]	12d
x	John Tickell, *clerk*, & wife	12d
x	Elizabeth [blank]	12d

[Total] £162 2s 4d

m. 3

The Land Rate

x	Mr. Richard Spicer for the house John Edwards lives in	8s
x	William Ball for a tenement in the possession of Francis Cooke	3s 4d
C	Mr. Henry Northleigh for severall tenements in possession of John Mitchell and others	7s 4d
x	The executors of John Rolle *esq.* for a tenement in possession of the said John Mitchell	4s
C	Mr. Isaac Cotten for a tenement in the possession of Abisha Brocas	3s 4d
C	Mr. Bartholomew Newcombe for a tenement in the possession of Edward Paynter	8s
x	John Lewes for a tenement in the possession of Thomas Hayman	3s 4d

Within the Close of St Peters

x	Mr. Joseph Hall for a tenement in possession of Judeth Pinckly widdow	8s
C	The Lady Cholmelhay for a tenement of Anthony Delton & others	4s
x	John Short *gent.* for severall houses in and belonging to the old Callenderhay	12s
x	Mrs. Mary Barons for a tenement in the possession of Joane Mills widow	5s 4d
C	Sir William Courtenay *knight* for a tenement in the possession of Thomas Shapcote *gent.*[1]	8s

Sum £4 6s 8d

Sum total £166 9s 0d

[1] Thomas Shapcott occupied what is now no. 7 The Close, the present Devon and Exeter Institution, which he held on a sub-lease from Sir William Courtenay (See E. Lega-Weekes, *Studies in the Topography of the Cathedral Close*, 176-7). Sir William held a lease from the Dean and Chapter, whose property it was.

Whereof is payd	
To the Sheriffe of the said Citty in mony	£111
For the Collectors Allowance	9s 3d
More on 10 Certificates as before	£28 10s
More to be defalcated out of 38 persons rates that are soe poore that they cannot pay the same before uncrossed, of whose poverty & insufficiency wee are certifyed by the aforesaid Collectors under their hands	£1 18s
More payd the Clarke for his allowance	9s 3d
More unpaid by Phillipp Shapcott *esq.* & his wife	£10 0s 6d
More unpaid by Cannon Bury 40s; and by Doctor Bidgood £10, hee having noe distresse but a Certificate from the university of Oxford	£12
More unpaid by Arthur Southcott *gent.*	£2
More paid by William Harry & William Follett in other parishes	2s

Sum totall of the payments & allowances is £166 9s 00d

PARISH OF ST. PETROCK

Nicholas Redwood
Robert Buckland *Collectors*

x	John Martyn, senior	£10
x	John Martin junior	10s
x	Katherine Martyn	12d
x	Jane Martin	12d
x	Sybil Clifte	12d
x	Joan Colcher	12d
x	William Sanford, sen. & wife	£5 0s 6d
x	William Sanford, jun., & wife	10s 6d
x	John Sanford	12d
x	Ann Sanford	12d
x	William Amye	12d
x	John Trowte	12d
x	Thomas Bennett	12d
x	Katherine Shoulder	12d
x	Mary Glover	12d
x	George Knowling & wife	£3 0s 6d
x	Susanna Follett	8s
x	William Wotton	12d
x	John Coombe	12d
x	Ann White	12d
x	Mary Baker	12d
x	John Ekynes	12d
x	Nicholas Redwood & wife	30s 6d
x	Christofer Ward	12d
[x]	Agnes Callamy widow	12d
[x	Robert] Callamy & wife	12d
m. 3d.		
[x	Ezeckiel W]ood & wife	12d
[x	Dorothy] Cradicke	12d
[x	Sarah] Gill	12d
[x]	John Bremblecombe & wife	12d
x	Sarah Bremblecombe	12d
x	Thomazine Bremblecombe	12d
x	George Thomas	12d
x	John Baylie	12d
x	Gilbert Hill	12d
x	John Colfox & wife	12d
	Samuel Sames	12d
	Angel Woodcocke	12d
	Margery Colfox	12d
	George Bodley & wife	12d
x	Philip Downing & wife	12d
x	Robert Harris & wife	12d
x	Richard Nott & wife	6s 6d
x	George Blochford	12d
x	George Trapnell	12d
x	Susanna Archepole	12d
x	Roger Manning & wife	12d
x	John Sames & wife	12d
x	John Dagg & wife	20s 6d
x	Samuel Smyth	12d
x	Thomas Curry	12d
x	Ann Elston	12d
x	Elizabeth Collye	12d
x	Elizabeth Dennys	12d
x	William Penny & wife	40s 6d
x	John Rowse	12d
x	James Gill	12d
x	Mary Rogers	12d
x	Margaret Carwithen widow	30s
x	John Carwithen & wife	10s 6d
x	Edward Prowse	12d
x	Elizabeth Cotten	12d
x	Henry Hugh & wife	4s 6d
x	George Tomes	12d
x	William Vinton	12d
x	Dorothy Fursdon	12d
x	John Bennett & wife	12d
x	Sarah Bennett	12d
x	Solomia Bennett	12d
x	Joan Tacke widow	40s
x	Edward Aishford & wife	10s 6d
x	Richard Harvye	12d
x	Thomas Tacke	12d
x	Ann Tacke	12d
x	Sarah Beard	12d
x	Ann Radcliffe	12d
x	Edward Anthony & wife	20s 6d
x	Benjamin Anthony	12d
x	Thomas Gilbert	12d
x	Samuel Beard & wife	10s 6d
x	Joan Shepard widow	4s
x	Hannah Dyer	12d

x	Edward Seaward	12d
x	Simon Trobridge	12d
x	Joan Beard	12d
x	Mary Luscombe	12d
x	Thomas Wilcox	2s 6d
x	Robert Buckland & wife	30s 6d
x	George Maton	12d
x	Hannah Allyn	12d
x	Agnes Addams	12d
x	Edward Starr & wife	50s 6d
x	Sarah Starr	12d
x	Francis Kingwell	12d
x	Mathias Nicholls	12d
x	Prudence Cursons	12d
x	John Starr & wife	15s 6d
x	Ellis Pinsent & wife	15s 6d
x	Christopher Snell	12d
x	James Lake	12d
x	Ann Birch	12d
x	John Mayne, *merchant*, & wife	£7 0s 6d
x	Christopher Ceely	12d
x	James Finey	12d
x	Richard Growdon	12d
x	William Beere	12d
x	Mary Liston	12d
x	Mary Whiddon	12d
x	Marcella Kempe	12d
x	Grace Sunter	12d
x	Rose Sampe	12d
x	Matthew Tanner & wife	12d
x	Joshua Jordaine	12d
x	Margaret Barons	12d
x	Joan Trescott widow	6s
x	John Colwill & wife	4s 6d
x	Ambrose Viccarye	12d
x	Margaret [blank]	12d
x	William Cowell & wife	2s 6d
C	Katherine Davidge widow	8s
x	Joan Tayler	12d
x	Dorothy Jefferye	12d
x	Mary Tirlinge	12d
x	James Brownsford & wife	2s 6d
x	Isaac Whitchalse	12d
x	Josiah Eveleigh	12d
x	Joan Lockyer	12d
x	George Evans & wife	12d
x	Elizabeth Evans	12d
x	Agnes Tapper widow	40s
x	Susanna Tapper	12d
	Nicholas Tapper	12d
x	Jason Pope	12d
m. 4.		
x	William Hooper & wife	30s 6d
x	William Hooper junior	12d
x	Joshua Austin	12d
x	Mary Stabb	12d
x	Susanna Dreton	12d
x	Jasper Radcliffe & wife	10s 6d
x	Jasper Radcliffe junior	6s
x	Elizabeth Radcliffe	12d
x	Michael Salter	12d
x	Robert Salter	12d
x	Ann Salter widow	12d
x	Ann Salter	12d
x	Joan Salter	12d
x	Isaac Maudit, sen., & wife[1]	40s 6d
x	Jasper Maudit	2s
x	Gilbert Yard	12d
x	Andrew Pike	12d
x	Hugh Morris	12d
x	Judith Fryer	12d
x	Andrew Quash & wife	40s 6d
x	Alice Quash	2s 6d
x	Rebecca Maudit	6s
x	Mary Bagglehole	12d
x	Susanna Day	12d
x	Hugh Coleman & wife	6s 6d
x	Mary Clarke	12d
x	John Gupwell & wife	20s 6d
x	Ellen Waldren	12d
x	Sarah Holditch widow	20s
x	Mary Wills	12d
x	Rebecca Chard	12d
x	Stephen Burton & wife	10s 6d
x	Thomas Turner	12d
x	Thomas Totle	12d
x	Sarah Tarlton	12d
x	Joan Baker	12d
x	Nicholas Totle & wife	12d
x	Elianor Tothill	12d
x	Thomas Humphry	12d
x	Margaret Veale	12d
x	John Rigge & wife	12d
x	Peter Irish & wife	12d
x	Grace Holwill widow	20s
x	William Murch	12d
x	Richard Smyth	12d
x	Sarah Marley	12d
x	Mary Macey	12d

The Land Rate

x	Mr. Budley for the tenement William Penny liveth in	8s
C	Mr. Richard Lant for 3 tenements in the possession of Edward Ashford, Samuell Beard & Edmond Starr	36s
x	Mr. Samuell Mayne for the tenement Mr. John Mayne liveth in	16s
x	Mr. John Hayne for the house Michaell Salter liveth in	5s 6d
x	Mr. Hooker for the tenement James Brownsford liveth in	5s 6d
x	Mr. John Blackall & Mr. John Jurdaine for the tenement William Sanford liveth in	16d

Sum Totall £68 14s 6d

[1] Isaac Maudit the elder owned the *Fountain Tavern* shown in the frontispiece to this volume.

Whereof is paid
To the Sheriffe of the said Cittie in mony £65 14s 6d
For the Collectors Allowance 5s 6d
More on 2 Certificates as before £2 4s
More to bee defalcated out of 5 persons rates that are soe poore that they cannot pay the same before uncrossed of whose poverty & insufficiency we are certified by the foresaid Collectors under their hands 5s
More paid the Clarke for his allowance 5s 6d

Sum totall of the payments & allowances £68 14s 6d

m. 4d.

[PARISH OF ST.] STEPHEN

Richard Freake
John Pearse *Collectors*

[x	Humphry] Wills & wife	12d
[x]	Alice Wills	12d
x	Henry Ford & wife	12d
x	Jane Hill widow	12d
x	Jane Hill the daughter	12d
x	Thomas Yard	12d
x	John Horman & wife	2s 6d
x	Stephen Hamlyn	12d
x	John Wilcox	12d
x	Antony Penny	12d
x	Ann [blank]	12d
x	Richard Cozens & wife	12d
x	Thomas Smith	12d
x	John Pearse & wife	8s 6d
x	Martha Buckingham	12d
x	Sarah Blagdon	12d
x	Mary Kempe	12d
x	Wilmot Boyes	12d
x	John Lee & wife	2s 6d
x	Mary Davy	12d
x	Elisha Fryer	12d
x	Grace Pottle	12d
x	Ann Williams	12d
	Mary Burgesse	12d
x	Nicholas Wood & wife	8s 6d
x	Thomazine Slade	12d
x	Jane Burch	12d
x	Henry Mills & wife	6s 6d
x	Ann Mills	12d
x	Christian Matherell	12d
x	Thomas Acland	12d
x	John Whitehorne & wife	8s 6d
x	Mary Whitehorne	12d
x	Elizabeth Clarke	12d
x	Roger Wood	12d
x	Mary Tinckcombe	12d
x	George Tompson & wife	2s 6d
x	Daniel Tompson	12d
x	Elizabeth Tompson	12d
x	Hannah Barret	12d
x	Rebecca Barrett	12d
x	Elizabeth Dymond	12d
x	Rachael Lang	12d
	Rebecca Harvy	12d
x	John Collins & wife	12s 6d
x	George Travers	12d
x	Ann Listen	12d
x	Christopher Trehan & wife	3s 6d
x	William King	12d
x	Elizabeth Hine widow	12d
x	Alice Knight	12d
x	Thomazine Midwinter widow	10s
x	William Follet & wife	12d
x	Gertrude Hore	12d
	Richard Tylly & wife	12d
x	Oliver Nevel	12d
x	John Harcourt	12d
x	John Guswell & wife	24s 6d
x	Thomas Guswell	12d
x	Susanna Guswell	12d
x	Hester Goswell	12d
x	John Hore	12d
x	Richard Bellewe	12d
x	George Tiller	12d
x	Walter Badcocke	12d
x	Ann Young	12d
x	Joan Guswell	12d
x	Katherine Shore	12d
x	Deborah Wills	12d
x	John Weekes & wife	12d
x	Ann Weekes widow	12d
x	Christopher Cooze & wife	12d
x	Thomas Avant	12d
x	Orlando Evans & wife	2s 6d
x	Ann Evans	12d
x	William Streete	12d
x	Ann Shapcote	12d
x	Solomia Thomas	12d
x	Humphry Staplyn & wife	12d
x	Peter Trosse *esq.*	£10
x	Peter Trosse the son	12d
x	Susanna Harris	12d
x	William Serle & wife	12d
x	Nicholas Pryer	12d
	Nathaniel Stangdon	12d
x	John Horwell	12d
m. 5		
	Richard Tallett	12d
x	John Tredenicke & wife	12d
x	Richard Reynolls & wife	2s 6d
x	Mary Burgoyne	12d
x	Elizabeth Sparke	12d
x	Mary Siverett	12d

x	Peter Payne	4s
x	Elizabeth Sainthill widow	4s
x	Dorothy Cornelius	12d
x	Dorothy Jackson	12d
x	Richard Guswell	12d
x	Nicholas Joice & wife	2s 6d
x	Lucy Hance widow	12d
x	John Triggs & wife	6s 6d
x	Alice Hooker	12d
	Nicholas Peeke	12d
x	Edward Peeke & wife	12d
x	Thomas Hockadye	12d
x	Philip Job	12d
x	Joshua Mapus	12d
x	Margaret Salter widow	12d
x	Richard Barnes	12d
x	Henry Baddiford	12d
x	Dorothy Bolt	12d
x	James Armestronge & wife	12d
x	Mary Darracott widow	12d
x	William Chowne	12d
x	George Pitts & wife	6s 6d
x	Mary Pitts	12d
x	Joan Hollens	12d
x	Robert Pearse	12d
x	John Fare	12d
x	John Savage & wife	12s 6d
x	[blank] Savage widow	12d
x	Abraham Savage	10s
	John Jones	6s
x	Christian Moore	12d
x	James Searle & wife	12d
	John Searle	12d
	Elizabeth Searle	12d
x	John Pasford	12d
x	John Webbar	12d
x	John Wise	6s
x	Philip Greedy & wife	2s 6d
x	William Bartlett	12d
x	Susanna Hingston	12d
	Grace Marsh widow	12d
x	Grace Parke	12d
x	Mary Johnson	12d
x	Jonathan Langcastle & wife	12d
x	Richard Reynell & wife	6s 6d
x	Richord Milles widow	6s
x	Thomas Collibeare	12d
x	Mary Patey	12d
x	Robert Hawkins	12d
x	George Stephens	12d
x	Margery Hawkins	12d
x	George Potter *merchant*	£5 10s
x	Arthur Acland & wife	£5 0s 6d
x	Thomas James	12d
x	Mary Wotton	12d
x	Richard Freake & wife	8s 6d
x	Hannah Freake	12d
x	Jeremiah Kinge	12d
x	Margaret Ball	12d
x	Frederick Stewer & wife	10s 6d
x	Mary Stewer	12d
x	Ebott Olliver	12d
x	Nathaniel Salter & wife	5s 6d
x	Samuel Salter	12d
x	Prudence Prowse widow	10s
x	Joan Jole	12d
x	Walter Full & wife	12d
x	William Horswell	12d
	Priscilla Waye	12d
x	Lewis Stuckley *clerk* & wife	20s 6d
x	Jane Harris	12d
x	Jane Castle	12d
x	Margaret Dymond	12d
	Wilmot Wyatt	12d
x	Thomas Powell *clerk* & wife	10s 6d
x	John Loosmore & wife	2s 6d
x	Nicholas Tapley	12d
x	Joan Loosmore	12d
	Mary Watkins	12d
x	Philip Pyne & wife	2s 6d
x	Thomas Moore & wife	2s 6d
x	[blank] Moore	12d
	Thomas Crutchley & wife	2s 6d
	Alice Wyott widow	12d
	Joan Blackmore	12d

Total £39 15s 6d

The Land Rate

x	The heires of Roger Mallacke *esq.* decd. for his tenement in the possession of George Pitts	16s
x	Robert Tristram for his Tenement in the possession of Grace Pottle widow	10s
[x]	Thomas Birdall[1] for his tenement in the possession of Orlando Evans	6s
[x]	Jane Hawkins widdow for the tenement Robert Hawkings dwelleth in	10s

[Total] 42s

Sum total [£]41 17[s] 6[d]

[1] Thomas Birdall, *brewer*, held a certain amount of city property also, including the Lamb Inn in Southgate Street. (See E.C.M. Book 190. Rental of City Property, 1671-76, fo. 21).

m. 5d.
[Whereof] is payd

[To the] Sheriffe in money	£40 8s 4d
[For] the Collectors allowance	3s 4d
More to be defalcated out of 14 persons rates that are soe poore they cannot pay their rates before uncrossed, of whose poverty & insufficiency we are certifyed by the foresaid Collectors under their hands	14s
More payd the Clarke for his allowance	3s 4d
More unpayd by John Jones 6s & Thomas Critchly 2s 6d	8s 6d

Sum total of the payments & allowances is £41 17s 6d

PARISH OF HOLY TRINITY

Abel Kinge
John Hawkes *Collectors*

x	Francis Mapowder & wife	5s 6d
x	Mary Randall	12d
x	James Clutterbuck & wife	2s 6d
x	John Dellamayne & wife	12d
x	Thomas Skynner & wife	5s 6d
x	Richard Bennett	12d
x	Edward Dolbeare	12d
x	Samuel Levett	12d
x	Mary Pope	12d
x	William Addams & wife	12d
x	Roger Stanfaire	12d
x	Richard Carfe & wife	5s 6d
x	John Carfe	12d
x	Olive Carfe	12d
x	Grace Farra	12d
x	Stephen Hele & wife	12d
x	Hester Pynny	12d
x	Abel King & wife	12d
x	Daniel Westlake	12d
x	Robert Baller & wife	12d
x	Thomas Pyne & wife	12d
x	Roger Cheeke sen.[1] & wife	£9 0s 6d
x	Susanna Cheeke	12d
	Dorothy Cheeke	12d
x	David Jones	12d
x	Thomas Guy	12d
x	William Turnepenny	12d
x	Elizabeth Turnepenny	12d
x	Robert Gunt & wife	12d
x	Joan Davies	12d
x	Elizabeth Johns	12d
	Wilmot Till	12d
x	John Pawlyn & wife	12d
	Thomazine Pawlyn	12d
x	John Gibbes & wife	12d
x	Henry Mathewe & wife	12d
x	John Gendle & wife	12d
x	William Williams	12d
x	Edward Coombe & wife	12d
x	John Saunders & wife	12d
x	John Robins & wife	12d
x	Samuel Beere & wife	12d
x	Edward Symes	12d
x	Thomas Prigg	12d
x	Henry Collyns & wife	12d
	John Trehane & wife	12d
x	Richard Mathewe & wife	12d
x	Mary Mathewe	12d
x	Nicholas Boyens & wife	12d
x	John Boynes & wife	12d
x	James Searle & wife	12d
	Thomas Lane	12d
x	William Pearse & wife	12d
x	Joan Pearse	12d
x	John Bradfeild & wife	12d
x	George Aggett & wife	12d
x	Martin Brothers & wife	12d
x	Thomas Slocombe & wife	12d
x	John Eastabrooke & wife	12d
x	William Card & wife	12d
x	Abraham Hacker & wife	12d
x	Moses Pinson & wife	12d
x	John Stripling & wife	2s 6d
	Richard Westcott	12d
x	Mary Callaway	12d
x	Robert Trott & wife	2s 6d
x	Thomas Lane & wife	12d
x	Henry Hooper & wife	12d
x	Robert Phillips & wife	12d
x	John Roberts & wife	12d
x	Robert Welsh & wife	12d
x	John Tomes	12d
m. 6		
x	Luke May & wife	12d
x	John Cocke & wife	12d
x	John Bannage & wife	12d
x	Robert Shepherd & wife	12d
x	John Tucker	12d
x	Nicholas Angell & wife	12d
x	John Weekes & wife	12d
x	Samuel Weekes & wife	12d
x	John Chard	12d
x	Richard Morrell & wife	12d
x	John Stavicke & wife	12d
x	William Bishopp & wife	12d

[1] Roger Cheeke, *brewer*, owned the *White Hart* in Southgate Street in 1649 (Izacke, *Memorials of the City of Exeter*, 1724 edn., p. 161).

x	John Rumbellowe & wife	12d
x	Walter Horwood & wife	12d
x	George Litleton	12d
x	William Mann & wife	12d
x	Robert Younge & wife	12d
x	John Bowdon	12d
x	Arthur Harris & wife	12d
x	Jane Dashwood	12d
	Lewis Floudd & wife	12d
x	John Style & wife	12d
x	Bernard Upcott & wife	12d
x	Zachary Hoskins & wife	12d
x	Philip Martyn & wife	12d
x	George Mudge & wife	12d
x	Edward Jessopp & wife	12d
x	John Langlon & wife	12d
x	William Offe & wife	12d
x	John Glanvill jun. & wife	12d
x	[blank] Dashwood & wife	12d
x	Katherine Wood	12d
x	John Glanvill sen. & wife	12d
x	Joseph Glanvill	12d
x	Beaton Glanvill	12d
x	Matthew Ferris & wife	12d
x	John Mutton	12d
x	John Eastabrooke	12d
x	John Rowe	12d
x	John Style	12d
x	John Locke	12d
x	William Glanfill	12d
x	Richard Payne	12d
x	Thomas Manley	12d
	Edith Glanvill widow	12d
x	Edith Glanvill the daughter	12d
x	Francis Ellis & wife	12d
x	John Tucker sen. & wife	12d
x	John Tucker jun. & wife	2s 6d
x	Roger Doddridge	12d
x	Thomas Seelye & wife	12d
x	Alexander Hayne & wife	12d
x	John Rumpson & wife	12d
x	George Sellicke	12d
x	Mary Sellicke	12d
x	Thomas Greedye & wife	12d
x	James Chambers & wife	12d
	George Deane & wife	12d
x	William Tucker & wife	12d
x	Ellis Goldsworthy & wife	12d
x	William Hollocke & wife	12d
x	William Major & wife	12d
x	James Glide & wife	2s 6d
x	Ambrose Breadon	12d
x	Thomas Breadon	12d
x	Katherine Rawlyn	12d
x	William Dyer jun. & wife	2s 6d
x	John [blank]	12d
	Elianor Abbott	12d
	Richard Westcombe, *merchant*, & wife	£5 0s 6d
	Judith Horswell	12d
x	William Ford & wife	2s 6d
x	Samuel Lymbery	12d

x	Nicholas Hooper & wife	12d
	William Wilcoxe	12d
x	John Goffe & wife	12d
x	Elizabeth Gosse	12d
x	Elizabeth Tunnage	12d
x	Walter Moore & wife	12d
x	Elizabeth Moore	12d
x	William Smyth & wife	12d
x	John Penny & wife	12d
x	Thomas Awdry & wife	12d
x	Robert Daniell & wife	12d
x	William Butler & wife	12d
[x	blank] Hamlyn	12d
[x	James] Jessopp	12d
m. 6d		
[x	Judith Doble]	[12d]
[x	John Payne & wife]	12d
[x	Edward Haydon]	12d
[x	Humphrey] (. . . phrus) Bawdon & wife	4s 6d
[x	Bartholomew] Webb	12d
[x]	Robert Webb	12d
[x]	Samuel Bucknell	12d
[x]	Sarah Michell	12d
x	Mary Michell	12d
x	Silfester Follett & wife	12d
x	George Follett	12d
x	Susanna Follett	12d
x	Sophia Follett	12d
x	John Blackmore & wife	12d
x	Grace Lethbridge	12d
x	Thomas Martyn	12d
x	John Darke	12d
x	John Peeke & wife	12d
x	Rebecca Peeke	12d
x	Mary Cholwill widow	12d
x	John Taylor & wife	12d
	John Ellyott & wife	12d
x	Ambrose Hooper & wife	12d
x	Richard Harris	12d
x	James Saunders & wife	12d
x	Edward Withall & wife	12d
x	Elianor Harris	12d
x	John Baker & wife	12d
x	William Baker	12d
x	Elianor Williams	12d
	Antony Bradfeild	12d
	Ann Bradfeild	12d
x	Arthur Thorne & wife	12d
x	John Searle	12d
x	William Penny	12d
x	John Coombe	12d
x	Elizabeth Bazell	12d
x	Abel King & wife	2s 6d
x	Joseph King	12d
x	James King	12d
x	Edward Cheeke & wife	12d
x	German Tilley & wife	12d
x	John Pyne & wife	12d
x	Arthur Harris & wife	12d
x	Richard Simons & wife	12d
x	Margery Symons	12d

x William Nurton & wife 12d
x John Grenfill & wife 12d
x John Saunders & wife 12d
x Christopher Cann & wife 12d
x Thomas Grendon & wife 12d
x George Browning & wife 10s 6d
x William Fowler 12d
John Upton 12d
x Thomazine Burnell 12d
x Ann Charles 12d
x Ann Northway 12d
x Hugh Fry & wife 12d
x Richard Nicks & wife 12d
x Richard Nicks the son 12d
x George Moore 12d
x Robert Richardson & wife 12d
Antony Richardson & wife 12d
x John Russell & wife 12d
x John Pitts & wife 12d
x Joan Chichester 12d
x Thomas Tilley & wife 12d
x John Gantony 12d
x Peter Gantony 12d
x Richard Gantony & wife 12d
x Daniel Butcher 12d
x John Hawkes & wife 12d
x Hannah Hawkes 12d
x John Tucker 12d
x John Fry 12d
x James Taylor & wife 12d
x William Dyer sen. & wife 10s 6d
x Dorothy Dyer 12d
x William Pride 12d
x John Helliar 12d
x Elizabeth Crispin 12d
x Hester Jenckins 12d
x John Tayler & wife 12d
x Nathaniel Farrant & wife 12d
x Thomas Dodson & wife 12d
x Henry Smurt & wife 12d
x Agnes Smurt 12d

m. 7

x John Crossman & wife 12d
x Robert Mogridge & wife 12d
x John Rawlyn & wife 12d
x John Woodward 12d
x Edward Collyns & wife 12d
x John Collyns & wife 12d
x Michael Rooke 12d
x John Purchase & wife 12d
x Edward Moodye & wife 12d
x William Humfry & wife 12d
x William Heath 12d
x William Knowsley & wife 12d
x Mary Purchase 12d
x Richard Kelland & wife 2s 6d
x Charles Michell 12d
George Crooke 12d
x Katherine Davies 12d
x John Perryman & wife 12d
x Stephen Helliar & wife 12d
x William West & wife 2s 6d
x Humphrey Locke & wife 2s 6d
x John Reymond & wife 12d
x Elizabeth Farmelowe 12d
x William Searle & wife 12d
x Nicholas Coffyn 12d
x Joseph Nosseter 12d
x Elizabeth Mathewe widow 2s 6d
x Elizabeth Mathewe 12d
x Alice Mathewe 12d
x John Mathew & wife 20s 6d
x William Pollard 12d
x William Rosser 12d
x Elizabeth Mountstephen 12d
x Katherine Nicholls 12d
x John Bowdon & wife 12d
x William Awdrey & wife 12d
x Margery Withernton 12d
William Bowdon & wife 12d
x Robert Bevean & wife 12d
x Edward Jones & wife 12d
x Thomas Crispyn jun. & wife 12d
x Ralph Ashley & wife 12d
x *Gen'* Rolston & wife 12d
x Thomas Saunders & wife 12d
x Richard Bray & wife 12d
x Stephen Thomas & wife 12d
x Thomas Kelland & wife 12d
x William Cape & wife 12d
x Thomas Powell 12d
x John Moore 12d
x John Wood & wife 12d
x William Guy & wife 12d
x William Michell & wife 12d
x Nicholas Bickley & wife 12d
Amy Munday 12d
x Zachary Preston & wife 12d
x Agnes Preston 12d
x Joan Jaques 12d
x Richard Warren & wife 2s 6d
x Gilbert Comyns 12d
Elizabeth Mathewes 12d
x Thomas Rowe & wife 12d
x John Ley & wife 12d
x William Page & wife 12d
x Henry Bradford & wife 12d
x Hugh Dodridge 12d
x James Downe & wife 12d
x Michael Furlonge 12d
x Joan Furlonge 12d
x William Hole & wife 12d
Katherine Hole 12d
x Mary Hole 12d

Total £33 12s 0d

The Land Rate

[x]	Docter Robert Hall for Mr. Richard Westcombes house	6s
	Mr. John Colliton for his Lands in possession of Thomas Hance & others	18s
[x]	Mr. Robert Ridler for a Tenement in the possession of George Browning	5s
m. 7d		
x	Mrs. Mary Blight for John Gantonys Tenement	18d
x	Mrs. Mary Blight for Wm. Turnepennys Tenement	12d
x	Mrs. Mary Blight for Joane Davyes Tenement	18d
x	The Churchwardens of the Parish Lands	18d
	Doctor Parry for his Lands	4s 6d
[x]	Mr. Robert Ridler for the Tenement Wm. Nurton lives in	2s
x	Mr. Robert Ridler for the Tenement Christopher Cann lives in	2s
x	Mr. Robert Ridler for John Sanders Tenement	18d
x	Mr. Robert Ridler for Thomas Grendons Tenement	12d
x	Mr. Robert Ridler for Hugh Fryes Tenement	12d
x	Mr. Robert Ridler for Richard Nicks Tenement	12d
x	Mr. Robert Ridler for Robert Richardsons Tenement	12d
x	Mr. John Thomas for the Tenement Mr. Francis Mapowder & others live in	8s
x	The said Mr. Thomas for the Tenement Edward Collyns liveth in	4s
x	The said Mr. Thomas for the Tenement John Rawlyns liveth in	16d
	Sum	£3 2s 0d

Sum totall £36 14s 0d

Whereof is payd	
To the Sheriffe of the said Citty in mony	£29 4s 4d
for the Collectors allowance	2s 4d
More to be defalcated out of 20 persons rates that are soe poore that they cannot pay the same before uncrossed, of whose poverty & insufficiency wee are certyfyed under the Collectors hands	£1
More payd the Clarke for his allowance	2s 4d
unpayd by John Colliton 18s & Doctor Parry 4s 6d for their Lands	2s 6d
More by Dorothy Cheeke & Elizabeth Mathew within age	2s 6d
More unpaid by Richard Wescomb & his wife	£5 0s 6d

Sum total of the payments & allowances aforesaid is £36 14s 6d

PARISH OF ST. SIDWELL

Roger Cheeke
Peter Clapp *Collectors*

x	Roger Hart & wife	12d
x	Philippa Hart	12d
	John Medon	12d
x	George Jennings	12d
x	Jeremy Codner & wife	12d
	Elizabeth Endecott	12d
x	Richard Clowter sen.	12d
x	George Barons	12d
x	Edward Shapley	12d
x	William Gravett & wife	7s 6d
x	Bartholomew Allyn	12d
x	Mary Goodwyn	12d
x	Ann Payne	12d
x	Christian Gravett	2s
x	John Trobridge & wife	12d
x	William Hatherly & wife	12d
	Edward Hopping	12d
x	Roger Hopping & wife	12d
x	Richard Jewell & wife	12d
x	Richard Jewell jun.	12d
x	Thomas Jewell	12d
	John Jewell	12d
x	Elizabeth Cooper	12d
x	Thomazine Turner	12d
x	Richard Templer & wife	12d
	Christopher Osmond & wife	10s
x	William Nurton & wife	12d
x	James Yeo & wife	12d
x	John Hockridge & wife	12d
x	John Wilkins & wife	12d
	Roger Bent & wife	12d
x	William Peeke & wife	12d
x	Robert Foxwill	12d
x	Richard Clowter jun. & wife	12d
x	Thomas Drake & wife	12d
x	Joan Baker, sen.	12d

m. 8

x	Joan Baker jun.	12d
x	Charles Rewallyn & wife	2s
x	John Brooking & wife	12d
x	Henry Addams & wife	12d
x	Nicholas Gloyne & wife	12d
	John Quash	12d
	Antony Wolland	12d
x	John Eveleigh	12d
	Richard Filmore & wife	12d
x	William Thomas & wife	12d
x	John Tombes & wife	12d
x	William Squire & wife	12d
x	Robert Coffyn	12d
x	Thomas Greene & wife	12d
x	Samuel Trust	12d
x	John Silley	12d
	John Payne	12d
x	William Gilbert	12d
x	Alexander Langman & wife	12d
x	John Symons	12d
x	Mary Jefferye	6s
x	Thomas Horwood	12d
	Elias Wheller & wife	12d
x	John Wheeler & wife	12d
x	William Bartlett	12d
x	George Roch	12d
x	Charles Blinckhorne & wife	5s 6d
x	Jasper Bishopp	12d
x	Zachary Kelley	12d
	Robert Parker	12d
	[blank] Tucker widow	5s
x	Edward Blackmore *alias* Helliar & wife	2s 6d
x	Frances Blackmore	12d
x	Elizabeth Blackmore *alias* Helliar	12d
x	Thomas Williams & wife	12d
x	Richard Jerman & wife	12d
x	John Collibeare & wife	2s 6d
x	John Jones	12d
x	George Commyns & wife	12d
x	Thomas Hamilton & wife	12d
x	John Baker & wife	8s 6d
x	William Fletcher & wife	12d
x	William Bunce & wife	12d
x	Alice Banbury	12d
x	Martha Anslye	12d
x	James Came & wife	12d
x	John Hutton & wife	12d
x	Thomas Jones & wife	12d
x	Mary Williams	12d
	Peter Lyndon & wife	12d
	John Gorford	12d
	Richard Floudd	12d
	Thomas Whiting & wife	12d
x	Ralph Porter & wife	12d
x	John Roope & wife	2s 6d
	Henry Tanner	12d
x	Thomas Spring	12d
x	John Whiting & wife	12d
	Richord Pentire	12d
x	Robert Bentie & wife	12d
x	Robert Bennett, jun.	12d
x	George Hooper & wife	12d
	Robert Legg, sen.	12d
x	George Sowden, sen., & wife	12d
	George Sowden, jun.	12d
	George Hawkins & wife	12d
x	Samuell Sowden & wife	12d
x	Tristram Pester & wife	12d
x	Thomas Gould	12d
x	Mark Gribble	12d
x	John Gribble	12d
x	Antony Gould	12d
x	James Freind	12d
x	Robert Humfry & wife	5s 6d
x	Elianor Silleye	12d
	William Jenckins	12d
x	Walter Jenkyns	12d
x	Jonas Bampfill & wife	12d
x	Charles Frost	12d
x	Edward Bicknall	12d
x	Francis Bidwill & wife	2s 6d
x	Nicholas Bidwell	12d
x	Margaret Burlace	12d
x	Richard Leacott	12d
	Antony Bodlye	12d
	Thomas Bicknell & wife	2s 6d
x	Edward Pyne	12d
x	Elizabeth Addams	12d
x	George Risdon & wife	12d
x	John Chapple	12d

m. 8d

	Joan Fowler, widow	12d
	Jane Fowler	12d
	Joan Fowler, jun.	12d
x	Susanna Mounsteven	12d
x	William Silley	12d
x	Geoffrey Mounsteven	12d
x	Hugh Averye & wife	12d
	Thomas Voysey	12d
x	Robert Burt, sen. & wife	12d
x	Robert Lackington & wife	5s 6d
x	Clement Triggs	12d
x	John Evans & wife	2s 6d
x	John Sparke & wife	12d
	Richard Filmore & wife	12d
x	Henry Filmore & wife	12d
x	John Mare & wife	12d
x	John Tucker & wife	12d
x	Robert Upcott & wife	12d
x	Solomia [blank]	12d
x	Robert Chaffe & wife	12d
x	Thomas Canes & wife	12d
x	Edward Washbeare & wife	12d
x	John Shepherd & wife	12d
x	Antony Cooke & wife	12d
	John Mounsteven & wife	12d
x	William Searle & wife	12d
x	Prudence Deymond	12d
x	Thomas Cheeke & wife	12d
x	George Seely, jun.	12d
x	Cristofer Seely & wife	12d

x	Humfrey Bury & wife	12d
x	Mary Bury	12d
	Grace Bury	12d
x	Lewis Pooke & wife	12d
	Charles Pearse	12d
x	Richard Bryant & wife	12d
	Richard Bryant the son	12d
x	Christopher London & wife	12d
	Nicholas Dunne & wife	12d
	Samuel Bodley & wife	12d
x	Robert Sainthill & wife	12d
	Richard Sainthill	12d
x	Cristopher Courtis & wife	12d
x	Henry Bealy	12d
x	William Jewell	12d
x	Joseph Drewe & wife	12d
x	Joseph Bowdon	12d
x	Rebecca Drewe	12d
	Thomas Baker	12d
x	John Izacke & wife	12d
x	Dorothy Dart	12d
x	Eleanor Allyn, widow	12d
	Roger Follett & wife	12d
	John Vile & wife	12d
x	Lewis Dell & wife	12d
x	George Dell & wife	12d
	Robert Reede	12d
x	Philip Strayer & wife	12d
	William Dele	12d
x	John Webber & wife	12d
x	Maurice Davye	12d
x	Nathaniel Izacke & wife	12d
x	Roger Cheeke, jun., & wife	£3 0 6d
x	Susanna Jewell	12d
x	Elizabeth Sylle, widow	12d
x	Mary Sylly	12d
x	James Seely & wife	12d
x	Edward Dymond & wife	12d
x	Susanna Elliott	12d
x	William Foxwill & wife	5s 6d
x	James Newton	12d
x	Richard Coaker	12d
x	Richard Elworthy	12d
x	Cristian Horwell	12d
x	Roger Crosse & wife	12d
	William Crosse	12d
x	Bernard Tempenny & wife	12d
	Thomas Lewes	12d
x	[blank] Jones & wife	12d
x	Richord Lee widow	12d
x	Humfrey Perry & wife	12d
x	Jane Keene	12d
	Philip Shapcott & wife	12d
	Thomas Ledge & wife	12d
x	Richard Symons & wife	12d
x	Edward Cheeke & wife	£3 10s 6d
x	Anne Cheeke, widow	20s

m. 9

x	Margaret Jellett	12d
x	Margery Godfree	12d
x	John Corham & wife	12d
x	John Andrewe	12d
x	William Johnson & wife	12d
x	Philippa (Pha') Burnell, widow	12d
x	Richard Jarman & wife	12d
x	James Stone & wife	12d
x	Richard Kneebone	12d
	Henry Richards	12d
x	John Frost & wife	12d
x	Juliane Payne, widow	12d
	John Hill & wife	12d
x	Jane Heath, widow	12d
x	James Rogers & wife	2s 6d
x	Alice Rogers	12d
x	Peter Humfry & wife	12d
x	Obediah Chapply & wife	2s 6d
x	Agnes Chapple	12d
x	Christofer Ley & wife	12d
	William Cooke & wife	12d
x	John Densham & wife	12d
x	Martyn Tarryn & wife	12d
x	Ismael Chapple & wife	2s 6d
	John Browning & wife	12d
x	William Floudd & wife	12d
	Zacharias Richards & wife	12d
	John Luxton & wife	12d
	Thomas Iverye & wife	12d
x	William Pearcey & wife	12d
x	Ralph Winter & wife	12d
x	Thomas Segar & wife	12d
x	William May & wife	12d
x	Thomas Densham & wife	12d
	Robert Staden & wife	12d
x	Mary Seelye	12d
	Grace Seelye	12d
x	James Horwood & wife	12d
x	William Boone & wife	12d
x	Thomas Worthing & wife	12d
x	John Hewett & wife	12d
x	[blank] Hewett, widow	12d
x	Sampson Thompson & wife	12d
x	Thomas Barrett & wife	12d
x	John Hore & wife	12d
x	John Clarke	12d
x	Oliver Horsey, jun.	12d
x	John Bennett & wife	12d
x	Robert May & wife	12d
x	John Horwill & wife	12d
x	Robert Jones & wife	12d
	Katherine Leonard	12d
x	Francis Williams & wife	12d
x	Richard Holland	2s
x	Charles Blishenton	12d
x	Mathew Penrose & wife	12d
x	Thomas Penrose & wife	12d
x	Robert Turner & wife	12d
x	Robert Greeneslade & wife	12d
x	Thomas Rigg & wife	12d
x	Thomas Broadbeare & wife	12d
x	Nicholas Bennett & wife	12d
x	John Blake	12d
	John Ash	12d
x	George Hart & wife	12d
x	John Stepling	12d

x John Smaleridge & wife 5s 6d
x Thomas Smaleridge 12d
x Susanna Smaleridge 12d
x John Kendor 12d
x Thomas Potter & wife 12d
x John Morgan & wife 12d
x Richard May 12d
[x] Hercules Jones & wife 12d
[x] Peter Mortimore & wife 12d
m. 9d.
[x William] Berrill & wife 12d
[x] George Squire & wife 12d
[x] Roger Blue 12d
John Foxwell 12d
x John Heaman & wife 5s 6d
x John Lavers & wife 12d
x Philip Pike & wife 12d
Robert Parsons & wife 12d
Robert Bunny & wife 12d
x John Smyth & wife 5s 6d
x Humfrey Smyth 12d
x Anne Smyth 12d
x Joseph Land & wife 12d
x Elizabeth Webber, widow £3 10s
x Dorothy Jargoe 12d
x Antony Pore & wife 12d
x John James 12d
x Thomas Bennett 12d
x John Hopping & wife 5s 6d
x George Hopping 12d
x Susanna Hopping 12d
x Susanna Baker 12d
x Peter Kinsman & wife 12d
x Hugh Andrewe & wife 12d
x Robert Roberson & wife 12d
Thomas Small & wife 12d
x Silvanus Baker & wife 12d
x John Hayman & wife 5s 6d
x Margaret Hayman 12d
x John Pottle & wife 12d
x Gawin Mathewe & wife 12d
x John Reynolls, jun., and wife 12d
x Mathew Upcott & wife 12d
x Robert Casely & wife 12d
Rebecca Evans, widow 12d
x John Hunney & wife 12d
x William Langdon, jun. & wife 12d
x Nathaniel Horsey & wife 12d
William Kempthorne 12d
x Robert Langdon & wife 12d
x Richard Allyn & wife 12d
x John Smyth, jun. 12d
William Kelley, sen., & wife 12d
x Robert Norrish & wife 12d
x William Kelley, jun. 12d
x John Beckett & wife 2s 6d
William Veale & wife 12d
x Peter Rennffe & wife 12d
x Thomas Smale & wife 12d
x John Gibbons & wife 12d
Edward Webber & wife 12d
Chrysostom Bricknall & wife 12d

Joan Bricknall 12d
Mary Bricknall 12d
x Christopher Cade & wife 12d
x Edward Burnbury & wife 5s 6d
x Richard Gale 12d
x John Gale 12d
x Sarah Gale 12d
x Grace Gale 12d
x Thomas Rennffe & wife 12d
x John Veale 12d
x Henry Carye 12d
x John Newcombe 12d
x Clemence Weekes & wife 5s 6d
x [blank] Wall 12d
x William Langdon & wife 12d
x Philip Blanchard & wife 12d
Philip James 12d
x John Paster & wife 12d
x Peter Clapp 40s
x Anne Croste 12d
James Baker & wife 12d
Robert Lowman & wife 12d
x Roger Hart, jun., & wife 12d
x William Davye & wife 12d
x John Smyth, sen., & wife 12d
m. 10
x George Smyth 12d
Lancellot Smyth 12d
x Roger Reede & wife 12d
x John Penny & wife 12d
William Minefye & wife 12d
x Robert Dorch & wife 12d
x Thomas Bampfill & wife 12d
x John Reynolls & wife 2s 6d
x Hannah Reynolls 12d
x Amos Butcher & wife 12d
x Richard Trunsham 12d
x Richard Thomas 12d
x Rebecca Casley 12d
x John Cood 12d
x Daniel Basse, jun., & wife 12d
x John Whiddon 12d
x John Humphry *Maulster* & wife 12d
x Hugh Fishmore & wife 12d
x Luke Baker & wife 12d
x Thomas Croste & wife 12d
x Robert Saunders & wife 12d
Thomas Brooke 12d
x Peter Huddy & wife 12d
x Mary Huddey 12d
x Abraham Davy & wife 12d
x John Chardon 12d
x Nicholas Phillips 12d
x Thomas Shilston 12d
x Giles Tremlett 12d
x Thomas Coombe 12d
x John Hopping & wife 12d
x Elizabeth Hobbes 12d
x William Lake & wife 12d
x Charles Bidnye & wife 12d
x Tobias Langdon & wife 12d
William Pike 12d

	Henry Hooper & wife	12d
	Prudence Stone, widow	12d
x	Zacharias Sweetland & wife	12d
x	William Comyns & wife	12d
x	Christofer Comyns & wife	12d
x	David Elworthy & wife	12d
x	Thomas Colwill & wife	12d
x	Edward Blight & wife	12d
	Benjamin Moore	12d
	Elizabeth Tucker, widow	12d
x	John Dare & wife	12d
x	John May & wife	12d
x	Cristofer Peard & wife	12d
x	John Hawkes & wife	12d
x	John Dart	12d
	Elizabeth Milles	12d
x	Thomas Balford	2s 6d
x	Elizabeth Angle	12d
x	Hugh Woodward & wife	2s 6d
	Nicholas Kinthorne	12d
x	Thomas Manford	12d
x	Robert Bunny & wife	12d
	John Bunney	12d
x	Philip Southard & wife	12d
x	Thomas Jagoe & wife	12d
x	Anastacia Jagoe	12d
x	William Weekes	12d
x	Cornelius Weller	12d
x	Oliver Horsey, sen., & wife	2s 6d
x	Ezechiel Smyth	12d
x	Peter Bolt & wife	12d
x	Henry Burne & wife	12d
x	John Kedge & wife	12d
	Henry Newcombe	12d
x	William Andrewe & wife	12d
	John Griffing	12d
x	John Humfry Baker & wife	12d
	Richard Daniell	12d
x	John Rumpson & wife	12d
	Daniel Treate & wife	12d
x	Richard Mathew & wife	12d
x	Aldred Baker	12d
x	Samuel Yebsley & wife	12d
x	John Payne	12d
x	John Wiles	12d
x	James Downe	12d
x	John Corne & wife	12d
x	Thomas Wyott & wife	12d
x	Thomas Tawton & wife	12d
x	John Clampitt	12d
m.	10d	
x	Thomas Chollacombe	12d
x	Philip Elworthy	12d
x	George Smyth & wife	5s 6d
x	Elianor Cornish	12d
x	George Manning & wife	12d
x	Thomas Dowdall & wife	2s 6d
x	Jane Dowdall	12d
x	Amy Weekes	12d
	Henry Tanner & wife	12d
x	John Stapling & wife	12d
x	John Reede & wife	12d
x	Thomas Owens & wife	12d
x	John Hill & wife	5s 6d
x	John Ellis & wife	12d
x	Henry Golsworthy & wife	12d
	Ephesian Shorte	12d
	Roger Phillipps & wife	12d
x	Urith Skynly, widow	5s
	Thomas Skinly	12d
x	Richard Miller	12d
x	William Rooper & wife	12d
x	Hubert Whiting & wife	12d
x	John Tuckfeild & wife	12d

Total £42 15s 6d

The Land Rate

x	Nicholas Reynoldes for his houses	5s
x	Robert Wilcox for his house	2s
	The Widow Jacob or Mr. Durant for a house & ground	2s
C	Mr. Henry White for a Close of ground called Jobs Parke	2s
x	John Isacke for his ground	8s
	Moses Tirrell for his ground	5s
C	Mr. White for another Close of ground	2s
x	Mr. Robert Carew for his ground	12s
	Mr. Dinham for his ground	4s
	Mrs. Boone for her ground	4s 6d
		£2 5s 6d

Sum total £45 1s 0d

whereof is payd	
To the Sheriffe of the said Citty in mony	£38 14s 2d
For the Collectors allowance	3s 2d
More to be defalcated out of 87 persons rates that are soe poore that they cannot pay the same before uncrossed of whose poverty & insufficiency wee are certifyed under their handes	£4 7s
More payd the Clarke for his allowance	3s 2d
Unpayd by Christopher Osmond 10s and the widdow Tucker 5s	15s
More unpayd by Moses Tirrell 5s, [blank] Durant 2s, [blank] Dinham 4s & Mrs. [blank] Boone 3s 6d as before for their Land rate	14s 6d
More to be allowed on Mr. Whites Certificate	4s

Sum total of the paymentes & allowances aforesaid is £45 1s 0d

m. 11.

West Ward

PARISH OF ST. MARY ARCHES

Samuel Cawley
Edward Heckman *Collectors*

x	Christopher Lethbridge *esq.* &c & wife	£10 0s 6d
x	Elizabeth Jurdaine	4s
x	James Pym	12d
x	Edward Crosse	12d
x	Thomas Lethbridge	12d
x	William Trevethicke	12d
x	John Lethbridge	12d
x	Thomas Lethbridge	12d
x	Katherine Conybee	12d
x	Judith Mundon	12d
x	Anne Giles	12d
x	Christopher Clarke *esq.* & wife	£10 0s 6d
x	Cristofer Clarke, jun.	12d
x	Elizabeth Clarke	12d
x	Agnes Pearse	12d
x	Thomazine Michell	12d
x	Margaret Westly	12d
x	Robert Walker *esq.* & wife	£10 0s 6d
x	Thomas Walker	10s
x	William Walker	12d
x	Robert Walker, jun.	12d
x	Margaret Walker	12d
x	Elizabeth Walker	12d
x	Mary Walker	12d
x	Francis Pease & wife	4s 6d
x	Elizabeth Hammett	12d
x	Susanna Muncke	12d
x	Richard Sweete *Alderman*	£5 0s 0d
x	Richard Crossing *esq.* & wife	£10 0s 6d
x	Peter Viney	12d
x	Joan Prudham	12d
x	Mary Eaton	12d
x	Jane Watts	12d
x	Thomas Owfeild	10s
x	Thomas Waterhouse, *Doctor of Medicine*, & wife	£10 0s 6d
x	Sarah Johns	12d
x	Richard Candish & wife	3s 6d
x	William Alden	12d
x	Mary Shamplyn	12d
x	Philip Markes	12d
x	Humphrey Stronge & wife	5s 6d
x	Antony Eveleigh	12d
x	Edward Eveleigh & wife	20s 6d
x	Edward Eveleigh, jun.	12d
x	Elizabeth Eveleigh	12d
x	Susanna Langdon	12d
x	Grace Macey, widow	20s 0d
x	Samuel Macey	12d
x	George Question	12d
x	Gilbert Wilton	12d
x	David Robinson	12d
x	Susanna Roppe	12d
x	Edward Heckman & wife	17s 6d
x	Edward Heckman, jun.	12d
x	Mary Geare	12d
x	Joan Marland	12d
x	Elizabeth Tucker, widow	£3 6s 6d
x	Geoffrey Tucker	20s 0d
x	Richard Tucker & wife	20s 6d
x	Eleanor Jotes	12d
x	Honor Dart	12d
x	William Bodly & wife	7s 6d
x	Elizabeth Reeve	12d
x	Francis Galhampton	12d
x	Joseph Chappell	12d
x	Elizabeth Inch	12d
x	Job Beard	2s 6d
x	John Boson	2s 6d
x	Mary Ellis	12d
x	Walter Radcliffe	12d
x	Abel Beardon & wife	4s 6d
x	John Atkins	5s 0d
x	John Arrundell & wife	16s 6d
m. 11d		
x	Sarah Arrundell	12d
x	Elizabeth Arrundell	12d
x	Thomas Atkins	12d
x	Elizabeth White	12d
x	Joseph Mawditt & wife	8s 6d
x	John Gardner	12d
x	John Drewe	12d
x	Judith Pope	12d
x	Jane Elston	12d

x	Susanna Giles	12d
x	Samuel Cawley & wife	10s 6d
x	William Kinge	12d
x	Nicholas Peris	12d
x	Mary Kingford	12d
x	Samuel Smyth	12d
x	A Blackmore servant	12d
x	Nicholas Bagwell & wife	5s 6d
x	Joan Bagwell	12d
x	Elizabeth Leach	12d
x	Joseph Fringston	12d
x	William Delve	12d
x	Abraham Gibbs & wife	20s 6d
x	John Dyer	12d
x	Jonathan Fryer	12d
x	John Gibbes	12d
x	William Bennett	12d
x	Elizabeth Bennett	12d
x	Mary Murch	12d
	Dorothy Pearse	12d
x	Elizabeth Chappell	12d
x	Elizabeth Beawill	12d
x	John Luchenson	5s
x	Elizabeth Sivvell	12d
x	Edward Smytall	7s 6d
x	Sarah Snytall	12d
x	Ralph Ireland	12d
x	Henry Menson	12d
x	Stephen Tottle	12d
x	Elizabeth Radd	12d
x	Judith Manlye	12d
x	Elizabeth Trosse	12d
x	Grace Levermore	12d
	Elizabeth Stoyle	12d
x	Mary Leigh	12d
x	Agnes Beare	12d
x	Margaret Venner	12d
x	Richard Triggs & wife	4s 6d
x	Judith Triggs	12d
x	William Fry & wife	12d
	Richard Ferris & wife	12d
x	Peter Ferris	12d
x	Elizabeth Clappe, widow	12d
	Mary Aron	12d
x	Nicholas Glovyer & wife	12d
x	John Legg & wife	12d
x	Obednih Wickington & wife	12d
x	Edward Perryman & wife	12d
x	Philip Gegell & wife	12d
x	Joan Skynner, widow	7s 6d
x	Richard Stacye & wife	12d
x	John Gill & wife	12d
x	Thomas Harris & wife	12d
x	Dorothy Bagwell	12d
x	Richard Langman & wife	4s 6d
x	John Langman	12d
m. 12		
x	Joan Coombe, widow	12d
x	John Crosse & wife	5s 6d
	William Harris	12d
x	Samuel Blake	12d
x	Bernard Commyns & wife	12d
	Elizabeth Commyns	12d
	Margaret Comyns	12d
x	Susanna Disten	12d
x	Elizabeth Growden, widow	12d
x	Francis Bickford & wife	12d
x	Thomas Pilley & wife	12d
x	Richard Chaffe & wife	8s 6d
x	John Chaffe	12d
x	Joseph Chaffe	12d
x	Jane Weale	12d
x	Philip Sparke & wife	12d
	John Northcott & wife	12d
x	Mary Rowland, widow	12d
x	William Rowland	12d
x	Mary Rowland, jun.	12d
x	Evan Williams & wife	12d
x	Richard Lawrence & wife	12d
x	James Tucker & wife	39s 6d
x	Elizabeth Tucker	12d
x	Hannah Dymond	12d
x	William Coombe & wife	12d
	Mathew Leonard & wife	12d
	Stephen Hamlyn & wife	12d
	John Gitt & wife	12d
x	William Tawman & wife	12d
x	Henry Spurr & wife	12d
	Caleb Luscombe & wife	12d
	John Watts & wife	12d
	Agnes King, widow	12d
x	Alice Blacklen	12d
	Richard Owen & wife	12d
x	William Browne & wife	12d
x	Henry Trevill & wife	12d
x	George Edmonds & wife	20s 6d
	Elizabeth Bicknall	12d
x	John Tucker, *merchant*, & wife	£3 0s 6d
x	Anne Ceelye	12d
x	Margaret Clatworthy, widow	40s
x	Grace Grudworthy	12d
x	Katherine Williams	12d
x	Joan Hackwill	6s 8d
x	Elizabeth Hakewill	6s 8d
x	Mary Hakwill	6s 8d
x	Rebecca Fowler	12d

Total [blank]

The Land Rate

C	William Davy *esq*. for the Tenement Edward Eveleigh liveth in	10s
x	Mr. [blank] Hunywood for the Tenement Mrs. Macey liveth in	10s
C	Mr. John Tuckfeild for parte of the Tenement Mrs. Macey liveth in	2s
x	Mr. Thomas Broking for the house William Coomb liveth in	2s
x	Mr. Mary Modyford for the house Richard Candish liveth in	4s
x	Mr. John Saunders for the house Walter Radcliffe liveth in	10s
C	Mr. Francis Lippingcott for the house Mrs. Trosse & Edmond Snytall live in	16s
		54s

Sum totall of the parish aforesaid is £90 11s 2d

whereof is paid	
To the Sheriffe of the said Cittie in money	£87 12s 6d
For the Collectors allowance	7s 4d
More on 3 Certificates as before	£1 8s
More to bee defalcated out of 16 persons rates that are soe poore that they cannot pay the same before uncrossed of whose poverty wee are certified under the Collectors hands	16s
More paid the Clarke for his allowance	7s 4d

Sum totall of the payments & allowances aforesaid £90 11s 2d

m. 12d.

PARISH OF ST. OLAVE

Philip Burgoyne
Robert Seaman *Collectors*

x	Nicholas Broking *esq*. & wife	£10 0s 6d
x	Margaret Broking	12d
x	Frances Broking	12d
x	Alice Brooking	12d
x	Dorothy Broking	12d
x	Hannah Broking	12d
x	Mary Crofte	12d
x	George Cole	12d
x	Elizabeth Goodridge	12d
x	John Acland, *merchant*, & wife	£5 0s 6d
x	Wilmot Ford	12d
x	Elizabeth Gould	12d
x	John Gandy	12d
x	Dorothy Bale	12d
x	Edward Cotten, Clerk	32s
x	William Pyne, *merchant*, & wife	£3 0s 6d
x	Margaret Rawling	12d
x	George Fox	12d
x	John Anthony, *merchant*, & wife	40s 6d
x	Frances Jurdaine	12d
x	Charles Peard	12d
x	Otho Bastard & wife	40s 6d
x	Mary Bastard	12d
x	Mary Heath	12d
x	Joseph Pearse	12d
x	Philip Burgoyne & wife	30s 6d
x	Joan Serle	12d
x	Mary Treslowe, widow	10s
x	Joan Tucker	12d
x	William Cove & wife	10s 6d
x	Elizabeth Taylor	12d
x	John Atwill & wife	8s 6d
x	Mary Atwill	12d
x	Susann Barnes, widow	10s
x	Robert Seaman & wife	5s 6d
x	Margaret ?Dare	12d
x	Mary Nurton, widow	12d
x	Grace Copleston, widow	5s
x	George Copleston	12d
x	Jane Copleston	12d
x	Ursula Copleston	12d
x	Edward Lane	12d
x	Robert Vinicombe & wife	12d
x	James Redman	12d
x	Joseph Miller	12d
x	Katherine Pyne	12d
x	Mary Lapp	12d
x	John Taylor & wife	12d
x	Marian Hadder, widow	3s
x	Mark Pansford	12d
x	John Fox	12d
x	Elizabeth Hawkinges, widow	12d
x	Elizabeth Hawkinges the daughter	12d
x	Mary Hawkinges	12d
x	Elizabeth Squire	12d
x	Katherine Burgesse	12d
x	John Lome & wife	8s 6d
x	Robert Edwardes	12d
x	Honor Richardes	12d
x	Henry Jacob	12d
x	William Bickton & wife	12d
x	Elizabeth Bickton	12d
x	Judith Morton	12d

x	John Mason & wife	12d
x	Arnold Golding	12d
x	John Barnes	12d
x	John Baker	12d
x	Thomas Elwood & wife	12d
x	Simon Pinckombe & wife	12d
	James Crosse	12d
x	John Parsons	12d
x	John Elwood & wife	12d
x	William Sanders & wife	12d
x	Elizabeth Elwood	12d
x	Elizabeth Barker, widow	12d
m. 13		
x	Jeremy Collier	12d
	Elizabeth Gray	12d
x	Robert Hawkinges & wife	12d
	Nicholas Williams	12d
x	Henry Hole & wife	5s 6d
x	Katherine Roch, widow	12d
x	Joan Hole	12d
x	Susannah Norris	12d
x	Richard Coles	12d
x	Peter Hex	12d
x	Jonathan Hawkinges & wife	12d
x	William Roch & wife	12d
x	Philip Cundy & wife	3s
x	Thomas Bond & wife	2s 6d
x	Richard Mayne	12d
	Lucy Peters	12d
x	David Crosse & wife	12d
x	Zacharias Crosse	12d
x	John Wacombe	12d
x	Thomas Wood & wife	4s 6d
x	William Bayly	12d
x	William Copleston & wife	4s 6d
x	Mary Statt	12d
x	Jonathan Langcastle	12d
x	William Norrish	12d
x	Roger Bolt & wife	12d
x	Richard Taylor & wife	12d
x	Jane Wattes	12d
x	Peter Acland	12d
x	Henry Parker & wife	12d
x	Lazarus Parker & wife	12d
x	Henry Hamblyn & wife	12d
x	John Jones & wife	12d
x	William Luckis & wife	12d
x	George White & wife	12d
x	Sarah White	12d
x	Richard Williams	12d
x	Walter Harford & wife	2s 6d
x	John Harford	12d
x	Thomas Castle & wife	12d
x	Rebecca Eggins	12d
x	Mathew Thomas	12d
x	Bartholomew Pridham & wife	12d
x	Anne Eastabrooke	12d
x	Mary Alford, widow	12d
x	Dionisia Gale	12d
x	Henry Westcot & wife	12d
x	John Pole	12d
x	Charles Basse & wife	12d

x	John Ashly & wife	12d
x	Barnard Gale & wife	3s 6d
x	Edward Richardes	12d
x	Agnes Paul, widow	12d
x	Agnes Paul the daughter	12d
x	Benjamin Stenlake	12d
x	Thomas Hawker, sen., & wife	12d
x	John Hawker	12d
x	Ferdinand Nicholls, *Clerk*, & wife	20s 6d
x	John Nicholls	12d
x	Mary Nicholls	12d
x	Elizabeth Reynoldes	12d
x	Margaret Fryer	12d
x	Ezechiel Paice & wife	3s 6d
x	Richard Tucker	12d
x	Richard Luxton	12d
x	Thomazine Snowe	12d
x	Thomas Michell	12d
x	John Plumpton	12d
x	Elizabeth Clappe	12d
x	Richard Dewdney & wife	10s 6d
x	Joan Collins	12d
x	George Turner	12d
x	Richard Trend & wife	20s 6d
x	Aunt Kittie	12d
x	Margaret Maddocke, widow	12d
x	Nathaniel Maddocke	12d
x	Alice Herle	12d
x	Sampson Giles & wife	12d
x	Thomas Ward & wife	12d
x	Walter Harford, jun., & wife	12d
x	Thomas Zellacke & wife	12d
x	Walter Palke	12d
x	John Wall	12d
[x]	William Sampson & wife	12d
	Thomas Munford	12d
[x]	George Dyer & wife	12d
m. 13d		
[x	Leonard] Cocke & wife	12d
[x]	Ann Grindle, widow	12d
x	George Richardes & wife	12d
x	George Barnes, *alien*, & wife	10s 6d
x	Philip Bartlet & wife	12d
x	William Mole & wife	12d
x	Malachias Bucknoll & wife	12d
	William Clatworthy & wife	12d
x	Elianor Matherell	12d
x	Thomas Hopkinges & wife	12d
	Joan Gardner, widow	12d
	Honor Townsend, widow	12d
x	Thomas Curry & wife	12d
x	Edward Bowerman & wife	12d
x	John Barret & wife	12d
x	Peter West & wife	12d
x	Joan Tucker	12d
x	Joan Parking	12d
	John Fowler & wife	12d
x	Lawrence Stripling & wife	12d
	Thomas Couch & wife	12d
x	Richard Pace	12d
x	Ralph Cooze, sen., & wife	12d

x	[blank] Daniel & wife	12d
x	Henry Minton & wife	12d
x	James Holditch & wife	12s 6d
x	Margaret Potter	12d
x	Susanna Hernaman	12d
x	Richard Lee	12d
x	Jonathan Hawkinges, jun.	12d
	Richard Madder & wife	12d
x	Stephen Codmer & wife	12d
x	Robert Ray & wife	12d
x	Dorothy Hollacombe, widow	12d
x	Thomas Martyn & wife	12d
x	Henry Stone	12d
x	Francis Martyn	12d
x	Thomas Woodwall	12d
x	Francis Hayman & wife	12d
x	Thomas Rapson & wife	12d
x	Mary Rapson	12d
x	John Beavis & wife	12d
	Richard Ward & wife	12d
x	Joseph Braunscombe & wife	5s 6d
x	Thomas Stavacke	12d
x	John Perriman	12d
x	Antony Marley & wife	12d
x	John Barter	12d
x	Peter Bastone	12d
x	William Hooke & wife	12d
x	William Burgesse & wife	12d
x	George Marsh & wife	12d
x	William Ellacombe & wife	3s 6d
	Racheal Leamon	12d
x	Robert Ellacombe	12d
x	James Stone & wife	12d
x	Philip Puddicombe	12d
x	John Macey	12d
x	Henry Holman & wife	12d
	William Olliver & wife	12d
	Thomazine Pole, widow	12d
x	Andrew Heard & wife	12d
x	Nicholas Fooke & wife	12d
x	Robert Calwood & wife	12d
x	Jonas Limbry & wife	12d

The Land rate

C	Sir John Yonge, *Knight*	26s
	Sir Thomas Mallett, *Knight*	16s
	Mr. John Colleton	16s
x	Mr. Robert Collins	8s 8d
C	Mr. Thomas Chaffe	12s
x	Mrs. Margery Taylor	4s
x	Mr. Malachy Dewdny	4s
x	The Corporation of Weavers & Fullers	4s
x	Mr. [blank] Eastabrooke, *Clarke*	7s
		£4 17s 8d

Sum totall £48 12s 8d

Whereof is paid	
To the Sheriff of the said Citty in money	£44 1s 4d
For the Collectors allowance	3s 8d
More for 2 Certificates as before	£1 18s
More to bee defalcated out of 14 persons rates that are poore & unable to pay the same being soe certified under the Collectors handes	14s
More to the Clarke for his allowance	3s 8d
More unpaid by Sir Thomas Mallett & Mr. Colleton for their Landes	£1 12s

Sum totall £48 12s 8d

m. 14

PARISH OF ALL HALLOWS ON THE WALLS

Joseph Pince
John Adams *Collectors*

x	Christopher Harris & wife	12d
x	William Till & wife	12d
x	Mary Till, widow	12d
x	John Woodall & wife	12d
x	Robert Pitcher & wife	15s 6d
x	Nicholas Glanvill	12d
x	Thomas Eastabrooke	12d
x	William Tamlyn	12d
x	Robert Pitcher, jun.	12d
x	Thomas Peverton	12d
x	James Tamson	12d
x	Thomazin Glanvill	12d
x	Grace Hatchly	12d
x	Thomazine Mountstephen, widow	12d
x	John Taply & wife	12d

x	John Mathew & wife	12d
x	John Minson & wife	12d
x	Henry Tayler & wife	12d
x	William May	12d
x	Elizabeth May	12d
x	James Hunt & wife	12d
x	John Addams & wife	4s 6d
x	Thomas Waters	12d
x	William Pearse	12d
x	John Trend & wife	12d
x	John Beare & wife	12d
x	William Heard & wife	12d
x	Richard Rider & wife	12d
x	John Nicholls & wife	12d
x	Mathew Worden & wife	12d
x	Leonard Luxton & wife	12d
x	Thomas Hayne & wife	2s 6d
x	Hugh Hayne	12d
x	Susanna Williams	12d
x	George Gibson & wife	12d
x	John Hooper & wife	12d
x	James Blatchford & wife	12d
x	Elizabeth Heard, widow	12d
x	George Penny & wife	12d
x	Henry Hole & wife	2s 6d
x	John Trescot & wife	12d
x	James Archapole & wife	2s 6d
x	Thomas Hayne & wife	12d
x	John Peeke & wife	12d
x	John Barnes & wife	12d
x	John Barnes, jun., & wife	12d
x	Roger Bolt & wife	12d
x	Ralph Luxton & wife	12d
x	Ralph Harbert & wife	2s 6d
x	Ralph Harbert, the son	12d
x	Nicholas Bolt	12d
x	Mathew Mediat & wife	2s 6d
x	Edward Hele & wife	12d
x	Richard Pole & wife	12d
x	John Pearse & wife	12d
x	Thomas Morrish & wife	12d
x	[blank] Parramore, widow	12d
x	Avitia Wheeler, widow	12d
x	Edward Pince & wife	20s 6d
x	Henry Clement	12d
x	Joseph Clare	12d
x	Jane Heydon	12d
x	Jennet Williams	12d
x	Joseph Pince	3s 0d
x	Thomas Burt	12d
x	William Trescot & wife	2s 6d
x	Samuel Trescot	12d
x	Susanna Trescot	12d
x	Edward Twigges & wife	12d
x	Michael Estridge & wife	12d
x	[blank] Howard, widow	12d
x	John Glanvill & wife	12d
x	John Hussey & wife	12d
x	John Poole & wife	12d
x	Simon Simons & wife	12d
m.	14d	
x	Arthur Twiggs & wife	12d
x	John Vann & wife	2s 6d
x	Thomas Jacob & wife	12d
x	Edward Vanstone & wife	12d
x	Antony Paige	12d
x	John Ludlow & wife	5s 6d
x	George Alam	12d
x	Mary Dench	12d
x	Jonathan Hodges	12d
x	Chapcot Tett	12d
x	William Barons & wife	12d
x	Mary Barons	12d
x	Thomas Carter	12d
x	Thomas Taylor & wife	2s 6d
x	William Yeo	12d
x	Robert Keene & wife	12d
x	Thomas May & wife	12d
x	Richard Streete & wife	12d
x	Stephen Moring & wife	12d
x	Richard Barons, jun., & wife	12d
x	Thomas Guest & wife	2s 6d
x	Katharine Lond	12d
x	William Bidgood & wife	2s 6d
x	Alice Driscombe	12d
x	Thomas Edgman	12d
x	John Pince & wife	2s 6d

Total £8 1s 6d

The Land Rate

Sir John Davy *Knight* for his Land	4s 6d
Thomas Achim *esq*, for his Land	4s
Mr. John Trosse for his Land	2s
Mrs. Sara Tothill for a house	5s
Mr. Thomas Orchard for his Land	2s
The executors of Mr. Sweetelandes house	2s
	19s 6d

Sum total £9 1s 0d

whereof is payd	
To the Sheriffe of the said Citty in money	£8 9s 2d
For the Collectors allowance	8d
More to be defalcated out of persons rates that they cannot pay the same before uncrost of whose poverty & insufficiency wee are certifyed under the Collectors hands	[nil]
More payd the Clarke for his allowance	8d
More to be allowed on three certificates as before	10s 6d

Sum total of the payments & allowances is £9 1s 0d

PARISH OF ST. EDMUND

Matthew Axe
Francis Mapowder *Collectors*

x	George Leach	£5 0s 6d
x	Gregory Legg	12d
x	Robert Styant	12d
x	Margaret Baker	12d
x	Elizabeth King	12d
x	John Stile & wife	12d
x	Thomas Bremilcombe & wife	12d
x	Jasper Serle & wife	12d
x	Roger Tether & wife	12d
x	Jane Tether	12d
x	John Hornabrooke & wife	5s
x	James Fabian	12d
x	Thomas Stile	12d
x	Thomas Sharpe	12d
x	John Chambers	12d
x	Agnes [blank]	12d
x	Joan Thomas	12d
x	John Collinges, sen.	4s
x	John Collinges, jun., & wife	2s 6d
x	John Clooman	12d
x	Philip Whetcombe & wife	12d
x	Thomas Arthur & wife	6s 6d
x	Elizabeth Arthur	12d
x	John Arthur	12d
x	John Hutchinges	12d
x	William White	12d
x	Richard Ford	12d
	George Bidard	12d

m. 15

x	John Davy & wife	12d
x	Anne Barons, widow	12d
x	Thomazine Waterfeild	12d
x	Roger Tuckfeild & wife	12d
x	Sybil Sunter	12d
x	Benjamin Bowdon & wife	12d
x	William Bussell	12d
x	Roger Harding	12d
x	Joan Herding	12d
x	Thomazine Herding	12d
x	Roger Woody & wife	12d
x	Anne Woody	12d
x	Nicholas Barons & wife	12d
x	John Bussell & wife	12d
x	Joan Bussell	12d
x	John Dymond & wife	12d
x	Hugh Doble & wife	12d
x	Thomas Mathew & wife	12d
x	John Northcot & wife	12d
x	Robert Rogers & wife	12d
x	William Coleridge & wife	12d
x	Sarah Mediat	12d
x	John May & wife	12d
x	Jane Serle, widow	12d
x	Anne Howell, widow	12d
x	John Callender & wife	12d
x	Roger Woody & wife	12d
x	Humfry White & wife	12d
x	Mathew Tipper & wife	12d
x	Mathew Tipper, jun.	12d
x	Sampson Deacon	12d
x	David Harvy & wife	2s 6d
x	Agnes Mathew	12d
x	Joan Stone, widow	12d
x	John Endicot & wife	12d
x	Andrew Strong & wife	12d
x	John Bolt	12d
	John Joseph	12d
x	Elias Shore	12d
x	James Howell & wife	12d
x	Samuel Howell	12d
x	Joan Howell	12d
x	Joan Simons	12d
x	Elizabeth Heaward	12d
x	Thomas Brothers & wife	4s 6d
x	Anne Brothers	12d
x	Mary Awton	12d
x	Margaret Kennicke	12d
x	Thomas Hole	12d
x	William Bishopp	12d
	Peter Shane	12d
x	John Raphell & wife	2s 6d
x	Susanna Raphell	12d
x	James Dally & wife	12d
x	Leonard Webb & wife	12d
x	Agnes Ashly	12d
x	Isaac Burch & wife	4s 6d
	Grace Harding	12d
x	Baldwin Drew	5s
x	Mathew Lacey	12d
x	John Pulling	12d
x	William Quicke	12d
x	James Boone	12d
x	Joan Fry	12d

x	Henry Hodge & wife	12d
x	William Cooke	12d
x	Thomazine Thomas	12d
x	Margaret Hamlyn	12d
x	Samuel Hugh & wife	12d
x	Thomas Caterly & wife	12d
x	John Martyn & wife	12d
x	Joan Hugh, widow	12d
x	Christofer Marker	12d
x	Constantine Hart & wife	12d
x	William Drescombe	12d
x	Elianor Cocke	12d
x	Henry Dart & wife	12d
x	William Balch	12d
x	Christofer Weekes & wife	12d
x	Henry Salter	12d
x	Thomas Hunt & wife	12d
x	Mathew Rogers	12d
x	Elizabeth Rogers	12d
x	Robert Cannon	12d
x	Hester Cannon	12d
x	John Weekes	12d
m. 15d		
x	William Haysom & wife	4s 6d
x	William Bayly	12d
x	James Collinges	12d
x	William White	12d
x	William Phillips	12d
x	Elianor Dyer	12d
x	Henry Hatherly & wife	12d
x	James Serle & wife	12d
x	Thomas Serle	12d
x	Vincent Trenaman & wife	12d
x	Elizabeth Mapis, widow	12d
	Margaret Mapas	12d
x	William Bennet & wife	12d
x	Sarah Lashbrooke, widow	12d
x	Katherine Clarke	3s
x	Christofer Bennet & wife	12d
x	Katherine Earle	12d
x	Thomas Fox	12d
x	George Budd	12d
x	Christopher Inam	12d
x	John Wills & wife	12d
x	Caritea Berriman	12d
x	Jonas Pinsent & wife	8s 6d
x	Elias Skibbow & wife	12d
x	Andrew Stephens & wife	12d
x	Robert Catford & wife	12d
x	Joseph Harvy	12d
x	Philip Balston & wife	12d
x	Walter Trescot	12d
	Elizabeth Gilbert	12d
x	Ambrose Paige & wife	5s 6d
x	Thomas Mayne	12d
x	Anne Partridge	12d
x	George Drew	2s
x	Margaret Symons, widow	12d
x	Mary Simons	12d
x	William Slade & wife	8s 6d
	Joan Liscrowe	12d
x	William Wind & wife	3s 6d
x	Germond Wollacot	12d
x	Joan Mathew	12d
x	Sarah Field	12d
x	Humphry White & wife	12d
x	Thomas Lacey & wife	12d
x	Mathew Austin & wife	12d
x	Isaac Woolland	12d
	William Luckis	12d
x	Radford Gill & wife	12d
x	Thomas Newman & wife	12d
x	Anne Jenkins, widow	12d
x	Samuel Tremlet & wife	12d
x	Richard Tattle & wife	12d
x	Alice Tothill	12d
x	Peter Gunstone & wife	2s 6d
x	William Rice	12d
x	Evan Lewes	12d
	William Rechell	12d
x	William White & wife	12d
	John Waters	12d
x	Thomas Horsham & wife	12d
x	William Horsham	12d
x	Tristram Ames & wife	12d
x	Edith Heyson, widow	12d
x	John Haysom & wife	12d
x	Thomas Rogers & wife	5s 6d
x	Susanna Leigh, widow	12d
x	Richard Rogers	12d
x	Richard Burch	12d
x	Henry Westcot	12d
x	Mary Grosse	12d
x	Robert Pewtner	6s
x	Joan Huggins	12d
x	Philippa Packer	12d
x	Roger Huggins	12d
x	Josias Bucknall & wife	20s 6d
x	John Sparke	12d
x	Mathew Simons	12d
x	Robert Cooke	12d
x	Robert Delbridge	12d
x	Robert Sparke	12d
x	John Gould	12d
x	Thomas Huggins	12d
x	Susanna Geane	12d
x	Morgan Philly & wife	20s 6d
x	Edward Pigion	12d
x	Katharine Rice	12d
x	John Dagworthy & wife	12d
x	Edward Skinner	12d
m. 16		
x	Joan Bevill	12d
x	Sarah Bevill	12d
x	Mary Bevill	12d
x	Henry Casely & wife	12d
x	Richard Jurden & wife	12d
x	John Peter & wife	12d
x	Samuel Fox & wife	12d
x	William Commings	12d
x	Robert Easton & wife	12d
x	Christian Acreman	12d
x	Roger Taylor & wife	12d
x	William Coombe & wife	12d

x	John Hawker & wife	12d
x	John Simmons & wife	12d
x	William Rule	12d
x	John Hewett & wife	12d
x	Thomas Casely & wife	12d
x	William Holder	12d
x	Stephen Reed	12d
x	Zacheus Crapp & wife	12d
x	Edward Strong & wife	12d
x	Philip Tamlyn & wife	2s 6d
x	Richard Tragoner	12d
x	Joan Courtis	12d
x	Thomas Salisbury & wife	12d
x	Richard Savage & wife	12d
x	Richard Axe and wife	12d
x	Katherine Martyn	12d
x	Robert Paige & wife	12d
x	Joan Warner	12d
x	Joan Austyn	12d
x	Richard Tamlyn & wife	2s 6d
x	Thomas Holwill	12d
x	Tristram Tragoner	12d
x	Mathew Axe & wife	30s 6d
x	Letitia Bennett	10s
x	Thomas Banckes	12d
x	Richard Coxe	12d
x	Richard Peach	12d
x	Fenies Preist	12d
x	Mary Bond	12d
x	Precilla Tuckfeild	12d
x	Margaret Holder	10s
x	Antony Mapowder & wife	5s 6d
	Elizabeth Gidley	4s
x	Henry Jeanes & wife	12d
x	Elizabeth Poe	12d
x	John Binmore & wife	12d
x	Hubert Griffen & wife	6s 6d
x	Charles Browning	12d
x	John Manley & wife	6s 6d
x	Margaret Townsend	12d
x	Richard Yennett	12d
x	Richard King & wife	12d
x	John Knight & wife	12d
	John Irish	12d
	John Snow	12d
x	Thomas Gully & wife	12d
	John Gillard	12d
	Mary Jervis	12d
x	Isaac Stone & wife	12d
x	John Holder	20s 6d
x	Nicholas Holder	12d
	Thomas Newman	15s
x	Agnes Pince	12d
x	Margaret Drake	12d
x	Richard Berdon	12d
x	Stephen Facey & wife	12d
x	Bartholomew Langly	12d
	Robert Beavill & wife	12d
x	Joan Gorring	12d
x	William Clogge & wife	12d
x	Margaret Hellier, widow	5s
x	Mary Pope, widow	12d
m.	16d	
x	John Pope	12d
x	Samuel Pope	12d
x	Elizabeth Rogers	12d
x	John Yelland & wife	4s 6d
x	Elianor Meadway	12d
x	Nicholas Bickford & wife	12d
x	Nicholas Bickford, jun.	12d
x	Peter Clarke	12d
x	Mary Poole	12d
	Rebecca Moone	12d
x	Margaret Atway	12d
x	Thomas Meade & wife	12d
x	George Fox & wife	12d
x	Margaret Fox	12d
x	Gilbert Keene & wife	5s 6d
x	Edward Brooke	12d
x	Randall Cane	12d
x	Ellianor Saunders, widow	12d
x	Josias Woollacot & wife	12d
x	Sarah Gale	12d
x	William Hele & wife	12d
	Mary Cole	12d
x	Elizabeth Catford	12d

Total £31 5s 0d

The Land Rate

C	Mr. William Wills for his rents	6s
x	Gregory Bonifant for his rents	2s 6d
C	The heires of Mr. Martyn of Lyndridge for his rentes	6s 9d
C	The heires of Hunt for his rentes	4s
x	Mrs. Alice Turner for her rent	2s
x	Mrs. Katherine Pyle for her Mills	48s
x	Mrs. Anne Gould for her rent	2s 6d
C	Mr. John Whiddon for his rent	2s
x	William Holcombe for his rent	6s
		£3 19s 9d

Sum total £35 4s 9d

Whereof is payd	
To the Sheriffe of the said Citty in mony	£33 6s 8d
For the Collectors allowance	2s 8d
More to be defalcated out of 14 persons rates that are soe poore that they cannot pay the same before uncrossed, of whose poverty & insufficiency wee are certified under the Collectors handes	14s
More payd the Clarke for his allowance	2s 8d
More to be allowed on fower Certificates as before	18s 9d
	£35 4s 9d

Sum totall of the paymentes & allowances aforesaid is £35 4s 9d

North Ward

PARISH OF ST. KERRIAN

George Tothill
John Starr *Collectors*

x	Elizabeth Westcombe, widow	£3 6s 8d
x	William Bruen, *merchant*, & wife	£5 0s 6d
x	Alan Lide	12d
x	Agnes Elwood	12d
x	Elizabeth Snell	12d
	Bridget Strong	12d
x	John Browne & wife	2s 6d
x	Christian Robinson, widow	12d
x	Thomas Robinson	12d
x	Mathew Robinson	12d
x	Nicholas Buckland & wife	10s 6d
m. 17		
x	Margaret Hill	12d
x	Isaac Maudit & wife	10s 6d
x	Mary Barter	12d
x	John Starr & wife	15s 6d
x	Nicholas Kendall	12d
x	Susanna Newell	12d
x	Elizabeth Yeo, widow	20s
x	Caritia Adams	12d
x	John Clapp & wife	12d
x	Walter Deeble, *merchant*	£6 0s 0d
x	Edward Giles, *gent.* & wife	20s 6d
x	Agnes Deeble	12d
x	Elizabeth Deeble	12d
x	John Weeks	12d
x	Susanna Dyer	12d
x	Grace Phere	12d
x	Rebecca Trosse, widow	£4 0s 0d
x	James Battyn, *gent.*, & wife	40s 6d
x	Ellianor Grigg	12d
x	Thomazine Skinner	12d
x	Joan Baker	12d
x	Jane Churchill	12d
x	John Geare	12d
x	William Shower, *merchant*, & wife	£3 0s 6d
x	Richard Hooke	12d
x	Joan Westcot	12d
x	Mary Allen	12d
x	Richard Paice, sen.	12d
	Richard Paice, jun.	12d
x	Francis Jewell & wife	12d
x	Roger Jewell & wife	12d
x	John Pratt	12d
x	John Wood & wife	12d
x	George Shapcot & wife	£4 0s 6d
x	Thomas Payne	12d
x	Christofer Guard	12d
x	Elizabeth Parsswell	12d
x	John Lavers & wife	2s 6d
x	James Marshall, *Alderman*, & wife	£5 0s 6d
x	Richard Marshall	12d
x	James Potter	12d
x	Blanch Vosse	12d
x	Francis Coombe	12d
x	Richard White, *merchant*, & wife	£4 6d
x	Bartholomew White	12s
x	William Cooke	12d
x	Sarah Aire	12d
x	Joan King	12d
x	Mark Downe & wife	12s 6d
x	Welthian Peeke	12d
x	Sarah Thomas	12d
x	Thomas Crispyn & wife	10s 6d
x	Andrew Jeffery	12d
x	Robert Coombe	12d
x	Christofer Hyne	12d
x	John Dudgell	12d
x	Margery Poe	12d
x	Grace Ipsly	12d
x	Barbara Seckham	12d
x	John Munckly & wife	15s 6d
x	Sarah Clether	12d
x	Elizabeth Pyle	12d
x	John Clarke & wife	12d
x	George Yeo & wife	2s 6d
x	Philip Wyett	12d
x	William Jarman	12d
x	Dorothy Dollyn	12d
x	Peter West	3s
x	Nicholas Mediat	12d
x	George Tuthill, *merchant*, & wife	40s 6d
x	Philip Billen	12d

m. 17d

x	Joan Drake	12d
x	Edward Crosse & wife	2s 6d
x	Thomas Corward	12d
x	Bernard Bartlett, *merchant*	£3 0s 0d
x	Mary Bartlet	12d
x	Thomazine Wyet	12d
x	Nicholas Kennicot & wife	20s 6d
x	Nicholas Dynham	12d
x	Nicholas Lavers	12d
x	William Davy	12d
x	John Ford	12d
x	William Millend	12d
x	Elizabeth Greene	12d
x	Nicholas Bolt & wife	6s 6d
x	Mary Drew	12d
x	Edward Prince & wife	2s 6d
x	Antony Dennys	2s
	Katherine Cutteford	12d

Total £55 3s 2d

Whereof is payd	
To the Sheriffe of the said Citty in money	£54 11s
For the Collectors allowance	4s 7d
More to be defalcated for persons rated that are extreame poore	3s
More payd the Clarke for his allowance	4s [7d]

Sum total of the paymentes & allowances is £55 3s 2d

PARISH OF ALL HALLOWS GOLDSMITH STREET

George Trippet
Thomas Gloyne *Collectors*

x	Elizabeth Gould, widow	£3 6s 6d
x	Joan Clarke	12d
x	William Howe & wife	12d
x	Thomas Foxwill & wife	4s 6d
x	John Foxwell	12d
x	Susanna Edwardes	12d
x	Thomazine Seaward	12d
x	Jerome Tothill & wife	12d
x	Philip Jerman & wife	10s 6d
x	Margaret Hart	12d
x	Peter Beavill	12d
	Henry Old	12d
x	Thomas Goosecott & wife	12d
x	Martha Goosecot	12d
x	William Young & wife	2s 6d
x	Edward Cockell & wife	2s 6d
x	Michael Cornish	12d
x	Stephen Vigures	12d
x	Joan Taylor, widow	20s
x	Anne Leach	10s
x	Simon Snow, *esq.*, & wife	£10 0s 6d
x	Anne Sanders	12d
x	Susanna Mountstephen	12d
x	Thomas Mills	12d
x	Simon Bayly	12d
x	James Richardes	4s
x	Dorothy Richardes	12d
x	Dorothy Stephens	12d
x	John Pym, *merchant*, & wife	£4 0s 6d
x	John Pope	12d
x	Edward Hayward	12d
x	Mary Taylor	12d
x	Pricilla Husway	12d
x	George Trippet	8s
x	Richard Periam	12d
x	Roger Tucker & wife	4s 6d
	John Northcot	12d
x	Judith Beere	12d
x	Katherine Dart	12d
x	Robert Eveleigh & wife	5s 6d
x	Robert Loveridge	12d
x	Joan Minterne	12d
x	Anne Palmer, widow	5s
x	Gabriel Holway	12d
	Elizabeth Land	12d
x	Thomas Gloyne & wife	6s 6d

m. 18

x	Gilbert Davy	12d
x	Margaret King, widow	12d
x	Mary King	12d
x	Robert Vilvaine, *Doctor of Medicine*	£10
x	Thomas Westlake, *gent.*, *Attorney*, & wife	£3 0s 6d
x	Joseph Baker	12d
x	William Mitchell	12d
x	Elizabeth Dingle	12d
x	Robert Tothill & wife	12d
x	Sarah Tothill	12d
x	Thomas Tothill	12d
x	William Browne & wife	2s 6d
x	Robert Crocker	12d
x	William Helwill	12d
x	Thomas Webb	12d
x	George Sainthill	4s 0d
x	Edward Sainthill	12d
x	Oliver Old	12d
x	Thomas Palmer & wife	12s 6d
x	Hannah Maddocke	12d
	Joan Drayton	12d
x	Richard March	2s 6d
x	James Daniel	12d
x	Jane Risdon, widow	£4
x	Peter Risdon	10s
x	Elizabeth Pynny	12d

x	Joan Berry, widow	12d
x	Katherine Berry	12d
x	Elizabeth Westcot, widow	24s
x	Thomas Westcot	12d
x	Hannah Westcot	12d
x	John Darke & wife	20s 6d
x	Mary Darke	12d
x	Anne Cater	12d
x	Arthur Isacke	10s
x	Daniel Gundry & wife	5s 6d
x	Mary Guest	12d
x	Joan Catford, widow	8s
x	Ferdinand Ware	12d
x	Thomas Collings	12d
x	Philip Kneebone	12d
x	Thomas Edmondes & wife	8s
x	Thomas Horne	12d
x	Joan Edmondes	12d
x	Joan Russell	12d
x	Henry Floud & wife	10s 6d
x	Richard Parrett	12d
x	Edward Parrett	12d
x	Richard Goffe	12d
x	Hugh Abell & wife	10s 6d
x	Elizabeth Abell	12d
x	Alexander Bennet	12d
x	William Noyes	12d
	Grace Greene	12d
x	William Ham & wife	2s 6d
x	Edward Bryant & wife	6s 6d
x	John Bryant	12d
x	John Pollard & wife	12d
x	John Stavicke	12d
x	John Nusser & wife	12d
x	Christian Flamber	12d
x	Anne Tapscot	12d
x	Nicholas Roades	12d
x	James Rogers & wife	2s 6d
x	William Warren	12d
x	Cipio Greenslade & wife	12d
x	Margaret Fletcher	12d
x	Dorcas Lush, widow	12d
x	Mary Yarcombe, widow	12d
x	George Bustyn & wife	12d
x	James Lillington	12d
x	Peter Cary	12d
x	John Bidwell & wife	2s 6d
x	Thomas Locke	12d
x	Thomas Gould & wife	2s 6d
x	Mary Osborne	12d
m. 18d		
x	Edward Ebdon & wife	3s 6d
x	Stephen Phillipps	12d
x	Thomas Cornish	12d
x	George Thomas & wife	12d
x	Benjamin Risdon	5s

Total £46 14s 2d

The Lana Rate

C	Mr. Thomas Prestwood for severall tenements in the possession of Mrs. Elizabeth Gould & others	14s
C	Bartholomew Newcombe for severall tenements Wm. Young & others live in	10s
x	Mr. John Cary & his wife for severall tenements in the possession of Jane Risdon & others	8s
x	Mrs. Anne Hert for Mrs. Johan Berryes rent	2s
x	Mr. Thomas Hart for severall Tenements in the possession of Peter Turner & others	8s
C	John Tuckfeild *esq.* for severall Tenements in the possession of Thomas Edmondes & others	4s
	Mr. Thomas Butson for a Tenement Mr. John Darke lives in	6s
		£2 12s

Sum total £49 6s 2d

Whereof is payd	
To the Sheriffe of the said Citty in mony	£46 19s 4d
For the Collectors allowance	3s 11d
To the Clarke for his allowance	3s 11d
More to be defalcated on six persons rates before uncrossed who are so poore that they cannot pay the same as we are certifyed under the Collectors handes	6s
More on three certificates as afore	£1 8s
More unpayd by Benjamin Risdon	5s

Sum total of the paymentes & allowances is £49 6s 2d

PARISH OF ST. PANCRAS

John Mongwell
Thomas Atherton *Collectors*

x	Elizabeth Flay, widow	£4 0s 0d
x	Richard Simons	12d
x	Philip Slocombe	12d
x	Margaret Easton	12d
x	Amy Filley	12d
x	Edward Foxwell & wife	£4 0s 6d
x	Margaret Burrington	12s
x	Margaret Foxwell	12d
x	Robert Taylor	12d
x	Anne Foxwell	12d
x	Ellianor Williams	12d
x	Philippa Summers, widow	5s
x	Thomas Savory & wife	10s 6d
x	Margaret Severicke	12d
x	Francis Sanders	12d
x	Grace Parr	4s
x	Susanna Parr	4s
x	Anne Parr	4s
x	Mary Foxwell, widow	5s
x	John Foxwell & wife	10s 6d
x	George Foxwell	12d
x	Anne Bickford	12d
x	Elizabeth Clatworthy	12d
x	Benjamin Beard & wife	7s 6d
x	Richard North	2s 6d
x	John Wills	12d
x	Peter Battishill	12d
x	Joan Rowcliffe	12d
x	Alice Martyn	5s
x	Edward Copleston	2s
x	Elizabeth Copleston	12d
C	Mary Prideaux, widow	£3 6s 8d
x	Dorothy Southard	12d
x	John Robins & wife	5s 6d
x	Mary Robins	12d
x	John Mongwell & wife	15s
x	John Passmore	12d
x	Edward Portbury	12d
x	John Mountstephen	12d
x	Thomas Atherton & wife	20s 6d
m. 19		
x	John Palmer	12d
x	Joan Coleman	12d
x	Giles Burchyoung	12d
x	Peter Taylor & wife	15s 6d
x	John Hayman	12d
	Anne Holsworth	12d
	Agnes Upton	12d
x	Peter Turner & wife	10s 6d
x	John Turner	12d
x	Susanna Turner	12d
x	Thomas Dix & wife	15s 6d
x	Susanna Gregory	2s
x	Thomas Dix, jun.	12d
x	John Brenly	12d
x	Thomas Macumber	12d
x	Anne Syms	12d
x	Edward Wood & wife	5s 6d
x	Zacheus Lee	12d
x	Elizabeth Wall	12d
x	Margery White	12d
x	George Rogers & wife	12d
x	Michael Mill	12d
x	Richard Evans & wife	12d
x	Honor Widwell, widow	12d
x	Thomas Somerton & wife	12d
x	William Somerton & wife	12d
x	Thomas Scorch & wife	12d

Total £21 13s 8d

The Land rate

Anthony Blagdon *gent.* for a tenement Thomas Dix liveth in	8s
John Estcot for severall tenements in the possession of Beniamin Beard & others	12s
	£1

Sum total £22 13s 8d

Whereof is payd	
To the Sheriffe of the said Citty in money	£19 1s
For the Collectors allowance	1s 6d
To the Clarke for his allowance	1s 6d
More to be defalcated out of two persons rates that are poore as wee are Certifyed under the Collectors handes	2s
More on a Certificate for Mrs. Mary Prideaux & her servant Dorothy Southard	£3 7s 8d

Sum totall of the paymentes & allowances is £22 13s 8d

PARISH OF ST. LAWRENCE

Thomas Savage
John Taylor *Collectors*

x	Thomas Savage & wife	8s 6d
x	Anne Savage	12d
x	William Hayter *gent.* & wife	40s 6d
x	Mary Jorden	12d
x	Mary Goffe	12d
	Thomas Baker	12d
x	[blank] Chapman	12d
	Andrew Stephens & wife	12d
x	Giles Newman	12d
x	Nicholas Worthyn & wife	12d
x	John Looman & wife	2s 6d
x	Henry Smith	12d
x	Francis Coffin	12d
x	Alice Lowed	12d
x	Sidwell Pinsent	12d
x	Thomas Long, *Clerk*, & wife	£1 0s 6d
x	Grace Martyn	12d
x	Mary Follett	12d
x	Mary Hamlyn	6s
x	Mary Corham	6s
x	Robert Catford & wife	4s 6d
x	Mary Satterly	12d
x	Robert Dawe & wife	7s 6d
x	John Tombs	12d
x	Joan Abbot, widow	12d
x	Richard Bayly	12d

m. 19d

x	William Stuckey & wife	5s 6d
	Robert Nicholl	12d
x	Christian Norrish	12d
x	[blank] Cornish, widow	12d
	Elizabeth Calender	12d
x	Edward Hill	12d
	John Sanders & wife	12d
x	Henry Rogers, sen.	2s
x	Philip Rogers	12d
x	John Pike	12d
x	Henry Rogers, jun., & wife	12d
x	John Rowe & wife	12d
x	Richard Harris	12d
x	Pricilla Chapple	6s
x	Joan Salter	12d
x	Thomas Day & wife	6s 6d
x	Elianor Adams	12d
x	Richard Pollard, *gent.*	6s
	Martyn Periman & wife	12d
x	Roger Humphry & wife	2s 6d
x	John Haydon & wife	12d
x	Richard Heath & wife	12d
x	John Taylor & wife	4s 6d
x	Zacharias Pearse	12d
x	Elizabeth Hutch	12d
x	Christopher Eithridge & wife	12d
x	Richard Martyn & wife	12d
x	John Dun & wife	12d
	Robert Awton & wife	12d
x	Thomas Hall, jun., & wife	2s 6d
x	William Wood	12d
x	Richard Robinson	12d
x	John Hamond	12d
x	Grace Joanes	12d
x	[blank] Giles, widow	5s
x	Grace Wood	12d
x	Edward Wood	8s
x	Elizabeth Lampry	12d
x	John Comminges & wife	2s 6d
x	John Cominges the son	12d
x	Samuel Higby & wife	12d
x	George Hooper & wife	12d
x	Charles Cox	12d
x	Humfry Finnimore & wife	3s 6d
x	Bridget Berry	12d
x	Dorothy Bigglestone, widow	8s
x	Rebecca Passmore, widow	12d
x	John Abbot & wife	12d
x	Thomas Dowdall & wife	2s 6d
x	Richard Berry	12d
x	John Dynning & wife	3s 6d
x	John Dynning the son	12d
x	Griffen Lewes & wife	12d
x	Elizabeth Shapcot	12d
x	Edith Winball	4s
x	Peter Winball	5s
x	Anne Scott	12d
x	Richard Dare & wife	12d
x	Edward Bradford & wife	2s 6d
	Katherine Samson	12d
x	Peter Hellier & wife	6s 6d
x	Philip Hellier & wife	12d
	Thomas Huish	5s
x	Zipora [blank]	12d
x	Nathaniel Clarke & wife	3s 6d
	Magdalen Swaffing	12d
x	William Waters & wife	12d
x	Margaret Waters	12d
x	Robert Sprauge & wife	12s 6d
x	Peter Baker	12d
x	Nicholas Coote	12d
x	Jane [blank]	12d
x	William Sidford & wife	12d
x	George Manning & wife	12d
	Joan Cooper	12d
x	John Tayler & wife	12d
	William Coffin & wife	12d
	Mary Coffin	12d

m. 20

x	John Baker & wife	2s 6d
x	William Baker	12d
x	Margaret Anderson	12d
x	Gertrude Robinson, widow	12d
	John Clarke & wife	12d
x	Gilbert Daniel & wife	12d
x	Thomas Windham & wife	12d
x	Andrew Raddon & wife	12s 6d
x	Elianor Raddon	12d
x	Ursula Isacke, widow	5s
x	Uusula Isacke the daughter	2s 6d
x	Anne Webb	12d
x	John Eithridge, *Attorney* &c.	£3

x	Joan Foale	12d
x	Thomas Bucknoll & wife	12s 6d
x	Nicholas Pidgeon & wife	2s 6d
x	George Pidgeon & wife	12d
x	Judith Dowrich	12d
x	Thomas Blake & wife	8s 6d
x	Thomas Blake, jun.	12d
x	Robert Ash	12d
x	Grace Essery	12d
x	Thomas Essery	12d
x	Joan Essery	12d
x	George Masters & wife	12d
x	Stephen Bickford & wife	12d
x	Judith Hatchly	12d
x	Zacharias Humphry & wife	12d
x	Margaret [blank]	12d
x	Richard Hingston & wife	2s 6d
x	Richard Hingston, jun.	12d
x	John Goodman & wife	12d
x	William Leight	12d
x	Mary Joanes	12d
x	Thomas Hall, sen.	4s
x	Edith Knight, widow	2s
	Willmot Beale	12d
x	William Trend & wife	12d
	Robert Grinking & wife	12d
x	Abraham Penrose & wife	12d
x	Scipio Crocker & wife	12d
x	Anne Crocker	12d
x	John Dart & wife	12d
x	Timothy Dart	12d
x	Ruth Dart	12d
x	Pricilla Dart	12d
x	Thomas Day, taylor & wife	5s 6d
x	John Wood	12d
x	Thomas Best	12d
x	Nicholas Lovell & wife	12d
x	Timothy Hore & wife	12d
x	[blank] Winball, widow	5s
x	William Wellman	12d
	Debora Daniell	12d
x	Paul Bradford	12d
x	James Hamlen & wife	12d
	William Bunhay & wife	12d
x	[blank] Shephard, widow	12d
x	John Greedy, sen., & wife	12d
x	Daniel Greedy	12d
x	John Greedy	12d
x	Beatea Greedy	12d
x	Thomas Dight & wife	5s 6d
x	Elizabeth Dight	12d
x	Katherine Pites	12d
x	John Smoote & wife	12d
x	Philip Vivian & wife	12d
x	John Richardes & wife	3s 6d
C	David Owen & wife	10s
	Anne Guddridge	12d
x	Hannibal Hayne & wife	2s 6d
m. 20d		
x	Hannibal Hayne, jun.	12d
x	Thomas Webber & wife	12d
	John Foster & wife	12d
	Wilmot Mathew, widow	12d
	Margaret Smoote	12d
x	Cicillia Pratt, widow	12d
x	Elizabeth Pratt	12d
x	John Robertes & wife	12d
x	William Winson & wife	12d
x	Elianor Hale, widow	12d
	Edward Nynnis & wife	12d
x	Nicholas Gribble & wife	12d
x	Gregory Hunt & wife	12d
x	Henry Humphry & wife	12d
	Andrew Robins & wife	12d
	Thomas Halse & wife	12d
x	Henry Glanvill & wife	12d
	Ruth Gannon	12d
x	[blank] Cary, widow	12d
x	Sarah Evans	12d
x	Thomas Holmes & wife	12d
x	Joan Herring	12d
x	John Best & wife	12d
	Richard Warren & wife	12d
x	Nicholas Slanning & wife	12d
x	Richard Luscombe & wife	12d
x	Alexander Hill & wife	12d
x	Philip Greedy & wife	12d
x	James Gallop & wife	12d
x	Thomas Gully & wife	12d
x	John Tarryn & wife	12d
x	Mary Greene, widow	2s 6d
x	Mathew Greene	12d
x	Hester Greene	12d
x	Elizabeth Greene	12d
	Julian Humphry	12d
x	Humfry Southcot & wife	12d
x	Anne Martyn	12d
	John Trott & wife	12d

Total £29 10s 0d

Land Rate

C	Sir Coplestone Banfeild Bart. for his tenementes	8s
x	Mr. William Clenson for his houses	8s
C	Thomas Orchard *gent.* for his houses	10s
C	Bartholomew Newcombe for his tenementes	6s
x	Mrs. Dorothy Cary for Andrew Raddons house	8s
x	Mr. Joseph Prowse for Mrs. Chapples house	8s
		48s

Sum total £31 18s

Whereof is payd	
To the Sheriffe of the said Citty in mony	£28 4s 4d
For the Collectors allowance	2s 4d
To the Clarke for his allowance	2s 4d
More to be defalcated out of 30 persons rates before uncrost who are soe poore that they cannot pay the same of whose poverty & insufficiency wee are certified under their handes	£1 10s
More to be allowed on 4 Certificates as before	£1 14s
More unpayd by Thomas Huish	5s

Sum total of the paymentes & allowances is £31 18s

PARISH OF ST. PAUL

John Bragg
Lewis Greenslade *Collectors*

x	Henry Gandy, sen., & wife	£8 0s 6d
x	Alice Gandy	12d
x	Judith Gandy	12d
x	Dorothy Shapcot	12d
x	Alice Ford, widow	£3 6s 8d
x	Anne Ford	10s
x	Mary Higgens	12d
x	Mary Leigh	12d
x	Katherine Stone	12d
x	Gertrude Ford, widow	40s
x	Elizabeth Copleston	12d
x	John Gandy & wife	40s 6d
m. 21		
x	William Ducket	12d
x	Nicholas Somerton	12d
x	Agnes Whitborough	12d
x	Agnes Tincombe	12d
	Agnes Trise	12d
x	John Southard & wife	12d
x	Richard Southard & wife	12d
x	Elizabeth Radford	12d
x	Sibyl Skinner	12d
x	Richard Carwithy	12d
x	Jane Phillipps	12d
x	Susanna Silly	12d
x	John Norman, *gent.* & wife	20s 6d
x	Bartholomew Canter	12d
x	Sarah Codner	12d
x	Robert Pafford & wife	12d
x	Thomas Kennicot	12d
x	Richard Ley	12d
x	Samuel Tuke	12d
x	Mary Fabian	12d
x	George Good & wife	12d
x	William Hill *Comber*	8s
x	Mary Hill	12d
x	Francis Leyman	12d
x	John Jackment & wife	12d
x	Mary Putt	12d
x	Thomas Herring & wife	12d
x	John Heath & wife	12d
x	Martin Chapple	12d
x	Christofer Parr & wife	12d
x	Susanna Parr	12d
x	Edward Woollcot, jun.	12d
	Thomas Bale & wife	12d
x	Hannah Bale	12d
x	Judith Bale	12d
x	George Ray	12d
x	Margaret Parnell	12d
x	Richord (*Rica'*) Williams	12d
x	Mary Williams	12d
x	Roger Mathew & wife	12d
x	Humphry Chubb & wife	12d
x	John Lyle & wife	12d
x	William Woollcot	12d
x	Henry Norrish & wife	12d
x	James Simons & wife	12d
x	Alice Lyle, widow	12d
x	John Daniel & wife	12d
x	John Pennington & wife	10s 6d
x	Thomas Pennington	12d
x	Katherine Bremilcombe, widow	12d
x	Christian Summers	12d
x	Edward Nurton & wife	12d
x	Anne Sheares	12d
x	Richard Missery & wife	12d
x	William Lewes	12d
x	George Markes & wife	12d
x	Richard Ledgingham	12d
x	Isaac Ledginham	12d
x	William Wotten & wife	12d
x	Dorothy Wills, widow	12d
x	Dorothy Wills	12d
x	Mary Wills	12d
	Thomas Bale, jun. & wife	12d
x	John Pasture & wife	12d
x	Elizabeth Pasture	12d
x	William Staplehill & wife	12d
x	Elizabeth Sheeres	12d
x	Joan Wolcot	12d
x	William Comminges & wife	12d
x	Peter Wills & wife	12d
x	George Hunny & wife	12d
x	Christobel Lightfoote	12d
x	Sarah Crocker	12d
x	Mary Crocker	12d
x	Martha Crocker	12d
x	Peter Irish & wife	12d
x	Peter Irish, jun.	12d
x	Elizabeth Irish	12d

x	Christopher Mountstephen & wife	12d
m. 21d		
x	Dorothy Ledgingham, widow	12d
x	Samuel Hutchinges & wife	12d
x	Thomas Manly & wife	12d
x	Hester Hayne	12d
x	Robert Pryn & wife	12d
x	Philip Hayne	12d
x	Lewis Greenslade & wife	10s 6d
x	George Greenslade & wife	12d
x	Gilbert Greenslade	12d
x	Lewis Greenslade, jun.	12d
x	Thomas Lasky	12d
x	William Rowing	12d
x	John Vigures	12d
x	Richard Fursse	12d
x	Nicholas Manly	12d
x	Humphry Chubb & wife	12d
x	Agnes Somerton	12d
x	Katherine Somerton	12d
x	Thomas Smith & wife	12d
x	John Cooze	12d
x	Elizabeth Joanes	12d
x	Simon Chubb	12d
x	Mary Wood, widow	12d
x	Mary Wood, jun.	12d
x	Tristram Stenlake & wife	12d
x	Simon Kelway & wife	12d
x	Henry Somerton & wife	12d
x	Andrew Ash & wife	12d
x	John Beard	12d
x	Elizabeth Smith	12d
x	Robert Shapcot & wife	12d
x	Christofer Tekle & wife	12d
x	Simon Ven & wife	12d
x	Thomas Downing & wife	12d
x	Joseph Ford & wife	12d
x	Thomas Simons	12d
x	John Dotten & wife	12d
x	Christofer Holland	12d
x	Henry Clarke & wife	12d
x	Henry Clarke, jun.	12d
x	Samson Mallacke	12d
x	Francis Hele & wife	12d
x	Elizabeth Williams	12d
x	Anne Tucker	12d
x	Sarah Luscombe	12d
x	Elizabeth Tucker	12d
x	Anne Sommers, widow	12d
x	Edward Dennys & wife	12d
x	Henry Hancocke & wife	4s 6d
x	Andrew Ebsly	12d
x	Thomas Keene & wife	12d
x	Charles Norrish & wife	12d
x	Charles Vigures & wife	12d
x	Ezekiel Stephens & wife	12d
x	Agnes Boeman, widow	12d
x	Andrew Boeman	12d
x	Peter Halstaffe, jun. & wife	12d
x	Ezekiel Dart	12d
x	Isaac Kendall	12d
x	John Watts & wife	12d
x	Michael Fudge & wife	12d
x	Joseph Tracey & wife	12d
x	William Arnold	12d
x	Margery Gibson	12d
x	John Endicot & wife	12d
x	Thomas Bownser & wife	12d
x	Joan Brooking, widow	12d
x	Alice Brooking	12d
x	Mary Payne, widow	12d
x	Jonathan Grinham	12d
x	William Perry & wife	12d
x	Christofer Edgcombe	12d
x	Susanna Draper	12d
x	Elizabeth Sanders, widow	12d
x	Sarah Bennet	12d
x	Richard Robinson & wife	12d
m. 22		
x	Susanna Reynolds, widow	12d
x	Susanna Reynolds, jun.	12d
x	Thomas Hales & wife	12d
x	Elizabeth Dale, widow	12d
x	Thomas Pafford & wife	12d
x	William Hill, *chandler*	12d
x	Andrew Pearse	12d
x	Richard Morris, *Doctor of Medicine*, & wife	£10 0s 6d
x	Honor [blank]	12d
x	Philip Bastard & wife	12d
x	Wilmot Bastard	12d
x	Bartholomew Anthony, *merchant*, & wife	40s 6d
x	Anne Payne	12d
x	William Hooker	12d
x	John Starr	12d
x	Anne Timelyng	12d
x	[blank] Crosby, widow	12d
x	Joan Barnes, widow	12d
x	Grace Barnes	12d
x	Katherine Evans, widow	£3 6s 8d
x	Katherine Crocker	10s 0d
x	Elizabeth Horwood	12d
x	Agnes Every	12d
x	Anne Holmes	12d
x	John Burgesse & wife	12d
x	Mary Burgesse	12d
x	Susanna Grendon, widow	12d
x	Edward Martyn	12d
x	Susanna Grendon, jun.	12d
	Robert Hunt	12d
x	Joel Reynolds	12d
x	Thomas Bancks & wife	8s 6d
x	Simon Lafers	12d
x	Peter Halstaffe, sen. & wife	12d
x	Stephen Tremlett	12d
x	Samuel Davy & wife	12d
x	George Gill	12d
x	Joan Gill	12d
x	Henry Taunton & wife	12d
x	Samuel Taunton	12d
x	Nathaniel Taunton	12d
x	Mary Paschoe	12d
x	Joan Barrett	12d

x	John Hodge & wife	3s 6d
x	John Packer	12d
x	Henry Lile	12d
x	William Sorrell	12d
x	Martha Stephens	12d
x	Joan Budd	12d
x	Hugh Flower	12d
x	Nicholas Mussell	12d
x	Anne Purchase	12d
x	David Powell	12d
x	Penelope Simons	12d
x	Elizabeth Grosse	12d
x	John Lowman & wife	2s 6d
x	Elizabeth Muxery	12d
x	Christofer Bruer	12d
x	Philip Jordaine	12d
x	Benedict Faro & wife	12d
x	Cristofer Palmer & wife	12d
x	Ralph Cooze & wife	12d
x	Cornelius Cooze Cooze & wife	12d
x	Lucy Thomas, widow	12d
x	Anne Jewell, widow	12d
x	Hannah Jewell	12d
x	Samuel Alford & wife	12d
	Elizabeth Alford	12d
	Dorothy Voysey	12d
x	Robert Bond & wife	5s 6d
x	Abel Heape	12d
x	Robert Reeve	12d
x	Katherine Watts	12d
x	Peter Pitts & wife	12d
x	William Powell & wife	12d
x	Tavernor Cockram	12d
x	Mary Venner	12d

m. 22d

x	William Warren & wife	12d
x	John Bunce & wife	12d
x	Edward Irish & wife	12d
x	Richard Williams	12d
x	Thomas Marker & wife	12d
x	Margaret Prise, jun.	12d
x	Edward Kathericke & wife	12d
x	John Bragge & wife	16s 6d
x	Michael Hide & wife	12d
x	Mary Coleman, widow	2s
	Ursula Jeffery	12d

Bradninch

x	Thomas Chudleigh *gent.* & wife	12d
x	Charles Collings	12d
x	Katherine Leare	12d
x	Dorothy Bassett	12d
x	Francis Child *gent.* & wife	10s 6d
x	Jane Lowde	12d
x	John Pitt & wife	12d
x	Mary Howard	12d
x	John Rooke & wife	10s 6d
x	Elizabeth Brooke	12d
x	Katherine Gifford	40s
x	James Rubyn	12d
x	Elizabeth Brian	12d
x	Honor Daniell	12d
x	Charles Cokin & wife	12d
x	Elizabeth Drewe	12d
x	Mary Gibbons, widow	8s
x	Mulier Johns	12d
x	Humphry Dyer & wife	12d

Total £52 6s 4d

The Land rate

x	Mr. John Webbe for his houses Thomas Kennicot & others live in	9s
C	John Hore *gent.* for his houses Joane Dight & others live in	7s 6d
x	Dun & Catfords Lands John Hodge & others live in	18s
x	John Larramore for his Land William Hill *chandler* liveth in	2s
		36s 6d

Sum total £54 2s 10d

Whereof is payd	
To the Sheriffe of the said Citty in money	£53 6d
For the Collectors allowance	4s 5d
To the Clarke for his allowance	4s 5d
More to be defalcated for persons rates befor uncrossed who are so poore that they cannot pay the same & of whose poverty & insufficiency wee are certifyed under the Collectors hands	6s
More on a Certificate for John Hore	7s 6d

Sum total of the payments & allowances is £54 2s 10d

PARISH OF ST. DAVID

James Marshall, jun.
Antony Gay *Collectors*

x	Robert Hungerford & wife	£4 0s 6d
	Joan Nigro	12d
x	Dorothy Davies	12d
x	Richord (Rica') Audry	12d
x	Elizabeth Jeffery	12d
x	Edward Branscombe	12d
x	Edward Salter	12d
x	Stephen Webber	12d
x	Peter Talby	12d
x	Philip Peeke & wife	12d
x	Elianor Trowte	12d
x	Henry Walker *gent.*	£3
x	John Deymond	12d
x	William Ford	12d
x	Joan Guest	12d
	Mary Scott	12d
x	Richard Seaward & wife	12d
m. 23		
x	Richard Sircombe	12d
x	William Macumber	12d
x	Joan Tucker	12d
x	John Perryam & wife	2s 6d
x	Grace Scott	12d
x	Mary Downing	12d
x	Charles Williams	12d
x	John Tremlett & wife	12d
x	[blank] Tremlet the daughter	12d
x	Robert White & wife	12d
x	Thomas Maynard & wife	12d
x	Robert Wilcox & wife	2s 6d
	William Reeves	12d
x	William Pitts	12d
x	Roger Wilcox	12d
x	Katherine Welsh	12d
	Mathew Knight	12d
	Charles Robins	12d
x	Abraham Mare	12d
x	Richard Greenslade	12d
x	John Drewe & wife	12d
x	Thomas Tucker & wife	2s 6d
x	William Risdon & wife	12d
x	[blank] Risdon the son	12d
x	Hannah Tremlet	12d
x	[blank] Tremlet	12d
x	Abel Hooper & wife	12d
x	Philip Dodridge	12d
	William Rogers	12d
x	Richard Best & wife	12d
	Hugh Shapcot	12d
	Samuel Coombe	12d
x	Elizabeth Jefford, widow	12d
x	Elianor King	12d
x	John Jole & wife	12d
x	Honor Prudham	12d
x	[blank] Hobbs	12d
x	John Chapple & wife	12d
	Margaret Hill	12d
x	Mathew Hill & wife	12d
x	Richard Rugg & wife	12d
x	Mary Davy, widow	12d
x	[blank] Davy the daughter	12d
	Digory Greedy & wife	12d
	Simon Curryer	12d
x	Nicholas Cripsey & wife	12d
x	James Edwards	12d
	Brigant Bonefee	12d
x	William Bennet	12d
x	John Evans & wife	12d
x	William Wood & wife	12d
	George Edwards	12d
x	Robert Snelling & wife	12d
x	John Sanders & wife	12d
x	Peter Edwards & wife	12d
x	Richard Golsworthy & wife	12d
x	Daniel Burnel	12d
x	John Pitts	12d
x	William Bennet & wife	12d
x	Elizabeth Bennet	12d
x	John Bennet	12d
x	Thomas Bennet	12d
x	Andrew Harris	12d
x	Simon Crocker & wife	12d
x	[blank] Crocker the daughter	12d
x	Wilmot Crocker	12d
x	Humphrey Owens	12d
x	John Boomer, jun. & wife	12d
	Robert Please & wife	12d
x	Gregory Woodward & wife	12d
x	Samuel Knight	12d
x	Robert Lyston	12d
x	Thomas Drake	12d
	Mary Senee	12d
x	Christofer Sparke & wife	12d
x	Digory Sparke	12d
x	Thomas Whithaire & wife	12d
x	Nicholas Cornish & wife	2s 6d
x	Josias Glanvill & wife	12d
x	Robert Glanvill	12d
x	Richard Pearse	12d
x	John Seller & wife	12d
x	Richard Prowse & wife	12d
m. 23d.		
x	[blank]	12d
x	Richard Gold & wife	12d
x	William Mitchell	12d
x	Henry Sanders	12d
x	Emanuel Stephens	12d
x	John Newberry	12d
	Agnes Coles	12d
	Mary Thomas	12d
x	John Arundell & wife	2s 6d
x	[blank] Wood, widow	12d
x	Robert Lisse & wife	12d
x	Henry Rolls & wife	12d
x	Theophilus Triggs & wife	12d
x	John Triggs	12d
x	George Lyssett	12d
x	[blank] Staplyn, widow	12d
x	Robert Hixe & wife	12d

x	John Battyn	12d
x	Benjamin Norcot	12d
x	John Hawkes	12d
x	John Keife & wife	12d
x	John Gitson	12d
x	Margaret Shorly	12d
x	Elizabeth Growden	12d
x	John Lake & wife	12d
x	Barnard Hodge	12d
x	Michael Heard	4s
x	Joan Heard	12d
x	William Chilcot & wife	12d
	William Parnell	12d
x	David Leary & wife	12d
	Thomas Ester	12d
x	John Lowman & wife	12d
x	George Rickson & wife	12d
x	John Tucker & wife	12d
x	Richard Sheares & wife	12d
x	Mathew Dambrell	12d
x	John Ladimore	12d
x	Arthur Tucker & wife	12d
x	Richard Bagnall	12d
x	Winifred Burrough, widow	24s
x	Martha Burrough	12d
x	Mary Whitton	12d
x	Richard Lysset & wife	12d
x	Peter Jewell & wife	12d
x	Robert Woolcot & wife	12d
x	John Tyller & wife	12d
x	Henry Thomas & wife	2s 6d
x	Solomy Tiller	12d
x	Peter Tucker & wife	12d
x	Samuel Marwood & wife	12d
x	Richard Wheeler & wife	12d
x	John Braydon	12d
x	Edward Foxwell	12d
x	[blank] Godfry, widow	12d
x	Henry Bolt & wife	12d
	Lewis Keife	12d
x	Edward Branscombe & wife	12d
x	Alice Webber	12d
x	Richard Mortimer & wife	12d
x	Robert Mogridge & wife	2s 6d
x	Elizabeth Haywood, widow	12d
x	Richard Jefford & wife	5s 6d
x	Thomas Jefford	12d
	John Addams	12d
x	Henry Best	12d
x	Nicholas Yeo	12d
x	John Rentfree & wife	12d
x	William Evans	12d
x	Michael Collibeare	12d
x	William Windeat & wife	12d
x	John Heath	12d
x	Richard Dart & wife	12d
x	John Chambers & wife	12d
x	Philip Grigg	12d
x	Henry Bone & wife	12d
x	William Hole & wife	12d
x	Salome Hole	12d
x	John Strang & wife	12d
x	Thomas Clannaborrowe	12d
x	Richard Tremlet & wife	12d
x	Antony Gervis & wife	12d
x	John Jellard & wife	12d
m. 24		
x	George Dart & wife	12d
x	Edward Clarke & wife	12d
x	Jeremiah Waters	12d
	John Triggs	12d
x	Anne Boone	12d
x	John Payne & wife	12d
x	Richard Scory & wife	12d
x	Thomas Tremlet & wife	12d
x	Peter Case & wife	12d
x	Emanuel Dart & wife	12d
x	Joan Dart	12d
x	James Marshall, jun. & wife	30s 6d
x	[blank] Walrond, widow	16s
x	Thomas Bicknall	12d
x	Tristram Loveridge	12d
x	George Stone	12d
x	Agnes Waldron	12d
x	Mary Stripling	12d
x	Susanna Williams, widow	12d
	Nicholas Peeke	12d
x	Susanna Peeke	12d
x	Barnard Watts & wife	12d
	Judith Babb	12d
x	Abraham Harward & wife	4s 6d
	Ursula Herder	12d
x	Elizabeth Buckly, widow	12d
x	Edith Jones	12d
x	Hugh Clarke & wife	2s 6d
x	John Williams	12d
x	Mary Gallaway	12d
x	John Glanvill & wife	12d
x	Abiza Maddocke & wife	12d
	John Ford & wife	12d
	John Smith	12d
	Antony Bodly	12d
x	Richard Upton & wife	12d
x	Rose Upton	12d
x	Nicholàs Manning & wife	12d
	Anne Zellake	12d
x	[blank] Zellake the daughter	12d
x	Nicholas Turner & wife	12d
x	Robert Stitson & wife	12d
x	Thomas Collings	12d
x	John Friersvargus & wife	12d
x	George Warne & wife	12d
x	Honor Warne	12d
x	Richard Webber & wife	12d
x	Humfry Gilbert	12d
x	Mary Barter	12d
x	Thomas Williams & wife	12d
x	Roger Light & wife	12d
x	John Ferrys & wife	12d
x	William Harbert	12d
	Thomas Eastabrooke	12d
x	Antony Guy & wife	5s [6d]
x	[blank] Guy, widow	12d
x	John Guy	12d

x Antony Squire 12d
x John Butt 12d
x Henry Langnill 12d
x Josias Follet & wife 12d
x John Davy & wife 5s 6d
x Gertrude Davy 12d
x Robert Venner & wife 12d
x William Triggs 12d
x John Slade, sen. & wife 2s 6d
x John Leader 12d
x Samuel Fowler & wife 2s 6d
Henry Holmeade 12d
x William Crosse 2s
x Nicholas Notwell 12d
x Anne Crosse 12d
x Marmaduke Waggot & wife 12d
x Margaret Light 12d
x Elizabeth Loveridge 12d
x Mary Morris 12d
x John Berry & wife 12d
x Lewis Keife 12d
x John West & wife 12d
x Joan West 12d
Julian Godes 12d
x Edward Redmills & wife 12d
Edward Redmill 12d
Charles Bayly 12d
m. 24d
x Walter Stockman & wife 12d
x Alice Slocombe, widow 12d
x Thomas Treherne 12d
x Thomas Fuen 12d
x Timothy Abbot & wife 2s 6d
x Edward Divis 12d
Robert Downing 12d
x Thomas Rattenbury & wife 12d
Grace Wood 12d
x Joan Ackey 12d
x [blank] Wood, widow 12d
x Rebecca King 12d
x William Stephens 12d
x Joan Land 12d
x Richard Fursdon & wife 12d
x Herbert Rider & wife 12d
x George Wood 12d
Elizabeth West 12d
x John Bruford & wife 3s
x Thomazine Bruford 12d
x Susanna Bale 12d
x Sibyl Wannell 12d
x William Harvy 12d
x William Buney 12d
x Peter Cooke & wife 12d
x Francis Ware & wife 12d
x Mary Tickle 12d
x Richard Warren & wife 12d
x John Northcot & wife 12d
x John Baker 12d
x Lewis Floate 12d
x William Strang 12d
x Thomas Mundy 12d
Margery Blackmore 12d
x John Sprauge & wife 12d
x Susanna Irish 12d
x George Reynolds & wife 12d
x Thomas Dare 12d
Grace Reynolds 12d
x Gabriel Pudson & wife 12d
x Arthur Dodge & wife 12d
Joan Fell 12d
Mary Arthur 12d

Total £28 2s 6d

The Land Rate

x Mr. Oliver Reed for his house & ground John Payne holdeth 12s
x The same Mr. Reed for land Thomas Hall holdeth 7s
C John Malet *esq.* for lands in possession of Isaac Maudit 24s
x Walter Horwood for his Land in the possession of Winifrid Borough 2s 4d
C Joan Dyer widdow for her Marsh at Cowlybridge 6s 8d
x Elliot Payne & Browne for their Marsh 5s 8d
x Mr. Richard Spicer for his ground called Starcombe 8s
x John Isacke for his ground 4s 9d
Nicholas West for his houses & ground 3s 2d
x Mr. Thomas Kendall for his ground 5s

£3 17s 7d

Sum total £32 0s 1d

Whereof is payd
To the Sheriffe of the said Citty in mony £27 19s 7d
For the Collectors allowance 2s 4d
To the Clarke for his allowance 2s 4d
More to be defalcated out of severall persons rates befor uncrossed, who are extreame poore, as wee are certified under the Collectors hands £2 3s
More on two certificates as before £1 9s 8d
More unpayd by Nicholas West 3s 2d

Sum total of the payments & allowances is £32 0s 1d

South Ward

PARISH OF ST. MARY MAJOR

John Gibbons
Thomas Cunningham
Adrian Hayman
Paul Bale *Collectors*

x	James Pearse *Alderman*	£5
m. 25		
x	Elianor Upton	6s
x	Rachel Pearse	12d
x	Jane Lunney	12d
x	Rebecca Blake	12d
x	Margaret Gilbert, widow	3s
x	Thomas Gilbert & wife	2s 6d
x	Simon Gilbert	12d
x	Grace Collings	12d
x	Henry Dodderidge & wife	12d
x	Robert Mugford	12d
x	William Fill & wife	2s 6d
x	Richard Gilbert	12d
x	John Westcot	12d
x	Joan Jones	12d
x	Eusebius Holmes, jun. & wife	2s 6d
x	John Venner	12d
x	Thomas Ellard & wife	12d
x	William Ward & wife	2s 6d
x	Giles Ward	12d
x	Thomas Dennys	12d
x	John Bale & wife	12d
x	Thomas Floud & wife	10s 6d
x	John Floud & wife	12d
x	Richard Pedler & wife	12d
x	John Stone	12d
x	Thomas Coward	12d
x	Cicillia May	12d
x	Richard Wood & wife	12d
	Mary Champion	12d
x	Richard Rattenbury & wife	12d
x	Richard Browse & wife	12d
x	Emanuel Luscombe	12d
x	Samuel Collings	12d
x	James Veale & wife	2s 6d
x	Grace Gullacke	12d
x	Daniel Mills & wife	2s 6d
x	John Crewes	12d
x	Nicholas Westcot	12d
x	John Palmer	12d
x	Roger Broadmead, jun. & wife	12d
x	Francis Holmes & wife	12d
x	John Archapole & wife	8s 6d
x	Anne Archapole	12d
x	John Crosse	12d
x	Elizabeth Lyde	12d
x	Samuel Beard	12d
x	Richard Welshford	12d
x	Nicholas Delve	5s
x	Gabriel Burch & wife	5s 6d
x	William Laskey	12d
x	Thomazine Bond, widow	12d
x	Henry Mitchell & wife	12d
x	Michael Mitchell	12d
x	Edward Penny	12d
x	Thomas Paddon & wife	12d
x	John Martyn & wife	12d
	Nicholas Randle & wife	12d
x	James Ellett & wife	12d
x	Christofer Fortescue & wife	12d
	Elizabeth Andrew, widow	12d
x	Sarah Hunniwill	12d
x	Robert Elwill & wife	12d
x	Thomas Carpenter & wife	12d
x	William Teape & wife	12d
x	Andrew Nicholls & wife	12d
	Cristofer Basely & wife	12d
x	John Towill	12d
x	Gabriel Watch	12d
x	Ureth Phillipps, widow	12d
x	Elizabeth Phillipps	12d
x	George Phillipps	12d
x	John Gillard & wife	12d
x	Robert Jerman	12d
x	William King & wife	12d
x	William Stephens & wife	12d
x	William Parker & wife	12d
x	Arthur Crafford & wife	12d
m. 25d		
x	Mary Essery	12d
x	Mary Beard	12d
	Elianor Windeate	12d
x	John Newcombe & wife	12d
x	Robert Webb	12d
x	Katherine Harris	12d
x	Argentine Twiggs	20s
x	Martyn Harris	12d
x	George Palmer	12d
x	John Foxwell	12d
x	Lawrence West	12d
x	Katherine Little	12d
x	Rebecca Barrett, widow	10s
x	Abraham Blackmore	12d
x	Robert Luke	12d
x	Mary Crossing	12d
x	Roger Broadmeade, sen. & wife	12d
x	Mary Broadmead	12d
x	Thomas Ching & wife	2s 6d
x	Richard Crosseman	12d
x	Susanna Rowe	12d
x	Richard Hooper & wife	20s 6d
x	John Lee	12d
x	William Coomer	12d
x	John Chase	12d
x	Lewis Page	12d
x	Mary Westlake	12d
x	Elizabeth Sherwill	12d
x	Edward Mathew & wife	12d
x	Robert Gooding	12d
x	Katherine Ball	12d
x	Joan Hellier, widow	12d
x	Richard Harris & wife	12d
x	Thomas Ball & wife	12d
x	Richard Hewett & wife	2s 6d
x	William Horwood	12d

x	Tristram Hawkings & wife	12d
x	John Minson & wife	12d
x	John Weekes & wife	12d
x	Mary Weekes	12d
	Phebe Heard, widow	12d
	John Somerton & wife	12d
	Elizabeth Blackmore, widow	12d
x	John Sowdon & wife	12d
x	John Drewe & wife	12d
x	John Reed & wife	2s 6d
x	Elizabeth Clarke, widow	2s 6d
x	Hannibal Ratcliffe & wife	12d
x	William Wreyford	12d
	Edward Mayo	12d
x	John Sanders & wife	12d
x	Robert Carter & wife	12d
x	Henry Magazen & wife	12d
x	Martyn White	12d
x	Peter Miller & wife	12d
x	Ezechiel Gribble & wife	12d
x	Mary Haydon	12d
x	George Cawly & wife	12d
x	Elizabeth Cawly	12d
x	George Clare & wife	20s 6d
x	Thomas Clare	12d
x	Richard Williams	12d
x	Ruth Clare, widow	12d
x	John Alford & wife	5s 6d
x	William Smallridge & wife	12d
	John Drake & wife	12d
x	Michael Yebbacombe	12d
x	Thomas Wolfe & wife	12d
x	Mary Wolfe	12d
x	Nicholas Hellier & wife	12d
x	Henry Edwards & wife	12d
x	Thomas Bishopp & wife	12d
m. 26		
x	John Downe & wife	12d
x	Henry Somerton & wife	12d
x	John Edye & wife	12d
x	John Fox & wife	12d
x	Samuel Pitts & wife	12d
x	Edward Hooper & wife	12d
x	Geoffrey Peeke & wife	12d
x	William Casely	12d
	John Turner & wife	12d
x	Dorothy Legg, widow	12d
x	Elianor Legg	12d
x	Richard Gobb & wife	12d
x	John Bowden & wife	12d
x	Richard Tucker & wife	12d
x	William Goffe & wife	12d
x	Audrey Sowdon, widow	12d
x	John Baker & wife	8s 6d
x	Anne Manning	12d
x	Thomas Cupper	20s
x	Richard Gibbons	20s
x	William Tibbolls	12d
x	Thomas Facey & wife	2s 6d
x	John Webber & wife	2s 6d
x	Roger Haydon	12d
x	Anne Berry	12d
x	Humfrey Spencer & wife	12d
x	Edward Hellier & wife	12d
x	Sarah Hellier	12d
x	Alexander Skinner & wife	12d
x	Winifred Lyddon	12d
x	Agnes Northcot	12d
x	Laurence Biddle & wife	12d
	Peter Tueker	12d
x	John Tremayne & wife	12d
x	George Hobbs	12d
x	Robert Hewett	12d
x	Cornelius Melhunna	12d
x	Thomas Melhuna	12d
x	Nathaniel Reeve & wife	2s 6d
x	Walter Strang	12s 6d
x	John Mumford	12d
x	James Brangwill	12d
x	Thomas Sumpter	12d
x	John Strang	12d
x	Owen Thomas	12d
x	Alice Pearse	12d
x	Elizabeth Strang	12d
x	Gilbert Leigh & wife	5s 6d
x	Nicholas Baker	12d
x	Richard Rake	12d
x	Joan Prawle	12d
x	Susanna Leigh	12d
x	Thomazine Alford, widow	2s [6d]
x	Bridget Alford	12d
x	Jane Alford	12d
x	William Knight & wife	4s 6d
x	Samuel Pitts, jun.	12d
x	Dorothy Knight	12d
x	Elizabeth Sanders	12d
x	Mary Bartlet, widow	12d
x	Susanna Bartlet	12d
x	Robert Wadge & wife	8s 6d
x	Robert Foster	12d
x	Robert Landry & wife	12d
x	John Luxton & wife	12d
	Joseph White & wife	12d
x	John Purchase & wife	12d
x	Henry Wolland & wife	12d
x	Thomas Blanchford & wife	12d
x	Nathaniel Palmer & wife	12d
x	Robert Denny & wife	5s 6d
x	Joan Eastabrooke	12d
x	Thomas Davy	12d
x	Nicholas Sanders & wife	3s 6d
x	James Wilcox	12d
x	Thomas Norrish	12d
m. 26d		
x	John Kennicke & wife	12d
x	Elizabeth Slee	12d
x	Stephen Phillipps & wife	12d
x	John Sanders & wife	12d
x	Thomas Dight	12d
x	John Hart & wife	12d
x	Richard Cudmore	12d
x	Thomas Quicke & wife	12d
x	Thomas Paul & wife	2s 6d
x	Katherine Paul, widow	12d

x	William White	12d
x	Mary Lethbridge, widow	20s
x	Zenobia Lethbridge	12d
x	Mary Lethbridge	12d
x	Mellisant Jefford	12d
x	Mary Ford, widow	12d
x	Anne Dodson	12d
x	William May & wife	12d
x	Robert Halstaffe & wife	12d
x	Mary Halstaffe	12d
x	John Pengelly & wife	12d
x	Mary Mapowder	12d
x	Mary Woodward	12d
x	Richard Thuel & wife	12d
x	John Shute & wife	12d
x	John Johnson & wife	12d
x	Paul Martyn & wife	12d
x	John Deymond & wife	12d
x	David Deane & wife	3s 6d
x	Mary Waldron	12d
x	Thomas Flavell, *clerk*, & wife	12d
x	Susanna Flavell	12d
x	George Davy & wife	12d
x	William Crute & wife	12d
x	Susanna Crute	12d
x	Peter Clawson & wife	10s 6d
x	Dorothy Webb, widow	15s
x	Hannah Husway	12d
x	Samuel Anthony & wife	5s 6d
x	Katherine Passmore	12d
x	Susanna Cockram	12d
x	Margery Wilson, widow	12d
x	Gilbert Wilson	12d
x	Richard Beavis	12d
x	George Atkins	12d
x	Philip Balston & wife	2s 6d
x	Philip Balston the son	12d
x	John Howe & wife	12d
x	William Redwood & wife	12d
x	Margaret Cuttery, widow	12d
x	Mary Cuttery	12d
x	Mary Sanders	12d
x	Joan Deymond	12d
x	Thomas Mawry & wife	12d
x	Elizabeth Perriman, widow	12d
x	Josias Burgesse & wife	12d
x	John Webber & wife	12d
x	William Foxwell & wife	2s 6d
x	Nicholas Brenly & wife	15s 6d
x	Alice Brenly	12d
x	Sarah Brenly	12d
x	Elianor Brenly	12d
x	Susanna Brenly	12d
x	Elizabeth Webber	12d
x	Mary Lumly, widow	2s 6d
x	Mary Burgesse	12d
x	Lancelot Burgesse & wife	12d
x	George Dowrich & wife	12d
x	Elizabeth Dowrich	12d
x	Thomas Hurly & wife	10s 6d
x	John Sanders & wife	12d
x	Robert Marks	12d

x	William Hawton	12d
x	Grace Potter	12d
x	Joan Dyer	12d
x	John Harding	12d
x	Roger Lyddon & wife	12d
x	Edith Bonford	12d
x	William Glyde, jun. & wife	5s 6d
x	Anasticia Arthur	12d
x	John Cann and wife	10s 6d
x	John Clutterbucke	12d
x	Joan Jessop	12d
m. 27		
x	Anne Wills, widow	5s
x	Protesa Pynny	12d
x	John Manning & wife	7s 6d
x	Hannah Gay	12d
x	Mark Browning & wife	2s 6d
x	Hugh Dyer	12d
x	Susanna Cornish	12d
x	Robert Carrell & wife	2s 6d
x	William Carrell	12d
x	Joseph Taunton & wife	4s 6d
x	Richard Parsons	12d
x	Henry Lovelace	12d
x	Edward Taunton	12d
x	Rebecca Taunton	12d
x	Elizabeth Taunton	12d
x	Avery Hayman & wife	5s 6d
	Mary Hall	12d
x	Charles Alden	12d
x	Peter Hellier & wife	2s 6d
x	Richard Hellier	12d
x	Henry Smith & wife	4s 6d
x	Thomas Ball	12d
x	Mathew Bennet	12d
x	Peter Hadgedot, sen.	10s
x	Elizabeth Hadgedot	12d
x	James Yeo & wife	2s 6d
x	John Jewell	12d
x	Alice Yeo, widow	12d
x	Walter Robins & wife	12d
x	John Body & wife	12d
x	John Dowdall & wife	12d
x	William Lydiat & wife	12d
x	Charles Lydiat	12d
x	William Atkins & wife	12d
x	Richard Lane & wife	12d
x	Antony Keife & wife	12d
x	William Gilbert, sen. & wife	12d
x	Elianor Caple	12d
x	Thomas Parkins & wife	12d
x	Mathew Tanner & wife	12d
x	Christofer Kennicke & wife	12d
x	John Blake & wife	12d
x	Nicholas Baker & wife	12d
x	Elizabeth Baker	12d
x	Nicholas Yeo & wife	12d
x	William Sanders	12d
[x]	Peter Maynard & wife	12d
	[Onesimus Na]nson	12d
	[John Davi]es	12d
	[William Rowse]	12d

x	Robert Blake & wife	12d
x	John Gosswell	12d
x	Richard Bowden & wife	12d
x	Aquilla Fooke & wife	12d
	Dorothy Chambers	12d
x	Wilmot Kiltree	12d
x	Paschoe Crutchett	12d
x	Christobel Kiltree	12d
x	Timothy Allyn & wife	5s 6d
x	James Edmay	12d
x	Hester Clutterbucke	12d
x	Jane Rosser	12d
x	Elizabeth Slanning	12d
x	William Bowden & wife	12d
	Richard Davy	12d
x	Isaiah Davy	12d
x	Antony Potter & wife	12d
x	John James	12d
x	John Clase & wife	2s 6d
x	Isaac Weekes & wife	12d
x	Mary Sampson, widow	2s
x	Margaret Sampson	12d
x	Adam Pearse & wife	20s 6d
x	Ezechiel Steede	12d
x	Elizabeth Shefford	12d
x	Samuel Pearse	10s
x	John Eyles	10s
x	Simon Mathew & wife	12d
	Ursula Mathewe	12d
x	Philip Guard & wife	12d
	Lidia Davy, widow	12d
x	Mary Davy	12d
x	John Randell	12d
	Richard Anger & wife	12d
m. 27d		
x	Bernard Sparke, *merchant* & wife	£5 0s 6d
x	Richard Clapp	12d
x	Robert Chapman	12d
x	Mary Wincliffe	12d
x	Joan Trapnel	12d
x	Antony Smith & wife	2s 6d
x	William Brooke	12d
x	Mary Hamvell	12d
x	Robert Norden & wife	12d
x	John Nosworthy & wife	30s 6d
x	Nicholas Barons	12d
x	Richord (Rica') Smalridge	12d
x	Christofer Farwell & wife	20s 6d
	John Talbot & wife	10s 6d
x	John Hawkes	12d
x	John Taylor	12d
x	Thomas Rigg	12d
x	John Jaques & wife	12d
x	Anne Dilling	12d
x	Malachias Pyne, *merchant* & wife	£4 0s 6d
x	Robert Hodges	10s
x	William Merrill	12d
x	Henry Browning	12d
x	Richard Thomas	12d
x	Jasper Thorke	12d
x	Anne Davies	12d
x	Caritia Shaply	12d
x	Tobias Allyn & wife	20s 6d
x	Thomas Greenway	12d
x	John Friend	12d
x	Elizabeth Allyn	12d
x	Anne Mountstephen	12d
x	Elizabeth Mountstephen	12d
x	Robert Atkins, *clerk*, & wife	12d
x	Thomasine Stilling	12d
x	Jane Lovering	12d
[x	Michael] Browne & wife	12d
[x	Elias Furse]	12d
[x	Abraham] Burridge & wife	12d
[x	William Towill] & wife	12d
x	Abraham Crosseman	12d
x	Bartholomew Becket & wife	12d
	John Baker & wife	12d
x	Peter Commings & wife	2s 6d
	Robert Eastabrooke	12d
x	William Prowse	12d
x	Thomas Hawkings	12d
x	Mary Lynn	12d
x	John Bawdon & wife	12d
x	Humfry Northen	12d
x	William Lumber	12d
x	John Drewe	12d
x	Nicholas Floud & wife	8s 6d
x	Arthur Horsham	12d
x	William Drew	12d
x	Robert Katkett	12d
x	Henry Floud	12d
x	Mary Miller	12d
x	Susanna Wood	12d
x	Edward Twiggs & wife	5s 6d
	Christofer Taylor	12d
x	Charity Dodge	12d
	Elizabeth Price	12d
x	Thomas Heath & wife	2s 6d
x	Thomas Ward	12d
x	Margaret Lillacrapp	12d
x	Margaret Howe	12d
x	Elizabeth Foster	2s
x	Dorothy Lane, widow	2s 6d
x	Walter Kerslake & wife	12d
x	Thomas Brockington & wife	2s 6d
x	William Yeo	12d
x	Nicholas Gun	12d
x	Robert Grenfeild & wife	2s 6d
x	William Grenfeild	12d
x	Henry Stoakes	12d
x	Thomas Durant & wife	12d
	Edward Rugg	12d
	William Cornelius & wife	12d
x	Henry London	12d
x	John Joanes & wife	12d
x	William Wincot & wife	12d
x	John Lane & wife	12d
x	John Hackwill & wife	12d
x	Nicholas Eveleigh & wife	40s 6d
x	Thomas Osmond	12d
x	Mary Aire	12d
m. 28		
x	Mary Rimer	12d

x	Thomas Salter & wife	12d
x	Peter Cole	12d
x	Elizabeth Clapp	12d
x	Mary James, widow	12d
x	Roger Endebrooke & wife	2s 6d
x	Thomas Ward	12d
x	Grace Hutchings	12d
x	Thomas Halstaffe & wife	12d
x	Edward Mallet & wife	2s 6d
x	George Hewet & wife	12d
x	Epaphraditus Holmes	3s 6d
x	Andrew Dodridge	12d
x	Elizabeth Holmes	12d
x	Joan Hawkins	12d
x	Thomas Waterman & wife	12d
x	John Harris & wife	12d
	Thomas Stanly & wife	12d
x	Thomas Keatly & wife	12d
x	Mathew Purkys & wife	12d
	Peter Crosse & wife	12d
	Robert Hare & wife	12d
x	Zacharias Sanders & wife	12d
x	Richard Parsons & wife	12d
x	William Hooper	12d
x	Roger Bowman & wife	12d
x	Thomas Twiggs & wife	12d
	Edward White & wife	12d
x	William Twiggs & wife	12d
	Mary Twiggs	12d
	John Hawkes & wife	12d
	John Penny & wife	12d
x	Arthur Binmore & wife	12d
x	John Crocker & wife	12d
x	Margaret Crocker	12d
x	John Lane & wife	7s 6d
x	Christofer Harris	12d
x	Jonathan Manly	12d
x	Richard Dawkins	12d
x	Rebecca Lane	12d
x	Eusebius Holmes, sen. & wife	2s 6d
x	Samuel Holmes	12d
x	Richard Oxenberry	12d
x	Elizabeth Holmes	7s 6d
x	Thomas Sampford & wife	12d
x	John Soper	12d
x	Richard Lare	12d
x	John Watkins	12d
x	Robert Pullyn & wife	10s 6d
[x	Christopher] Herdman	12d
[x	Elizabeth Ellard]	12d
[x	Mary Lu]scombe	12d
[x	Margaret] Hammond	12d
x	William Oldman & wife	12d
x	Edward Courtis & wife	12d
	Cassandra Arundell, widow	12d
x	Paul Bale & wife	40s 6d
x	Christofer Bale	5s
x	Malachia Bale	12d
x	Lancelot Westcot	12d
x	William Millford	12d
x	Antony Bagwill	12d
x	Edward Edwards	12d
x	Elizabeth Wolland	12d
x	Edward Tozer & wife	5s 6d
x	William Pretty	12d
x	Mary Tozer	12d
x	Elizabeth Tozer	12d
x	Jane Norcot	12d
x	Jane Hagon, widow	12d
x	John Nurton & wife	12d
x	Nicholas Jeanes	12d
x	Mary Michell	12d
x	Mathias Purkyns & wife	12d
x	Mathew Cobb & wife	12d
x	John Gill & wife	12d
x	Gilbert Binmore	12d
x	Mathew Serle & wife	12d
x	Josias Clarke	12d
x	John Browning & wife	12d
x	Anne Duke	12d
x	Sarah Duke	12d
x	Anne Moone, widow	12d
x	John Coke & wife	12d
x	Richard Moone & wife	12d
x	Richard English & wife	12d
	Antony Heard & wife	12d
x	Peter Chaple & wife	12d
x	Humphry Berry & wife	12d
m. 28d		
x	Robert Bishopp & wife	12d
x	Amyas Webber	12d
	Elizabeth Webber	12d
x	Daniel Clapp & wife	12d
x	John Bawdon & wife	12d
x	Robert Treding & wife	12d
x	John Bath & wife	12d
	Ellianor Collings, widow	12d
	John Harris & wife	12d
x	Andrew Collings & wife	12d
x	Thomazine Collings, widow	12d
x	Thomazine Tottle	12d
x	Clara Bassill	12d
x	Zacharias Lumly & wife	10s 6d
x	Digory Prowte	12d
x	Mary Nettle	12d
	Joan Downe	12d
x	Philip Warren & wife	10s 6d
x	Richard Stitson	12d
x	Mary Draper	12d
x	Mary Clogg	12d
x	Elizabeth Thomas	12d
x	George Browning	12d
x	Richard Moone, jun.	12d
x	Nicholas Browne & wife	2s 6d
x	William Halstaffe	12d
x	John Browne	12d
x	Angel Sparke & wife	4s 6d
x	Joan Lake	12d
x	John King & wife	12d
x	William Dynning	12d
x	Elizabeth Dynning	12d
x	Henry Harnesse & wife	12d
	[Dorothy] Thomas, widow	12d
[x	William] Johns & wife	2s 6d

[x	Mary Ki]ngdome	12d
x	Antony Pafford & wife	12d
x	Nathaniel Wills & wife	12d
x	Richard Burrowe & wife	12d
x	Martin Hopkins & wife	12d
x	Bartholomew Heathman	12d
x	Antony Kiltree	12d
x	John Bowden & wife	12d
	Marian Passemore, widow	12d
x	Peter Passmore & wife	6s 6d
x	Christofer Tucker	12d
x	Samuel Glover	12d
x	John Binham	12d
	Honor Crutchet, widow	12d
x	Mary Crutchet	12d
x	Elizabeth Hopkings, widow	12d
	Silvanus Hust	12d
x	Laurence Broadmead & wife	12d
x	Robert Coombe	12d
x	Owen Davy & wife	12d
x	Hannah Salter	12d
x	Robert Blitchenden & wife	2s 6d
x	Margaret Coles	12d
x	Richard Lee & wife	12d
	William Morgan	12d
x	Michael Toose & wife	12d
x	Antony Michell	12d
x	John Mabor & wife	6s 6d
x	Grace Crispyn	12d
x	William Glyde, sen. & wife	20s 6d
x	Elizabeth Glide	12d
x	Nathaniel Blake	12d
x	Anne Legg	12d
x	William Smith & wife	12d
x	Mary Thomas	12d
x	Arthur Serle & wife	12d
x	Walter Trend & wife	12d
x	David Rice	12d
x	Thomas Paige & wife	12d
x	Francis Jaquet, widow	25s
x	Elizabeth Jaquet	12d
x	Zenobia Morrish	12d

m. 29

x	Elizabeth Pitman	12d
x	Joan Reepe	12d
x	Francis Hooper	12d
x	Jane Hooper	12d
x	Nicholas Palmer & wife	6s 6d
x	Robert Morgan	12d
x	Henry Palmer	12d
x	Agnes Hall	12d
x	James Salter & wife	5s 6d
x	Richard Hore	12d
x	Elizabeth Paynter	12d
x	Richard Deeble & wife	12d
x	Samuel Johns	12d
x	Mary Deeble	12d
x	John Cleake & wife	12d
x	Elizabeth Blake	12d
x	Richard Pawling & wife	12d
x	John Jarmyn & wife	12d
x	James Shute & wife	12d
x	Mathew Payne & wife	12d
x	Thomas Minifie	12d
x	Richard Pope	12d
	Alice Pope	12d
x	Margaret Lyde, widow	12d
x	Rebecca Chard	12d
x	George Dowe & wife	12d
x	Alexander Stretchly & wife	12d
	Susanna Stretchly	12d
x	Charles Bussell	12d
	Joan Hooper	12d
x	John Sanders & wife	12d
x	John Sanders, jun.	12d
x	Andrew Glanfill & wife	5s 6d
x	Timothy Martyn	12d
x	Elizabeth Takell, widow	8s
	Thomas Hollman	12d
x	Anne Wills	12d
x	Richard White & wife	2s 6d
x	Cicilia Hornbroke, widow	8s
x	Thomas Hornbrooke	12d
x	Robert Bazill	12d
x	John Hornbrooke & wife	2s 6d
x	Joan Reed, widow	12d
x	John Townsend	12d
x	Peter Townsend	12d
	[Margar]et Silvester, widow	12d
[x	John Sa]lter & wife	12d
[x	John P]ope & wife	12d
[x	John] Hughes & wife	12d
[x	William] Sainthill	12d
	Christofer Weekes	12d
	John Parsons	12d
x	Thomas Joye & wife	12d
	Katherine Pollard	12d
	Nicholas Skirry	12d
x	Anne Davies	12d
x	Simon Bazill & wife	12d
x	Thomas Peddericke & wife	12d
x	Christian Fish	12d
x	Nicholas Bond & wife	2s 6d
x	Daniel Gifford	12d
x	John Gifford	12d
x	Joseph Peeke & wife	12d
x	Thomas Peeke	12d
x	Elizabeth Weekes	12d
x	Philip Reeve & wife	12d
x	George Hayne & wife	12d
x	Philip Pearse & wife	12d
x	Elizabeth Ballamy, widow	12d
x	Agnes Pitts, widow	12d
x	John Pitts & wife	12d
x	John Glyden & wife	12d
x	Henry Stephens & wife	12d
	Robert Farrant	12d
x	Robert Paige & wife	12d
	Ralph Harbert	12d
x	Mary Stephens, widow	12d
x	Aron Randle & wife	12d
x	William Gale	12d
x	Thomas Northam & wife	12d
x	John Wilkings & wife	12d

x	Jane Gill	12d
	Richard Seager	12d
x	William Morrish & wife	12d
x	John Medland	12d
x	John Thrasher & wife	12d
m. 29d		
x	Richard Richards	12d
x	Robert Brewer	12d
x	Daniel Tiggens	12d
x	Thomas Fry & wife	12d
x	Grace Fry	12d
x	Mary Fry	12d
	Grace Bussell	12d
x	Hugh Callaway	12d
x	John Pomeroy & wife	5s 6d
x	Barnard Mervyn	12d
x	Elizabeth Ratcliffe	12d
x	Elizabeth Bartlet	12d
x	John Hyne & wife	12d
x	John Hyne, jun.	3s
x	Peter Hyne	12d
x	James Clarke	12d
x	Roger Drewe	12d
x	Elizabeth Hyne	12d
x	Anne Hyne	12d
x	Anne Boyer, widow	12d
x	Richard Boyer & wife	12d
x	Grace Vinsent, widow	12d
x	Walter Bath & wife	12d
x	Elias Foxwell & wife	5s 6d
x	Zacharias Foxwell	12d
x	Elias Foxwell, jun.	12d
x	John Haycroft	12d
x	Isaac Hake	12d
x	Mary Foxwell	12d
x	Honor Juns	12d
x	Agnes Parnell	12d
x	Philip Foxwell	12d
x	Gregory Wonstone & wife	5s 6d
x	Elizabeth Smith, widow	2s
[x]	John Warren & wife	12d
[x	Mary] Warren, widow	12d
[x	Thomas] Cunningham & wife	30s
[x	Richard Cun]ingham	12d
[x	Elizabeth Br]owne	12d
x	Stephen Toller	40s 6d
x	John Bagwell	12d
x	Jane Welshford	12d
x	Elizabeth Sparke	12d
x	Jonathan Carter & wife	2s 6d
x	Elizabeth Hannaford	12d
x	Richard Pidsly & wife	8s 6d
x	William Moore	12d
x	Elizabeth Lacey	12d
x	Samuel Seager	12d
x	Robert Hutchings & wife	2s 6d
x	Grace Hutchings	12d
x	Rebecca Olliver	12d
x	Joan Hill	12d
x	Grace Wood, widow	12d
x	Damore Baker	12d
x	William Jones & wife	12d
x	Henry Whiterow & wife	12d
x	William Keagle & wife	12d
x	Richard Paunsford	12d
x	Charles Eveleigh & wife	40s 6d
x	Margaret Bennet	12d
x	Sarah Hannaford, widow	12d
x	John Fistle	12d
x	Ralph Sheares	5s 6d
x	Elizabeth Lacey	12d
C	Jane Maddocke, widow	10s
x	Elizabeth Maddocke	12d
x	John Lavers & wife	2s 6d
x	John Lavers, jun.	12d
x	Frances Sherland	12d
x	Jane Sinckleare	12
x	John Elwill & wife	£4 0s 6d
x	Rebecca Elwill	12d
x	Robert Blatchford	12d
x	Henry Fulford	12d
x	Anne Durham	12d
x	Grace Wheeler	12d
x	Jacob Paul	12d
x	John Gibbons & wife	50s 6d
x	Joan Bishopp	12d
x	William Bolitha	2s
x	Leonard Tresloe	12d
x	Charles Cunningham	12d
m. 30		
x	Lewis Chilcot	12d
x	Joan Darracot	12d
x	Jane Gorge	12d
x	Christofer Burton & wife	4s 6d
x	Mary Mathew	12d
x	Elizabeth Lawrence, widow	5s
x	Robert Dabinet & wife	10s 6d
x	Elizabeth Ellett	12d
x	Joan Newman	12d
x	Robert Parsons & wife	2s 6d
x	Anne Berry, widow	12d
x	Robert Bridgman & wife	12d
x	William Warren & wife	5s 6d
x	Joan Deymond	12d
x	Pricilla Gribble	12d
x	Thomas Whiterow & wife	12d
x	Thomazine Humphry	12d
x	William Nicholls	12d
x	Henry Lynscot & wife	20s 6d
x	Elizabeth Sparke	12d
x	Edward Leamon	5s
x	Joshua Reynolds & wife	12d
x	Mary Reynolds	12d
x	Francis Pengelly & wife	5s 6d
x	Alice Batten	12d
x	Acchiah Brocas & wife	2s 6d
x	Humphry Facy & wife	12d
	Jane Morrish	12d
x	Rebecca Roberts, widow	12d
x	Francis Jewell & wife	2s 6d
x	Robert Mitchell	12d
x	Susanna Eachim	12d
x	Hannibal Ratcliffe & wife	10s 6d
x	Agnes Sheares	12d

	William Courtis	5s
x	Elizabeth Champnies, widow	12d
x	Hester Eveleigh	12d
x	Mathew Bennet & wife	12d
x	Pricilla Bennett	12d
x	Lucy Bennet	12d
x	Susanna Bennet	12d
x	James Moore & wife	12d
x	Elizabeth Foxwell, widow	12d
x	Mary Foxwell	12d
[x	Richard Gunt] & wife	12d
[x	Mary Newcombe]	12d
[x	blank] [Shilston] widow	12d
[x	Thomas Searle] & wife	12d
[x	George] Jiles *gent., Attorney* & wife	£3 0s 6d
[x]	Anne Dennys	12d
x	John Whiddon & wife	5s 6d
x	Elizabeth Whiddon	12d
x	Frances Greenwood	12d
	Rebecca Day	12d
x	Dorothy White	12d
x	John Dennys & wife	12d
x	Samuel Johns & wife	12d
x	Stephen Parris	12d
x	Anne Anderton	12d
x	Henry Hernaman & wife	12d
x	Thomas Codner & wife	12d
x	Nicholas Jagoe & wife	12d
x	Margary Hellyer, widow	12d
x	Juliana Towte	12d
x	Edith Towte	12d
x	John Pare & wife	12d
x	William Fry & wife	12d
x	John Hart	12d
x	Elizabeth Jones, widow	12d
x	Henry Gale & wife	12d
	John Walker & wife	12d
	William Bishopp & wife	12d
	Anastacia Newcombe	12d
	Mary Goldsworthy	12d
x	Rachel Palmer	12d
x	Charles Taylor *Attorney* & wife	£3 0s 6d
x	Anne Parker	12d
x	Richord Curson, widow	30s
x	John Curson	6s
x	George Curson	4s
x	Ruth Greedy	12d
x	John Cooke *merchant* & wife	£4 0s 6d
x	William Bishopp	12d
x	Elizabeth Minson	12d
m.	30d	
x	Richard Isacke *esq.* & wife	£10 0s 6d
x	Grace Harcombe	12d
x	Laurence Ward & wife	12d
x	John Addams & wife	12d
x	Bridget Humphry, widow	12d
x	George Kingdome	12d
	Thomas Mudd & wife	12d
x	Robert Parsons, sen. & wife	10s

Total £135 8s 6d

The Land Rate

x	Mrs. Katherine Pyle for the house John Elwill liveth in	10s
x	Mr. Robert Ridler for severall houses in the possession of Peter Passmore & others	10s
C	Mr. Henry White for his houses in the possession of Peter Hadgedot & others	20s
x	Mrs. [blank] Tucker for the house Mr. Nicholas Brenly liveth in	7s 6d
x	Thomas Bennet for the house William Glide the elder liveth in	4s
C	Mr. Hunt for the house Zachary Lumly liveth in	8s
x	Anne Trowte for the house Wm. Keagle & Henry Whiterowe live in	6s
x	Mr. Humphry Wilcox for the tenement Francis Pengelly lives in	3s
C	Mr. [blank] Shaply for the Innehouse at the Marmayde	2s
x	Mr. [blank] Birch, *Clarke*, for the houses Achaiah Brocas & Joshua Reynolds live in	6s

Sum £3 16s [6d]

Sum total £139 5s 0d

whereof is payd	
To the Sheriffe of the Citty in money	£132 1s [6d]
For the Collectors allowance	11s
For the Clarks allowance	11s
More to be defalcated out of 66 persons before [un]crossed who are soe poore that they cannot pay [the same &] of whose poverty & insufficiency wee [are certified under] the Collectors hands	£3 6s
[More unpayd by John] Talbot *gent.* 10s 6d & Wm. Cortis 5s	15s 6d
[More on 4 Certificates] as before	£2

[Sum total of the] payments & allowances £139 5s 0d

PARISH OF ST. GEORGE

Francis Westlake
Thomas Prigg *Collectors*

x	Augustine Drake & wife	32s 6d
x	Alexander Reynolds	12d
x	Thomas Hellier	12d
x	Prudence Jewell	12d
x	Thomazine Moore	12d
x	Richard Rich & wife	40s 6d
x	Nicholas Rich	12d
x	Christofer Payne & wife	20s 6d
x	William Hart	12d
x	William Wills	12d
x	Anastasia Till	12d
x	William Spiller & wife	10s 6d
x	Edward Perryman	12d
x	Thomas Willys	12d
x	Hugh Bidwell	12d
x	Richard Collings	12d
x	Anne Cheeke, widow	10s
x	Daniel Polton	12d
x	Alice Chorly	12d
x	Richard Shilston & wife	20s 6d
x	Joan Addams	12d
x	Joseph Yeo & wife	4s 6d
x	Thomas Crosse	12d
x	Elizabeth Yeo	12d
x	John Lome, sen. & wife	15s 6d
x	William Thomas	12d
x	John Sanders	12d
x	Jane Lyde	12d
x	Susanna Hopping, widow	20s
x	Charles Hopping	4s
x	Richard Hole	12d
x	John Locke	12d
x	Francis Dynning	12d
x	Susanna Putt	12d
x	Thomas Hance & wife	10s 6d
x	Honor Dowridge	12d
x	Agnes Tucker, widow	10s
x	Elizabeth Tucker	4s
x	Jane Prigg, widow	15s
m. 31		
x	Alice Prigg	4s
x	Thomas Prigg & wife	6s 6d
x	Christofer Mathew & wife	10s 6d
x	Elizabeth Mathew	12d
x	Margaret Blackinston, widow	8s
x	John Bowden & wife	4s 6d
x	Richard Bucknoll	12d
x	Peter Bryant	12d
x	Edward Lake	4s 6d
x	Elianor Eithridge	12d
x	Francis Westlake	4s
x	Henry Sheares & wife	3s 6d
x	George Goswell & wife	4s 6d
x	Amy Ware	12d
x	Mary Evans	12d
x	John Parris	12d
x	John Mannington & wife	2s 6d

x	Edward Bragg	12d
x	Antony Westcot & wife	4s 6d
x	John Payne & wife	4s 6d
x	Richard Westcot & wife	4s 6d
x	Robert Penny & wife	4s 6d
x	John Penny	12d
x	Elizabeth Penny	12d
x	John Salisbury	12d
x	Peter King	12d
x	Richard Gould & wife	4s 6d
x	William Geale	12d
x	John Rowe	12d
x	Joan Cole	12d
x	Thomas Kennicot & wife	2s 6d
x	Joan Bragg	12d
x	Joan Somerton, widow	5s
x	William Reepe & wife	12d
x	Laurence Lillicrapp & wife	12d
x	Joseph Jarman & wife	12d
x	John Heyward & wife	12d
	Christofer Pasmore & wife	12d
x	William Hayne & wife	12d
[x	Eleanor Sparke] widow	12d
[x	Sarah Sparke]	12d
[x	David Hilman] & wife	12d
[x	Thomas Macey] & wife	12d
[x	Richard Macey]	12d
x	Hannah Griffen	12d
x	John West & wife	[12d]
x	Richard Hooke & wife	[12d]
x	Edward Lemet & wife	[12d]
x	Edward Greene & wife	[12d]
x	Margaret Rich, widow	[12d]
x	George Bully & wife	[12d]
x	Edward Warren	12d
x	John Cotten & wife	12d
x	Richard Walters & wife	12d
x	Christofer Blake	12d
x	Honor Collings	12d
x	Rebecca Birdall	12d
x	[blank] Chard, widow	12d
	Roger Bridges & wife	12d
x	William Mathew & wife	12d
x	Augustine Drew & wife	12d
x	Edward Wills & wife	12d
x	Thomas Mortimer	12d
x	Mathew Wyet	12d
x	John Wills & wife	12d
x	John Eastabrooke & wife	12d
x	Katherine Withers, widow	12d
	Joseph Boole & wife	12d
	Richard Palmer & wife	12d
x	John Bagwell, sen. & wife	12d
x	John Bagwell, jun. & wife	12d
x	Robert Upton & wife	12d
x	Robert Upton the son	12d
x	Agnes Ford, widow	12d
x	Edward Parret & wife	12d
x	Elizabeth Worth, widow	12d
x	Robert Worth	12d
x	Honor Worth, widow	12d
x	John Takle & wife	12d

x Richard Takle 12d
m. 31d
x Margery Takle 12d
x Peter Gale & wife 12d
x Elizabeth Lumbard 12d
x John Lumbard 12d
x Henry Loxton & wife 2s 6d
x John Reeve 12d
x Digory Harch 12d
x Cicilia Thomas 12d
x Robert Gay 12d
x William Lapp 2s
x Thomas Hacker & wife 12d
x Andrew Reynolds & wife 12d
x Martyn Dunston 12d
x Margeret Taylor 12d
x James Gale & wife 12d
x John Gale 12d
x James Gale 12d
x George Vildey & wife 12d
x Ruth Moos 12d
x Richord (*Rica*') Beavis, widow 2s
x Samuel Jorden & wife 2s 6d
x Richard Rendell & wife 12d
x Edward Jerman & wife 12d
x Abel Worth & wife 12d
x Elizabeth May 12d
x William Clarke & wife 12d
x William Deeble & wife 12d
x Alice Bastard [12d]
x Moses Deeble [12d]
x Robert Carter & wife [12d]
x Winifred Carter [12d]
x Philip Richards & wife [12d]
x Sarah Hunny [12d]
[x] Margaret Follet, widow 12d
[x Ursula Tise] 12d
[x Edward May] 12d
[x John Awdry] & wife 12d
[x Samuel Michell] & wife 12d
[x Bartholomew Harvey] 12d
[x] John [Palmer] & wife 12d
x Jane Macy 12d
x Arthur Glanvill & wife 2s 6d
x Deborah Leach 12d
x Humfrey Kneebone 12d
x Robert Gale 12d
x Mary Drake 12d
x Henry Lawry & wife 12d
x Mary Lawry 12d
x William Poe & wife 12d
x Simon Stannaway & wife 12d
x Isaac Wolland & wife 12d
Rebecca Paddon 12d
x Dorothy Paddon 12d
Christofer Wolland 12d
x Edward Southard & wife 12d
x Henry Lawry, jun. 12d

Total £22 13s

The Land Rate

x Mr. [blank] Berry for Thomas Hance his tenement 4s
x Johan Hilliard for Richard Rich his tenement 2s
x John Garland for Edward Lakes tenement 6s
x Grace Langworthy for Richard Hookes tenement 4s
x Mr. Lippingcot for Abel Worths tenement 4s

20s

Sum total £23 13s 0d

Whereof is payd
To the Sheriffe of the said Citty in mony £23 4s 2d
For the Collectors allowance 1s 11d
To the Clarke for his allowance 1s 11d
More to be defalcated out of 5 persons rates before uncrossed that are so poore that they cannot pay the same, of whose poverty and insufficiency wee are certifyed under the Collectors hands 5s

Sum totall of the payments & allowances is £23 13s

m. 32

PARISH OF ST. MARY STEPS[1]

John Giles
John Ball *Collectors*

x	Edward Hill & wife	10s 6d
x	Mary Packe	12d
x	Christofer Payne & wife	5s 6d
x	John Horsey	12d
x	Thomas Turner	12d
x	Robert Westmacot & wife	2s 6d
x	John Welsh	12d
x	Thomas Dokes	12d
x	John Norcot	12d
x	William Nicholls & wife	2s 6d
x	Mary Tinckcombe	12d
x	George Gunstone & wife	18d
x	Andrew Tinckcombe & wife	18d
x	Evan Lewes & wife	12d
x	Joan Pridham, widow	12d
x	Agnes Gilbert, widow	12d
x	Thomas Wotten & wife	12d
x	Christofer Slade	12d
x	John Caunter & wife	4s 6d
x	Margery Caunter	12d
x	John Commings & wife	6s 6d
x	Peter Bowdon	12d
x	Richard Gilbert	12d
x	Thomas Willing	12d
x	Anne Gill	12d
x	Philip Mayo & wife	2s 6d
x	John Basse & wife	12d
x	Richard Kennell & wife	12d
x	Robert Pooke & wife	2s 6d
x	William Snelling & wife	12d
x	James Slade & wife	30s 6d
x	William Varly & wife	2s 6d
x	William Daymond & wife	12d
	Elianor Robins, widow	12d
x	Elianor Robins the daughter	12d
x	James Taylor & wife	18d
x	Mark Potter & wife	12d
x	William Rice & wife	12d
	Susanna Stenning, widow	12d
x	George Edwards & wife	12d
x	Cadwallader Gilbert & wife	12d
x	Rebecca Barons, widow	12d
x	Alice Barnes	12d
	& wife	12d
		2s 6d
	& wife	2s 6d
		12d
	& wife	2s 6d
		12d
	well & wife	2s 6d
	Lake	12d

	Manly & wife	12d
	Walter Reed	
	Robert Basse & wife	
x	Francis Basse	
x	William Pranket	
x	Rebecca Paige	
x	Richard Miller & wife	12d
x	Sarah Miller	12d
x	John Patey	12d
x	Richard Walter	12d
x	Thomas Barons & wife	3s 6d
x	Peter Pearse	12d
x	Henry Dabynet & wife	10s 6d
x	Joan Chilcot	12d
x	William Collings & wife	3s 6d
x	Richard Payne	3s
x	Mary Payne	12d
x	John Densham & wife	2s 6d
x	Sibyl Densham	12d
x	John Bewse & wife	12d
x	Agnes Yarcombe	12d
x	Richard Wood & wife	12d
x	Robert Legg & wife	12d
x	John Herring & wife	2s 6d
x	Joan Herring	12d
x	Mary Herring	12d
x	Elizabeth Herring	12d
x	John Herring, jun.	12d

m. 32d

x	Nicholas May & wife	12d
x	John Allumbricke & wife	12d
x	Henry Keene & wife	4s 6d
x	James Fooke	12d
x	Roger Minson	12d
x	Arthur Moore	12d
x	William Hayward	12d
x	Thomas Nossiter	12d
x	Elianor Bricknall	12d
x	Ann Powle, widow	4s
x	John Powle	12d
x	Mary Powle	12d
x	Katherine Powle	12d
x	Elizabeth Stone, widow	12d
x	Abraham Stone & wife	2s 6d
x	Richard Jones	12d
x	John Truman & wife	2s 6d
x	Elizabeth Stephens	12d
x	John Hawker & wife	4s 6d
x	Susanna [blank]	12d
x	Richard Mediat & wife	12d
x	Wilmot Mediat	12d
x	Sarah Mediat	
x	John Mediat	
x	Walter Head	
x	Anne Clarke, widow	
	Richard Fill & wife	
	[Joan ?] Fill, widow	
	[William ?] Mudge & wife	12d

[1] Both the Exeter copy and the Public Record Office copy of the assessment for St. Mary Steps are somewhat decayed with the result that some gaps cannot be filled from either.

	Cocke & wife	12d
	an	12d
	nan & wife	12d
		12d
	& wife	12d
		12d
	varthy	12d
		12d
	& wife	12d
x	William Morrish & wife	12d
x	Thomas Godderidge & wife	12d
x	John Owens & wife	12d
x	Peter Huggins & wife	12d
x	Mary Jones	8s
x	Elianor Murch	12d
x	George Poe & wife	2s 6d
x	Dorothy Holmes	12d
x	Hugh Bidwell & wife	8s 6d
x	John Yetman	12d
x	James Gold	12d
x	Katherine Oger	12d
x	Edward Virgil & wife	2s 6d
x	Charles Hooper & wife	12d
x	James Clarke & wife	12d
x	Thomas Holman & wife	2s 6d
x	Nathaniel Guest & wife	2s 6d
x	Susanna Lipscombe	12d
x	[blank] West, widow	12d
x	Robert Jones & wife	12d
x	John Bicknall & wife	3s 6d
x	Mary Hawkings	12d
x	Jasper Hayne & wife	2s 6d
x	Anne Hayne	12d
x	Katherine Dendall	12d
x	Katherine Bond, widow	12d
x	Edward Langly & wife	12d
x	Dorothy Lynn	12d
x	Thomas Fooke & wife	12d
	Curitia Fooke	12d
x	Richard Hore	12d
x	Hugh Bent & wife	12d
x	John Trend & wife	12d
x	John Hodges	12d
x	Mark Reeve & wife	12d
x	Susanna Reeve	12d
x	John Lillington & wife	12d
x	Henry Lillington	12d
x	Edward Grove & wife	12d
x	Hugh Bolt & wife	12d
x	Roger Leaman & wife	12d
x	Thomas Souther	12d

m. 33

x	Anne Hunnycombe	12d
x	Anne Hunnicombe the daughter	12d
x	Thomas Bartlet & wife	4s 6d
x	Alice Claniver	12d
x	Thomas Baker & wife	12d
x	John Burges & wife	12d
x	Anne Scutt, widow	12d
x	Michael Yebbacombe & wife	12d
x	John Penny & wife	12d
x	Thomas White & wife	4s 6d
x	Elizabeth Merdon	12d
x	Elizabeth Tayler, widow	12d
x	Elizabeth Tayler the daughter	12d
x	John Giles & wife	2s 6d
x	Richard Courde	12d
x	Joan Giles	12d
x	John Ball & wife	3s 6d
x	Mary Ball	12d
x	Agnes Ash	12d
x	Richard Cassell	12d
x	William Budd & wife	2s 6d
x	John Gudding & wife	2s 6d
x	William Pearse & wife	12d
x	Richard Mediat & wife	2s 6d
x	Grace Wollacot	12d
x	John Pyne & wife	3s 6d
x	Elizabeth Commins, widow	3s
x	Elizabeth Little Johns	12d
x	Peter Preist	12d
x	Susanna Markes, widow	12d
x	Jacob Perkins & wife	12d
x	Joan Westcot, widow	12d
x	Henry Dagworthy & wife	12d
x	Joan Reed	12d
x	Thomas Tooll & wife	12d
x	Henry Stampro & wife	2s 6d
x	William Richards	12d
x	Roger Mitchell & wife	2s 6d
x	John Trend & wife	12d
x	Thomas Downe & wife	12s 6d
x	Anne Downe	12d
x	Barbara Downe	12d
x	John Barten & wife	12d
x	Katherine Gale	12d
	Robert [Burt] & wife	12d
[x	John Sudderd]	12d
[x	Frances] [blank]	12d

Total £18 13s 6d

[*Land*] *Rate*

[x	Robert Way] for severall houses in the possession [of Henry Dabynott] & others	[5s]
x	Mrs. [Hunt of London] for severall tenements in the p[ossession] of John Canter & others	[12s]
x	Gregory Bonifant for Richard Millers house	[2s]
x	Thomas Avery for John Lillingtons house	[3s]
x	The heires of Mr. Martyn of Lyndridge for a Tenement John Foxwill holdeth	[3s]
x	Robert Ridler for Cricklepit Mills	20s
x	Thomas Birdall for the like	20s
		£3 5s

Sum total £21 18s 6d

Whereof is payd
To the Sheriffe of the said Citty in mony £21 10s
For the Collectors allowance 1s 9d
More to be defalcated out of 5 persons rates being soe poore that they are not able [to pay] the same before uncrossed, of whose poverty and insufficiency we are certifyed under the Collectors hands 5s
To the Clarke for his allowance 1s 9d

Sum total of the payments & allowances is £21 18s 6d

PARISH OF ST. JOHN'S BOW

John Lee
Daniel Skibbowe *Collectors*

x	William Pearse & wife	4s 6d
x	John Avery	12d
x	Richard Chilcot & wife	12d
x	Thomas Sutten	12d
x	Richard Templer & wife	8s 6d
x	Margaret Cuttiford	12d
x	Alice Brooke	12d
x	John Beere	12d
m. 33d		
x	Richard Blake	12d
x	Nicholas Collings & wife	4s 6d
x	Mary Bisse	12d
x	Thomas Rich & wife	4s 6d
x	Robert Kenton	12d
x	Dionisia Pearse, widow	2s
	Elizabeth Woollcot, widow	8s
x	Susanna Luscombe	12d
x	Andrew Stabbacke & wife	10s 6d
x	John Cockrum	12d
x	Robert Roberts & wife	3s 6d
x	Joan Roberts	12d
x	Philip Hunt	12d
x	John Sampson & wife	2s 6d
x	Anne Whitemore	12d
x	Roger Sumers & wife	10s 6d
x	Thomas Sommers	12d
x	Elizabeth Summers	12d
x	John Courtney	12d
x	Sidwell Rope	12d
x	John Edgman & wife	2s 6d
x	William Champion & wife	12d
x	Benjamin Olliver & wife	£5 0s 6d
x	Benjamin Olliver, jun.	12d
x	Thomas Reeve	12d
x	Robert Ridler	[12d]
x	Joseph Clarke	[12d]
x	James Cater	[12d]
x	Mary Legg	[12d]
x	Joan [Bissan]d	12d
x	John [Hingston] & wife	5s 6d
x	[Ann Hingston]	12d
[x	John Hingston, jun.]	12d
[x	Jane Blackmore]	12d
[x	Henry Newcombe and wife]	5s 6d
[x	Daniel Force]	12d
x	John Prancket	12d
x	William Chapman	12d
x	Edward Maye	12d
x	Mary Newman	12d
x	Margaret Bennet	12d
x	Robert Trescot	10s
x	Daniel Sckibbow & wife	2s 6d
x	George Pyne & wife	4s 6d
x	William Skibbow	12d
x	Mary Skibbow	12d
x	John Dennys	12d
x	Joseph Wood	12d
x	William Lobb	12d
x	William Titherly	12d
x	John Wood	12d
x	Margaret Lendon	12d
x	Elizabeth Marly	12d
x	Anne Glyde, widow	12d
x	Thomas Glide	2s 6d
x	Alice Mills	12d
x	Nowell Pearse, jun. & wife	12d
x	Henry Taylor & wife	18d
x	Thomazine Martyn, widow	12d
x	Emlyn Martyn	12d
x	Mary Seaman, widow	5s
x	Alice Pearse	12d
x	John Boyland & wife	5s 6d
x	John Hardy	12d
x	Samuel Boyland	12d
x	John Payne	12d
x	Joshua Loring	12d
x	Elizabeth Boyland	12d
x	Elizabeth Reed	12d
x	Richard Southard	2s
x	James Halse & wife	12d
x	John Hunnicombe	12d
x	Thomas Morrish & wife	12d
x	Thomazine Morell, widow	12d
x	John Hooper, jun. & wife	12d
x	William Clement & wife	12d
x	Richard Pavyer & wife	12d
x	John Eveleigh	12d
x	John Palmer	12d
x	Nowell Pearse & wife	12d
x	Peter Powell & wife	12d
x	John Hooper, jun. & wife	3s 6d
m. 34		
x	Jonas Waldron & wife	12d
x	Thomas Moore & wife	2s 6d
x	Antony Berrill	12d

x	Thomas Cotten & wife	12d
x	John Roberts & wife	12d
x	Richard Johns & wife	2s 6d
x	Katherine Harris	12d
x	Susanna Cary	12d
x	Robert Phipps & wife	£4 0s 6d
x	Philip Cheeke	12d
x	Elizabeth Clapp	12d
x	Mary Coyle, widow	12d
x	Liddia Williams	12d
x	Richard Mountstephen & wife	8s 6d
x	James Westcot	12d
x	Robert Bowyer	12d
x	Mathew Brag	12d
x	Mary Redwood	12d
x	Nicholas Weekes & wife	12d
x	John Acland	12d
x	William Olliphew & wife	12d
x	John Olliphew	12d
x	Bennedict Wade	12d
x	Edward Pafford & wife	12d
x	Hugh Pafford	12d
x	William Ebsly	12d
x	Richard Bowen	12d
x	Edward Skingly & wife	12d
x	Francis Derud	12d
x	Stephen Oliphew & wife	£3 0s 6d
x	Florence Casely	12d
x	William Harris & wife	3s 6d
x	Richard Damerell	12d
x	Elizabeth Sherae	12d
x	John Tremlet & wife	12d
x	Roger Wills	12d
x	Humfrey Greene & wife	12d
x	Johanna Corne	12d
x	John Tony & wife	18d
x	James Tony	12d
x	John Larramore & wife	12d
x	Thomas Basse & wife	5s 6d
x	Grace Basse	12d
x	Richard Comins	12d
[x	Wilmot ? Rissan]	12d
[x	James Ratcliffe & wife]	12d
[x	John Johnson & wife]	12d
[x	Roger Foxe & wife]	12d
[x	Susanna Foxe]	12d
[x	blank Spurrier] widow	12d
[x	William Cotton & wife]	12d
[x	John Waye]	12d
[x	Christopher Waye]	12d
[x	Elizabeth Waye]	12d
[x	William Barber] & wife	12d
[x	Alice Aishly]	12d
[x]	John Wyet & wife	12d
x	Henry Hawkins & wife	18d
x	Johanna Snelling	12d
x	Crispin Wyet & wife	12d
x	Abel Ward & wife	12d
x	John Deymond & wife	12d
[x]	John Moore & wife	2s 6d
[x]	Thomas Hunt & wife	4s 6d
[x]	Mary Reeve	12d
[x]	Emmanuel Hodge & wife	3s 6d
[x]	Sarah Lemon	12d
[x]	James Crocker	12d
[x	Nicholas] Mathew & wife	2s 6d
[x	John] Triggs	12d
[x	Elizabeth Cooke]	12d
[x	Mary Webber]	12d
[x	John Lee]	10s
[x	Joan Warren]	12d
[x	Mary Madder]	12d
[x	Thomas Golsery]	12d
[x	Thomas Dagworthy] & wife	12d
[x]	Mary [Addams, widow]	12d
[x]	William [Dunne & wife]	12d
[x	Anthony Tayler]	12d
[x	Robert Soper & wife]	12d
[x	John Scare & wife]	12d
m. 34d		
[x	Nicholas Whitmore & wife]	12d
x	[William Williams & wife]	18d
x	Mary [Bremblecombe]	12d
x	Mary [Lidyett]	12d
[x]	Thomas [Potter & wife]	18d
[x	blank] [Ward] widow	12d
[x	James Michell] & wife	12d
[x	Edward May & wife]	12d
	[John Prince]	12d
[x	Eleanor Trescott] widow	12d
[x	Richard Williams] & wife	12d
[x]	Susanna Williams	12d
[x	John] Daniel & wife	18d
[x]	John (?) Bond (?) & wife	12d
[x]	Richard Prower & wife	12d
[x]	Francis Virtue & wife	12d
[x	blank] Lemon, widow	12d
[x]	John Lemon	12d
x	Rachel Lemon	12d
x	Richard Oake & wife	12d
x	John Burgesse & wife	12d
x	John Hooper	12d
x	John Tayler & wife	2s 6d
x	Nicholas Taylor	12d
[x]	John Robins & wife	12d
[x]	John Tagford & wife	12d
[x	William Maye] & wife	12d
[x	John Crow] & wife	12d
[x	Richard Browne] & wife	12d
[x	Thomas Hole] & wife	12d
[x	blank] [Willes, widow]	12d
[x	Elizabeth Pentire]	12d
[x	Joan Pentire]	12d
[x	Hugh Tinge & wife]	12d
[x	Thomas Paule]	12d
[x	Susanna Teane, widow]	12d
[x	Humphrey Snowe & wife]	12d

Total £28 14s 6d

The Land Rate

C	*Sir* John Yong *knight*	8s
C	Thomas Achim *esq.*	6s
x	Mr, Richard Sanders	5s
x	Mr. Thomas Pitts	3s
		22s

Sum total £29 16s 6d

Whereof is payd	
To the Sheriffe of the said Citty in money	£28 7s 10d
For the Collectors allowance	2s 4d
More to be defalcated out of two persons rates that are soe poore that cannot pay the same of whose poverty & insufficiency wee are certyfyed under the Collectors hands before uncrossed	2s
More on two certificates as before	14s
More unpayd by Elizabeth Woollcot	8s
To the Clarke for his allowance	2s 4d

Sum total of the payments & allowances is £29 16s 6d

Sum totall of the monies paid to the Sheriffe is	£893 10s 3d
Sum of the Allowances	£108 12s 3d

Sum totall £1002 2s 6d

Christopher Lethbridge *Maior*
Simon Snowe
Christopher Clarke
Richard Crossing
Nicholas Broking

John Acland
John Mayne

Ralph Herman
John Martin
Henry Gandy

Wm. Bruen *Sherriff*

4. THE HEARTH TAX OF 1671.[1]

m.1

A List or Schedule of all Hearths and Stoves in the severall Houses in all the Parishes within the said Cittie of Exeter and Comitie of the said Cittie.

TRINITIE PARISH

Edward Templar	4
Robert Page	3
John Hayman	3
John Grenfeild	3
John Barons	13
William Chard	1
William Baker	2
Widow Warringe	3
John Beavys	3
John Wood	10
Widow Searle	4
John Saunders	2
John Mathew	8
Margarett Cattary	3
Widow Hayman	3
Ezekiel Gribble	3
John Tucker	3
Morrish Williams	2
Walter Horwood	2
Francis Wolfe	2
Daniel Clerke	2
John Glanvill	2
Morgan Philly	2
William Cape	2
Nathaniel Blight	7
John Soper	3
Thomas Pike	2
William Edwards	2
Samuel Philipps	2
Thomas Mortymore	3
William Drake	1
Robert Gunt	1
William Turnepenny	2
Thomas Pyne	2
Widow Cheeke	7
Abell Kinge sen.	3
Jermon Tilly	3
Edward Guest	1
Thomas Skinner	7
Francis Mapowder	4
John Mannington	7
John Bawdon	7
Nicholas Coffen	4
John Arden	4
Anthony Smyth	7
Henry Fitzwilliams	7
Henry Petit	5
Cabel Lowdon and tenants	11
John Collings	6
James Clutterbrooke	8
Widow Kinge	4
Johan Cheeke	2
Arthur Thorne	4
Christopher Cann	2
Joseph Hoyte	2
Andrew Reynolds	23
Richard Nickes	3
John Russell	2
John Norton	5
Thomas Humphrey	2
John Nichols	2
Andrew Bidwell	2
Hugh Dennys	2
Robert Shoulders	2
Nathaniell Farrant	2
John Hingston	6
William Dyer	6
John Hawkey	3
Josias Burges	2
Richard Ganthony	2
William Butler	6
John Bagwell	1
William West	2
Richard Mathew	2
John Boynes	2
William Atkins	1
William Legitt	2
Thomas Prigge	2
Robert Daniell	3
Thomas Heath	10
Stephen Harris	1
William Butler jun.	1
Nicholas Yeo	3
William Glanfill	2

[1] E.C.M., Misc. Rolls No. 74.

George Clare for his tenement	1
George Clare	5
William Yard	2
William Saunders	2
Martin Hopkins	1
John Lowman	3
Humphry Bawdon	10
Peter West	2
John Glanvill	2
Thomas Martin	2
Gabriell Byrch	3
George Reed	1
William Pyke	1
m.1d.	
Henry Fitzwilliams	3

Total 355

The poore of the said parish

Dorcas Williams	1
Timothy Abbott	1
John Rumbelow	1
Silvester Follett	1
Widow Bowdon	1
Widow Whitlocke	1
John Robins	1
Joan Flood	1
William Morris	1
Ann Bowdon widow	1
James Hore	1
Robert Edwards	2
William Morrish jun.	1
John Drake	1
Thomas Thomas	1
Peter Tucker	1
Mary Leigh	1
Lawrence Bidwell	1
John Peddericke	1
Philipp Wotten	1
Henry Tanner	1
Richard Gaydon	1
John Style	1
Widow Smith	1
Widow Hopkins	1
Philipp Martin	1
Richard Ward	1
Mary Chambers	1
Robert Auton	1
Thomas Whiddon	1
John Pearse	1
Gabriell Comings	1
John Bampfield	1
Peter Shepheard	1
Henry Campe	2
Henry Bradford	2
William Tucker	1
George Mudge	1
Widow Symons	1
William Viccary	1
Peter Radford	2
Thomas Row	2
Hex Dashford	2
Henry Rolles	2
Symon Light	1
Anthony Boatfield	1
James Yeo	1
Martin Brothers	1
Nicholas Bickley	1
Edward Jessop	1
John Langnler [Languler ?]	1
Thomas Prydeaux	1
Hugh Vivian	1
John Hore	1
Zachary Haskins	1
John Gibbs	1
Philipp Mugford	1
William Thomas	1
Mathew Ganthony	1
Roger Ganthony	1
John Floud	1
Abisha Mawditt	2
George Awton	2
Thomas Hare	1
Samuel Weeks	1
Widow Munday	1
William Macey	1
Widow Olliver	1
John Goffe	1
Ralph Clerke	1
Rebecca Mathew	1
John Gibbs	1
Widow Mathew	2
Widow Sloman	1
Widow Polin	1
Thomas Grindon	1
Hugh Playe	1
Widow Cuningham	1
Andrew Gitsham	1
Edward Raye	1
John Dart	1
Widow Greenham	1
Thomas Dotson	1
William Michell	1
Thomas Bonny	1
Agnes Hearth	1
Widow Jenkins	1
Edward Coombe	1
Cornelius Mollen	1
Widow Maye	1
John Pinn	1
John Blake	1
Widow Lay	1
Edward Edwards	1
Robert Kent	1
Robert Moggridge	1
Susanna Shoulder	1
Robert Welch	1
Thomas Lennington	1
Bartholemew Kennicke	1
Widow Boynes	2
Bartholemew Webb	1
Robert Richardson	1

Thomas Crispin	1
Anthony Richardson	1
Ambrose Walker	1
John Ellett	1
Edward Whithall	1
Abraham Sloman	1
Symon Ven	1
Richard Wilkins	1
Nicholas Furlong	1
m.2	
Dorothy Davy	1
William Ley	1
Ambrose Hooper	2
Widow Roul	1
Thomas Laskey	1
James Downe	1
Nicholas Ley	1
Henry Edwards	1
Widow Deane	1
Charles Lissett	1
Luke May	1
Thomas Johnson	1
Achia Pritty	1

Total 137

ST. SIDWELLE PARISH

Thomas Bicknell & Tenements	4
Christopher Courtice	3
William Grigg	2
Christopher Silly	1
Christopher London	2
Widow Bryant	2
Robert Humphrey	3
Jonas Bonfield	3
Robert Sainthill	1
Thomas Hooper	4
Roger Cheeke	8
George Linington	1
William Silly	1
John Webber	2
Anthony Gould	2
Nathaniel Isaacke	2
Gregory Hooper	2
Mathias Lant	1
Widow Dart	6
Thomas Jones	3
Widow Pitts	9
Richard Jerman	2
John Bowdon	1
Edward Blackmore	6
Edward Ridmills	1
Robert Catford	2
Thomas Weeks	1
Thomas Bartlett	2
Elias Wheeler	2
Luke Mathew	2
Robert Carter	27
Nicholas Pinton	2
John Brokin	1
James Silly	2
John Dinninge	2
Robert Hore	3
Evill Foxwell & Tenants	7
Henry Norton	1
Widow Leigh	1
Christopher Ellett	2
Richard Symons	1
Edward Cheeke	6
John Hill	3
Thomas Rogers	2
John Mounstephyn	1
Thomas Segar	1
Hugh Carraway	2
Alexander Langman	1
John Hewett	4
John Humphry	3
John Smalridge sen.	2
Amos Butcher	2
John Smalridge jun.	2
Thomas Smalridge	2
Thomas Towton	1
Anthony Pole	2
Thomas Mayne	4
Hugh Andrews	2
William Sweetland	5
Robert Loman	2
Robert Saunders	2
Edward Banbury	6
Richard Allyn	2
Nathaniel Hossey	1
Richard Langbridge	1
Robert Grenshald	2
Thomas Kaines	1
Robert Upcott	2
Daniell Smalridge	1
Henry Filmore	1
Stephen Hayne	1
Roger Reed	1
John Penny	1
Richard Penny	2
William Slade	1
John Reynolds	1
Thomas Pitfield	6
Peter Clapp	4
John Hoose	1
Widow Bennett	6
James Horwood	10
Widow Tucker	2
James Cham	2
Lewes Gyles	1
William Pyke	11
m.2d.	
John Ellys & Tenements	10
Philipp Southard	2
John Berry	2
Bernard Timpany	2
Richard Jewell	2
William Frost	2
Widow Baker	2
John Vile	2
Thomas Tilly	7

Richard Adams & Tenements	6
Jeremiah Cudmore	2
John Withars	5
Thomas Broadbeer	3
Edward Ellett	2
Thomas Bowdall sen.	4
George Smyth	3
Thomas Pitts	1
John How	4
John Carne	4
Widow Weekes	2
John Smyth	3
John Foxwell	1
Richard Westcott	1
George Bussell	1
Thomas Potter	2
John Reynolds	1
Richard Sweetland	3
Robert Daw for his Tenements	4
Widow Bidney	2
John Hoppinge	1
George Hoppinge	1
Luke Baker	4
Thomas Waterman sen. (−1)	2
John Collibeer	5
Thomas Crosse	1
Charles Rewallen	4
Daniell Tiggins	5
Mathew Wyott	4
Israel Mitchell	5
Nicholas Somerton	1
John Tuckfield sen.	1
Arthur White	1
Anthony Salter	5
John Moore	1
William Thomas	1
John Wheeler	1

Total 374

The poore of the parish of St. Sidwelle

Hugh Shapcott	1
Widow Mounstephyn	1
Edward May	1
Widow Isaacke	1
Roger Follett (−1)	2
John Shepheard	1
Robert Burt	1
Hugh Avery	1
Christopher Neels	2
Israel Court	1
Samuel Gyles	1
Thomas Bonfield	1
John Scanes	1
John Lowdon	1
Walter Ratcliffe	1
Elizabeth Ponnsford	1
George Traverse	1
William Hooper	1
Thomas Whitinge	1
Widow Tucker	1
Arthur Bilmore	2
George Reynolds	2
John Coram	2
Widow Slocombe	1
Widow Petty [Potty ?]	1
Lewes Baker	1
Peter Shafe	1
Widow Kittle	1
Ralph Doddridge	1
Bridgett Browne	1
Philipp Pyke	2
William Tucker	1
Widow Bodley	2
Widow Shafe	1
John Luxon	1
James Hodder	1
Nicholas Dunn	1
John Eastabrooke	1
Widow Goolfery	1
Robert Turner	2
John Hart	2
John Paddy	1
Widow Legge	1
Hercules Johns	1
Peter Mortimore	1
John Turner	1
Bernard Hatherley	1
John Andrew	1
John Jenkins	1
George Squyer	1
m.3	
Humphry Payne	1
Peter Payne	2
Genny Mathew	1
Thomas Cholwell	2
John Baker	1
Tristram Hare	1
Robert Dart	2
John Smith	2
Roger Hart	1
Widow Reynolds	1
Olliver Horsey	1
William Triggs	1
Richard May	1
Widow Bricknell	1
Julian Washbeare	1
Widow Gibbons	2
John Gibbons	1
John May	1
Richard May	2
William Langdon	1
John Washbeare	1
John Squyre	1
Thomas [blank]	1
Richard Randell	1
Robert Davy	1
Thomas Penrose	1
Nicholas Wannell	2
John Clerke	1
Christopher Battyn	2
Ciprian Center	1

William Mynifie 1
William Comings 1
Walter Cuddifer 1
Thomas Ridge 1
Peter Langdon 1
Widow Jones 1
John Rumpson 1
Robert Goldsworthy 1
John Cudmore 1
Widow Follett 1
Elianor James 1
John Hurlestone 1
John Hooper 1
Ralph Luxon 1
Thomas Ledge 2
Widow Bodley 1
George Bickham 1
Widow Silvester 1
Widow Shafe 1
Widow Butler 1
Bartholemew Hopkins 1
Richard Cocher 1
John Jewell 1
William Cooke 1
James Adder 1
Ralph Kinsman 1
Roger Cann 1
John Manly 1
Nicholas Bennett 1
John Chadner 1
Nicholas Dunn 1
John Eastabrooke 1
Philipp Tucker 1
Daniell Tedder 1
Peter Huddy 1
Widow Neels 1
Widow Seaward 1
Mary White 1
Robert May 2
Henry Tozer 2
George Goldsworthy 2
William Pearse 1
Robert Parsons 1
John Pottle 1
John Bond 1
John Frost 2
John Reed 2
Samuel Tregell 1
Robert Kestey 1
John Clerke 1
William Blake 1
Joseph Harris 1
Thomas Oynes 1
William Ellis 2
Thomas Barrett 2
John Pope 1
Richard Jerman 1
William Hatherley 1
George Pitfield 1
Valentine May 1
William Mallett 1
Widow Pidgeon 1
Widow Thomas 1
Edward Rutley 1
Edward Whitinge 1
Grace Shapley 1
Sampson Tompson 1
Ann Silly 1
Francis Weare 1
Robert Norris 1
Thomas Dunsham 1
Thomas Clement 1
James Perry 2
George Linnington 1
John Gunt 1
Leonard Irish 1
Nicholas Johnson 1
Thomas Liedgier 1
Peter Crosse 1
Abigal Ledge 1
Joan Herringe 1
William Savery 1
Elizabeth Slocombe 2
m.3d.
Christopher Pester 1
John Sally 1
Widow Lee 1
Thomas Bridgman 1
Widow Bennett 2
Widow Shapley 2
Peter Harris 2
Peter Hellyer 1
John Stephens 2
Philipp Fisher 2
William [Boson ?] 1
John Rumpson 1
David Ellary 1
John Ridge sen. 1
John Ridge jun. 1
William Andrew 1
Thomas Gedge 1
Thomas Broach 2
Christopher Comings 2
John Butson 2
John Band 1
[Blank] Trechan
Richard Balle 2
Robert Bonny 1
Zachary Sweetland 1
Henry Hooper 2
Joseph Drew 1
Nathaniel Baker 1
Widow Burnell 2
George Richards 1
Silvester Baker 1
David Jones 1
Thomas Croope 2
Thomas Drake 1
Hechabard Small 1
Widow Crocker 1
Otho Channell 1
Joseph Jerman 2
Widow Brockba 1
John Norman 1

Saunder Gitt	1
Hubert Whitinge	1
Christopher Mortymore sen.	1
Christopher Mortymore jun.	1
George Follett	1
Zachariah Buckpitt	1
Edward Whitcombe	2
Nicholas Hunt	1
Roger Slocombe	1
John Reader	1
Roger Kempe	1
Richard Cooke	1
John Carter	2
John Clerke	1
George Butchford	1
Thomas Pitford	1
William Woolcott	1
Mary Swert	1
Margarett Swert	1
John Cove	2
George Hoppinge	1
Richard Westcott	1

Total [268 in margin]

ST. PETROX

Ellize Pinsent	5
Edward Starr	8
Robert Buckland[1]	10
William Pinny	5
John Carwithen	10
Elizabeth Hugh	2
Edward Ayshford	7
Thomas Wood	5
John Guswell	8
John Atkins	6
Richard Nott	5
John Bayly	4
John Webber	1
Thomas Harris	2
Ezekiel Wood	2
William Jones	4
Widow Redwood	5
George Knowlinge	4
William Sanford *esq.*	8
John Mayne	8
Josias Eveleigh	3
Widow Bartlett	4
Mathew Payne	2
George Cary	2
Thomas Guswell	2
Thomas Turner	2
Joseph Pearce	2
John Martin	10
Stephen Burton	4
Ralph Bennett	9
William Norrish	5
Andrew Quash	4
Gilbert Yard	4
Ralph Sheers	5
Gyles Wood	2
William Hooper	6
Nicholas Savery	7
Agnes Tapper	5
Peter Battishill	2
Elianor Tothill	1

Total 191

m.4

The poore of the parish of St. Petrox

Widow Bowdon	1
William Poole	2

Total [3 in margin]

THE CLOSE

Anthony Lord Bishopp of Exon	17
William Beard	2
William Glyde	9
Nicholas Eveleigh	5
Chancellor Tompkins	7
Robert Chilcott	4
Mrs Greedy	3
Elizabeth Slaninge	1
Francis Courtney	2
Chaunter Bold	7
James Pearse	5
Nicholas Cooke	4
Widow Bowden	2
George Cary Deane	16
Widow Sainthill	3
Widow Cooke	4
Widow Cursons	7
Peter Trosse	4
Francis Jewell	4
Richard Izacke	3
Francis Pengelly	3
John Reynolds	3
Widow Linscott	4
Thomas Ellard	2
William Warren	4
John Macy	4
Richard Spicer	3
William Warren jun.	2
Christopher Brodridge	5
Robert Seamer	5
Widow Hopwood	3
Judeth Chubb	2
John Gare	3

[1] Probably the owner of the *Vintage Tavern,* now represented by No. 192 High Street. So the assessor is starting at Parliament Street and proceeding down High Street towards North Street.

Thomas Crossinge	2
William Humphry	2
John Johnson	2
Peter Gale	2
Richard Williams	1
Christopher Codner	1
John Dennys	3
David Powell	4
John Bareford	3
Thomas Moore	3
Henry Humfry	2
John Whiddon	2
Henry Gale	2
Robert Parsons	5
Jonathan Hawke	2
Jeremiah Johns	2
Widow Salter	2
John Jewell	1
Francis Cooke	4
John Mayne	7
Samuel Izacke sen.	7
Charles Taylor	4
Widow Cooke	2
Jane Hooper	2
John Snell	9
Mary Mapowder	1
Mrs Ducke & Tenements	5
John Slade	2
Nicholas Webber	7
Hannibal Ratcliffe	5
Thomas Lane	3
Thomas Holmes	4
Henry Harris	2
Jeremiah Kinge	6
John Warren	7
Thomas Wearman	7
John Force	5
Philipp Atherton	4
Richard Greedy	2
John Glanvill	3
Olliver Mustion	3
Widow Magent	2
John Bidgood	8
Thomas Wright	7
William Eastchurch	7
Symon Grymes	4
John Palmer	9
Richard Ashley	1
Robert Rouse	4
John Chichester *esq.*	8
Doctor Fulwood	8
Nicholas Isacke *Alderman*	9
Anthony Dolton	8
Christopher Sandford	7
Doctor Cotton	10
Baldwyn Acland *Treasurer*	16
Zachary Dashwood	7
John Loosemore	6
Canon Naylor	7
Doctor Morrish	6
Thomas Shears	6
Widow Blissington	3

Total 437

The poore of the Close

Nicholas Jagoe	2
Lancellot Burges	2
William Saunders	2
Francis Hill	2
Mary Macye	2
Henry Humphry	2
Philipp Hayne	2
Michaell North	2

Total [16 in margin]

m.4d.

ST. KIRYANS PARISH

Widow Ford	8
John Browne	3
George Yeo	2
Peter Risdon	6
Susanna Buckland	2
Peter Parr	4
Thomas Pafford	2
Peter West	3
Thomas Crispen	10
Bartholemew White	4
William Bodley	5
Richard White	6
Widow Marshall	10
Edward Edgecombe	3
Widow Brinly	4
George Shapcott	8
Dorcas Showers	7
Rebecca Trosse	7
Bartholemew Anthony	9
John Clapp	2
Richard Tucker	6
John Starr	13
Endymion Walker	7
George Tuthill *esq.*	6
Widow Crosse	2
George Ducke	2
John Clerke	2
Ann Colfox	1
Nicholas Kennicott	8
Nicholas Bolte	3
John Williams	10
John Turlinge	6

Total [171 in margin]

The poore of the parish of St. Kiryans

John Pratt	1
Roger Jewell	1
Richard Place	1
Widow Kneebone	1
Francis Jewell	1
John Adams	1

Total 6

ALLHALLOWS PARISH UPON THE WALLES

John Willes	2
John Hooper	1
Hugh Heant	3
George Gibson	1
John Pope	2
Andrew Heard	1
Temperance Penny	1
Roger Warner	2
Nicholas Medyatt	1
James Archipole	2
Thomas Payne	2
John Barons	1
Roger Bolte	2
Nicholas Snell	3
Mathew Medyatt	2
John Dinninge	1
Richard Pole	1
Humphry Morymore	1
John Bond	4
George Knowlinge	3
Edward Pince	6
Widow Michell	2
James Wescott	3
Richard Payne	2
John Keefe	4
William Trescott	3
Edward Pince	3
Henry Hole	3
Widow Jewell	1
Robert Foster	4
Robert Pitcher	7
John Daniell	2
Widow Mounstephen	1
Thomas Barons	5
John Woodwall	2
Susanna Harris	2
John Pince	3
Widow Bidgood	2
John Pyke	1
Richard Barons	2
William Barons	2
Nathaniel White	2
Nowel Pearse	5
Robert Martin	3
Jonathan Poe	2
Henry Dagworthy	2

Total 110

m.5

The poore of the parish of Allhallows on Walls

Edmond Barons	1
Lewes Hale	2
John Barrell	1
John Walters	1
Roger Smyth	1
George Carpenter	1
Robert Circum	2
Mary Guswell	1
James Blannchford	2
William Heard	1
Robert Light	1
Reynolds Marshall	1
William Elmes	1
Richard Job	1
John Coombe	1
Michaell Satchfield	1
Daniell Hodge	1
John Hooper	1
John Harper	1
Widow Hodge	1
Thomas Symons	1
Mathew Leonard	1
Thomas Jacob	1
Widow Mathew	1
John Tapley	2
Henry Gibbs	1
Widow Luxton	1
Nicholas Barons	1
Francis Breakbacke	1
Widow Larme	1
Stephen Hingstone	1
Thomas Baker	1
Widow Hawkings	1
Thomas Barons	1
Richard Jacob	1

Total 39

ST. DAVIDS PARISH

Abell Beardon	9
Richard Webber	2
John Janny	6
James Marshall	9
Thomas Rayson	2
Widow Bennett	1
Nathaniell Edwards	3
Thomas Maynor	1
Thomas Fooke	2
John Bennett	2
Symon Landman [Laudman ?]	1
Symon Tracy	2
George Woodwall	2
Nathaniell Ford	2
Edmond Tracy	2
John Seller	1
Nathaniell Ford	2
Henry Walker	4
John Hart	2
Zachary Tothill	2
Christopher Geard	3
Peter Tucker	5
James Knolton	2
Richard Shears	5
Thomas Rayson	2
Widow Tucker	1
Richard Davy	2

George Pole	2
John Knott	1
Hugh Woodwall	3
John Knott	5
David Holman	4
John Birdall	1
John Perryman	3
Edward Hungerford[1]	6
Robert Hungerford	1
John Wood	2
George Tuthill *esq.*	3
Nathaniell Holman	2
Thomas Speare	1
Nicholas Cornish	2
William Roper	4
Mrs Jordan	1
Robert Spicer	2
Thomas Hardy	2
John Pitts	1
Gabryell Howard	2
Samuel Knight	2
John Arundle	2
Widow Borough	5
Widow Hole	5
William Dinny	4
Henry Thomas	2
Samuel Marwood	4
George Rixon	2
Thomas Crispen	2
John Slowman	2
Gregory Woolcott	1
Robert Moggridge	1
Jeffery Pyke	2
Henry Bone	2
Stephen Tremlett	2
William Wyndeatt	2
Abell Hooper	2
George Flaye	2
John Payne	2
John Rentfree	1
Widow Jefford	1
Widow Davy	4
John Hill	1
Thomas Trescott	5
Anthony Gaye	3
m.5d.	
William Gilbert	3
James Lyde	2
Thomas Williams	2
Luke Falvey	7
John Ferris	1
Digory Greedy	1
George Robinson	6
John Bruford[2]	20
William Stuckey	15
William Welman	2
Robert Venner	4
John Barons	3
George Masters	4
Widow Egby	5
Widow Cawsey	2
John Hale	1
Widow Coffin	2
John Crosse	2
Thomas Williams	2
William Audry	2
Nicholas Gloyne	8
George Morcombe	4

Total 285

The poore of the said parish of St. David

John Northcott	2
Thomas Windham	2
Ralph Winter	2
John Coles	2
Hugh Woodward	2
Richard Best	2
Robert White	2
Peter Edwards	2
John Lugg	1
Richard Rugg	1
William Wood	2
Thomas Bristow	2
Michael Fooke	1
Malachy Bucknoll	1
Ephraem Short	1
John Tugbert	1
John Saunders	1
James Edwards	2
Theophilus Triggs	2
Isaac Sloman	2
Widow Keefe	2
William Carpenter	1
John Tidder	2
John Tucker	2
Richard Bagwell	1
Robert Pleace	2
Anthony Coxe	1
John Strange	2
Robert Lisle	2
Richard Dart	2
John Chambers	1
John Pollard	2
William Hare	2
William Crispin	2
Richard Wheeler	2
George Dyer	1
John Ford	1
Thomas Lee	1
George Dart	1
Christopher Divers	1
Thomas Tremlett	1
Joseph Jerman	1

[1] Barton Place, near Cowley Bridge, held by the Hungerfords on a lease from the Chamber.
[2] Probably the Oxford Inn, on the site of which the New London Inn was erected in 1794. The site is now covered by the Savoy Cinema.

Widow Dart	2
John Foxwell	2
John Hartnall	2
Peter Case	1
Nicholas Turner	2
Nicholas Manninge	1
Richard Triggs	2
Robert Woolcott	1
William Hole	1
James Blannchford	1
Edward Hobbs	1
George Lucy	1
John Lake	1
Mathew Kinge	1

Total 85

ST. JOHNS PARISH

Daniel Skibbow	4
John Boyland	6
Sir Beniamyn Olliver *knt.*	11
Roger Somers	7
John Sampson	3
Andrew Stavicke	5
Widow Pratt	3
Thomas Rich	6
Nicholas Collings	4
Richard Templar	10
m.6.	
William Pearse	6
William Harris	2
William Olliver	4
Robert Roberts	4
Ann Glyde	3
Henry Tayler	1
Thomas Martin	1
Widow Seamer	6
William Lobb	6
Richard Southward	2
John Pole	3
Peter Powell	1
Thomas Moore	3
John Cary	3
Robert Phipps	7
George Guswill	12
Richard Mountstephin	2
Ann Jones	1
Thomas Potter	1
Widow Kinge	3
John Lee	7
Nicholas Mathew	4
Edward Sloman	2
John Moore	2
Richard Lemett	1
John Cotton	2
Christopher Wyatt	2
John Cockerham	1
James Wescott	4
John Wyatt	1
Thomas Basse	2
John Tremlett	2
Christopher Harris	1
George Goffe	1
John Tayler	2
Mrs Lake	2

Total 166

The poore of the said parish of St. Johns

Thomas Paddon	1
Widow Edmond	1
Anthony Tayler	1
Isaack Wheeler	1
Nowell Pearse sen.	2
Widow Hole	1
Thomas Weeks	1
Widow Shears	2
William Dame	2
Richard Browne	2
William Hawkes	1
Widow Lemon	2
Edward May	2
Henry Minton	1
Richard Williams	2
John Roberts	2
Francis Vertue	2
Richard Oake	1
Raynold Watkins	1
Widow Payne	1
John Williams	1
Widow Martin	1
Thomas Paddon jun.	1
William Torringe	1
Richard Roberts	1
William Campton	1
Edward Pafford	1
Henry Saunders	1
Hugh Bolte	1
William Lumber	1
Widow Robinson	1
Elianor Trescott	1
Richard Prowcer	1
John Robyns	1
Nathaniell Williams	1
Richard Coles	1
Hugh Whitmore	1
John Burges	1
Richard Williams	1
Susanna Janes	1
Richard Willes	1
Moses Pinsent	1
Mary Harris	1
William Barber	1
Joan Solly	1
Thomas Willes	1
Katheryne Wythers	1
Christopher Wyatt	1
Thomas Cooper	1

William Williams	2
Alexander Pearse	1
Widow Stephens	1

Total 62

ST. MARY ARCHES PARISH

Robert Walker *esq.*	13
Thomas Walker *esq.*	4
Charles Alden	3
Edward Eveleigh	9
Hugh Abell	8
Edward Hickman	4
James Slade	9
Mrs Joan Lethbridge	12
Edward Crosse	3
John Boson	3
Richard Crossinge	9
Job Beard	5
John Tarleton	3
William Wotton	3
Richard Langman	3
Leonard Prince	4
Christopher Clerke	7
John Crosse	4
John Boson	6
Johan Hakewill	4
William Trevecke	1
m.6d.	
Jonathan Battishill	2
Nathaniell Bart	1
Thomas Green	1
Widow Gibbs	7
Samuel Calle	5
William Fry	2
Widow Bagwell	4
Joseph Mawditt	5
John Arundell	5
Mrs Clatworthy	5
Philipp Gaydon	1
Mrs. Skinner	1
George Sanford	5
John Crosse	3
Henry Trevill	1
William Tanman	2
Joseph Chafe	2
Francis Bigford	1
William Crumpton	3
William Coombe	2
Edward Berryman	2
Roger Giles	2
Widow Lake	2

Total 181

The poore of the parish of St. Mary Arches

John Delve	1
John Gill	1
John Hayman	1
Widow Growdon	1
Widow Pillye	1
John Northcott	1
Walter Harper	2
Philipp Sparke	1
Robert Parker	1
Evans Williams	1
Humphry Snowe	1
Ambrose Sumpter	2
John Kitt	1
Henry Spurr	1
Thomas Dare	1
John Watts	1
John Delve	1
Richard Lawrence	1
Richard Light	1
Obadiah Wigginton	1
John Leigh	1
Francis Bickford	1

Total [none given]

ST. PAULES PARISH

Joseph Yeo	2
Jonathan Walrond	2
John Lavers	8
James Pope	2
George Ducke	1
Cornelius Cooze	3
Philipp Bastard	1
Philipp Paty	1
Henry Cudmore	8
Robert Gale	2
William Gale	3
John Joyce	1
Samuel Browne	2
John Chubb	2
Walter Payne	2
Widow Grindinge	2
John Lavers jun.	2
Samuel Davy	1
Richard Hole	3
Katharyne Evans	7
Henry Saunders	2
John Hodge	13
Widow Barons	2
Widow Brakyn	1
Francis Hole [Hele ?]	2
Thomas Bouncer	2
Thomas Cooch	1
John Chase	4
Edward Dennys	3
[blank] Luscombe	4
Philipp Moore	2
Roger Bolte	1
Symon Carraway	1
John Dawton	2
Robert Atkins	3
Lewes Grenslade	5

Ezekiel Stevens 2
Samuel Hutchings 1
Jasper Yorke 2
Mrs Moulton 1
Peter Irish 3
John Loyde 4
John Butler 6
Widow Penington 6
William Toll 3
John Percy 1
m.7
William Harvy 1
John Jackman 2
William Hill 5
John Norman 8
John Rooke 10
Francis Child 6
Mr. Seaward 10
Walter Deeble 7
John Webb 4
Mary Lethbridge widow 8
John Gandy 13
Malachy Pyne 21
John Fare 3
John Hardinge 7
John Loyde 3
Abraham Trowte 6
William Lewes 4
Tavernor Cockerham 5
Edward Mathews 3
George Payne 2
Widow Martin 1
William Staplin 3
Daniel Gifford 2
John Browne 5
Ralph Cooze 3
John Jones 3
Samuel Alford 2
Robert Bond 5
Peter Pitts 3
The Bridewell 15
Joseph Cooze 2
Thomas Northcott 2
Robert Foxwell 2
Philipp Commings 1
John Brady 2
Thomas Halse 1
Richard Templer 2
Edmonde Kinge 3
Andrew Bowman 4

Total 321

The poore of St. Paules

Thomas Bale 1
Widow Draper 1
William Perry 2
William Keen 1
Michaell Fugg 1
Joseph Tracy 1
Widow Endicott 2
Thomas Keyne 1
Widow Baker 1
William Norris 1
Thomas Webb 1
George Thomas 1
Henry Somerton 1
Andrew Aysh 1
Thomas Timothy 1
Thomas Manly 2
George Markes 1
Richard Ledgingham 1
Christopher Mounstephin 1
Richard Misery 1
Thomas Bale 1
Andrew Small 1
Peter Willes 1
Thomas Baker 1
George Haven 1
Roger Muffers 1
Christopher Turner 1
William Whitrow 1
Richard Symons 1
George Ray 1
Ambrose Wall 1
William Byshopp 1
John Heath 1
Christopher Takell 1
Richard Hurly 1
Elizabeth Radford 1
Mary Northcott 1
George Bustyn 1
Edward Cautricke 1
Cipio Greenslade 1
Samuel Carsewell 1
William May 1
Nicholas Manley 1
William Smyth 1
Jonathan Downe 1
William Bilmore 1
Allen Hackwell 1
John Sams 1
Jonas Wolrond 1
John Packer 1
Caleb Luscombe 1
John Gill 1
Samuel Davys 1
Peter Pole 1
Josias Follett 1
Richard Balle 1
Robert Glanvill 1
Ann Gibson 1
Nicholas Winsor 1
Grace Pole 1
Walter Fynimore 1
John Ellys 1
William Pomroy 2
John Daniell 1
William Arnell 1
Thomas Manly 1
Digory Downinge 1
Edward Woolcott 1

Widow Chubb	1
William Lumber	1
m.7d.	
Thomas Morgan	1
James Mounstephin	1
Widow Medland	1
Richard Tucker	1
Peter Halstaffe sen.	1
John Heath	1
John Jonas	1
Widow Barons	1

Total [82 in margin]

ST. EDMONDS PARISH

Robert Wolland	2
Samuel Tabonlett	2
George Wood	2
The Tuckinge Milles	1
Edward Strange	2
Isaac Mawditt	8
Ambrose Paige	6
Joseph Pince	10
Aries Shore	1
Edward Hill	2
John Endicott	1
Widow Smalridge	2
Joseph Rouse	1
Jane Perriman	2
John Style	1
Thomas Arthur	3
Widow Harvy	2
Mathew Tipper sen.	2
John Denham	1
Joan Hardinge	1
Benjamin Bowdon	2
Edward Clerke	5
Widow Plumpton	3
Samuel Howell	2
William Leevs	2
John Tipper	1
Widow Well	2
Isaac Burch	2
Robert Sloman	1
William Wolland	1
Henry Hodge	2
Thomas Browne	2
Thomas Saterly	1
Vincent Tinman	2
Roger Ridder	2
Henry Dart	3
Thomas Hole	2
Isaac Wolland	6
Mathew Lacy	2
Christopher Wolland	1
William Yeo	1
William Haysome	4
Richard Tucker	6
Widow Hall	2
John Collinges	4
Mathew Symons	1
John Arthur	3
Christopher Ames	1
Widow Haysome	2
Thomas Haysome	3
John Sparke	9
Robert Easton	2
Roger Taylor	4
Zacheus Crabb	1
Thomas Huggins	2
Philipp Tamlyn	3
John Searle	1
Arthur Celler	1
Anthony Mapowder	4
Richard Tamlyn	3
Robert Delbridge	4
Isaac Wolland	1
Richard Jones	1
Hubert Griffen	5
Isaac Stone	1
Nicholas Bickford	2
Widow Made	2
Edward Basse	2
John Raphell	3
Widow Bayliffe	2
George Burd	2
William Parsons	2
Henry Keen	2
John Yolland	3
William Clogge	1
John Turner	1
Widow Holder	6
Richard Gore	1
Jonas Pinsent	4
John Hornabrooke	4
Widow Downe	1
Thomas Brothers	8
Henry Casely	2
Widow Tamlyn	2
John Hacker	1
Joan Warner	1
m.8.	
Widow Yarcombe	2
Christopher Bussell	1
Walter Reed	1
John Manly	2

Total 223

The poore of St. Edmonds

Richard Tothill	2
Widow Jenkyns	2
John Davys	1
Margaret Drake	1
Thomas Bremlecombe	1
Robert Burte	1
Elizabeth Huske	1
Widow Albyn	1
John Bond	1
Andrew Stephens	1

Joan Barons	1
Roger Tipper	1
John Satterly	1
Widow Northcott	1
Sarah Eedy	1
Mathew Mustion	1
Roger Woody	1
John Callender	1
John Coleman	1
Ann Richards	1
Widow Medyatt	1
Widow Cann	1
Thomas Hunt	1
Thomas Mathew	1
Peter Dyer	1
Widow Hatherly	1
James Searle	1
James Dally	1
William Bennett	1
Edward Lee	2
Richard Savage	1
Richard Axe	1
Widow Skibbowe	1
Robert Paige	2
John Hewett	1
John Hacker	1
Richard Mayne	1
Thomas Browne	1
Nicholas Bucknell	1
Edward Skinner	1
Richard Mead	1
Mathew Rogers	1

Total [not given]

ST. MARY STEPPES PARISH

Richard Payne	4
William Gamon	2
William Male	2
Lewes Rice	1
Robert Legg	1
John Carter	2
Elianor Dabynott	3
Philipp May	1
Richard Miller	4
Robert Basse	4
Widow Pole	1
Francis Basse	1
William Morgan	3
John Gale	1
John Goodinge	3
Abraham Stone	2
John Backwell	2
Richard Medyatt	2
Widow Tremlett	1
William Varley	3
John Horsey	1
Widow Bidd	1
William Slade	10
Widow Westmacott	4
Christopher Payne	3
Edward Hill	6
Henry Tanner	5
Edward Hill	2
Andrew Tincombe	1
Widow Canter	2
Widow May	1
John Guswell	2
Cadwallador Gilbert	2
Agnes Clerke	3
John Truman	4
William Mudge	1
Thomas Pudson	2
Henry Bolch	1
Thomas Goodridge	1
Peter Huggins	1
Henry Rice	1
Walter Trescott	1
Solomon Tedder	1
John Weeks	1
Rice Lewes	2
David Wall	2
John Wood	5
Thomas Wotton	1
John Midiacke	2
Stephen Reed	1
John Trescott	2
William Nicholls	2
John Basse	1
Ralph Barber	1
John Balle	3
John Gyles	3
m.8d.	
John Payne	1
Thomas White	2
George Pridham	3
John Lenington	3
Marke Reevs	2
George Adams	2
Robert Mugford	2
Hugh Bunt	2
Edward Longly	1
Widow Markes	3
Henry Stamprow	2
Roger Michell	2
Widow Downe	5
Robert Coombe	3
Edward Birdall	7
Thomas Holman	2
Hugh Bolte	1
Widow Tayler	1
Hugh Bidwell	5
Charles Hooper	2
Richard Rogers	2
Widow Jones	1
Daniel Reeve	2
Philipp Job	1
Jasper Hayne	3
Christopher Trelyne	1
Thomas Tayler	1
John Cocke	1
John Wood	1

Thomas Hayne	1
Constantine Hart	1

Total 191

St. Mary Steppes poore

Edward Barman	1
William May	1
John Bewis	1
John Herringe	1
James Foot	1
William Hayward	1
John Allimbridge	1
Richard C[blank]	1
John Potter	1
John Pole	1
Sarah Lewis	1
William Snellinge	1
Widow Fill	1
Widow Seinge [? Senige]	1
John Oynes	1
Mary Hoskins	1
Thomas Frye	1
Joseph Foxwell	2
John Knight	1
Henry Foxwell	1
William Bewis	1
John Walker	1
Robert May	1
Elizabeth Kenmill	1
Edward Gouldsworthy	1
Widow Honycombe	1
Aquila Fooke	1
Michael Whetcombe	1
Widow Herd	1
John Jones	1
Malachy Bucknell	1
Stephen Facy	1
Ralph Tarbert	1
Thomas Wotton	1

Total [not given]

ST. GEORGES PARISH

William Bellew	13[1]
Francis Westlake	7
Widow Salter	4
Thomas Hance	5
Richard Takell	2
John Penny	1
Robert Penny	3
Anthony Oxenbury	2
Widow Poe	8
John Row	2
John Takell	2
John Payne	5
Samuel Salter	2
Christofer Payne	5
William Deeble	1
James Salter	7
Philipp Richards	2
Philipp Downinge	2
Peter Clawson	3
John Bowden	3
Edward Lake	5
Samuel John	4
John Lewis	2
Richard Birdall	4
Widow Lome	4
Henry Westcott	1
m.9	
Richard Shuter	2
Richard Gould	3
Thomas Holman jun.	1
Widow North	2
Thomas Holman sen.	2
Thomas Kennicott	2
Widow Spiller	3
Widow Cheeke	2
Christopher Mathew	2
Bernard Gale	1
William Reep	4
Richard Walters	2
Susanna Hoppinge	10
Mathias Coombe	2
Thomas Browne	2
Francis Kingewell	4
Edward May	1
John Williams	1
Samuel Barons	1
Richard Macy	2
Thomas Hunt	2
Widow Sparke	1
Thomas Guest	5
Henry Newcombe	5
Symon Stanaway	2
George Veldue	2
Henry Lawry	3
Humfry Kneebone	2
Edward Jerman	1
Widow Prigg	2
David Crosse	4
Edward Searle	12
Zachary Humphry	3
Thomas Hacker	1

Total 193

St. Georges poore

Edward Tayler	1
Walter Hole	1
Widow Arundell	1

[1] Probably King John's Tavern, which stood near the top of South Street, on the W. side.

Walter Rawlinge	1
Jonas Limbry	1
Joseph Browne	1
Martha Hole	1
Widow Grigg	2
Widow Cotton	1
Widow Browne	1
James Downes	1
William Mathew	1
Widow Tenny	1
Roger Burges	1
George Bally	1
Roger Loman	1
Lawrence Lillicrop	1
John Hayward	1
Widow Jerman	1
Christopher Pasmore	1
Widow Hayne	1
Widow Adams	1

Total [not given]

ST. MARY THE MOORES PARISH

John Elwill	7
Richard Pidesley	4
Richard Pounsford	6
Andrew Lody	6
Arthur Searle	5
John Dowdall	2
Abraham Horwood	1
James Yeo	3
Arthur Glanvill	3
John Hayne	3
Thomas Cuningham	3
Elias Foxwell	3
Gregory Wolstone	3
Charles Cuningham	3
Elias Foxwell	3
Henry Whittrow	3
Stephen Toller	6
Jonathan Carter	4
Robert Hutchings	2
William Keagle	6
Robert Parsons	3
Christopher Burton	3
John Gibbons	8
Robert Dabynott	6
Grace Pottle	3
Elizabeth Perryman	3
Marke Browninge	1
Richard Leigh	1
John Butson	9
George Dowrich	2
Thomas Gloyne	19
Thomas Bayly	1
John Larramore	2
William Bennett	3
Mathew Perkins	2
John Case	4
John Webb	8

Widow Johns	1
George Davy	1
Thomas Collibear	2
John Kennicke	2
Nicholas Saunders	3
John Saunders	1
Thomas Hall	14
Thomas Salter	3
m.9d	
Lawrence Broadmead	3
Marke Browninge sen.	8
Widow Maninge	1
George Greenslade	2
John Fewell	2
Mathew Ferris	5
Thomas Waterhouse	6
Thomas Quicke	2
John Hart	1
William Toller	3
Peter Hellyer	3
Henry Smyth	9
Thomas Bartlett	3
John Sparke	8
William Glyde sen.	6
John Coombe	1
Francis Fryer	2
George Thomas	1
John Bagwell	2
Nicholas Palmer	3
Widow Jackett	7
George Blackford	3
William Jones	2
Henry Palmer	2
Robert Bassell	1
James Bolte	1
George Daw	1
Thomas Forward	1
Andrew Glandvill	5
Ezekiell Cleake	1
Roger Dixon	5
John Langworthy	1
Widow Veale	1
John Gay	2
Humfry Berry	1
John Tresher	2
Nicholas Browne	3
Angell Sparke	5
William Johns	6
Peter Pasmore	6
George Kingdome	1
Owen Davy	1
John Hugh	1
Widow Hooper	1
Joan Snickler	1
John Gifford	1
John Greedy	1
Peter Townesend	7
John Gadgecombe	1
Peter Pitts	2
Anthony Kifte	2
Richard Norris	1
Widow Frye	2

George Browninge	14
George Leach	7
Richard Rouse	15
John Kinge	1
Mathew Perkins	2
Henry Harris	1
Thomas Perkins	1
Thomas Hopkins	2
Henry Martin	2
Widow Hornabrooke	4
Richard White	2
Widow Moone	2
Peter Perkins	2
Zachary Saunders	3
William Holman	1
John Weeks	2
Thomas Northy	7
Epaphroditus Holmes	3
Widow Holmes	1
Edward Mallett	3
Roger Endibrooke	3
Walter Dinninge	2
Thomas Brockington	3
Walter Kerslake	1
Richard Dawkins	1
Joseph Taunton	2
Eusebius Holmes	2
Thomas Hawkins	1
Widow Gilbert	5
Henry Dodridge	1
John Hardy	6
Henry Slade	6
Joseph Wood	6
John Harris	6
Robert Grenfield	2
Martin Harris	2
Richard Collings	2
William Gale	2
William Laskey	3
William Penny	5
John Martin	3
William Milford	2
George Hewett	6
John Cooke	2
Christopher Kennicke	3
George Follett	1
Mary Tozer	4
Paul Bale	4
Edward Courtis	1
Thomas Somers	2
Thomas Sanford	2
Widow Holmes	4
Nicholas Glanvill	5
Robert Kennicke	2
William Brankett	1
Digory Sparke	1
Jasper Ratcliffe	6
John Archipole	5
m.10	
Daniel Mills	2
Edward Foxwell	1
Richard Gilbert	2
John Short	6
John Floud	1
Thomas Crosse	3
Theophilus Ford	1
Richard Laskey	1
Samuel Bricknall	1
John Balle	2
James Elwood	2
Widow Newcombe	2
Argenton Twiggs	3
John Liberton	2
Thomas Chinge	2
Richard Hooper	6
Richard Hewett	2
Nicholas Tayler	2
John Foxwell	4
Andrew Jeffery	7
Christopher Tayler	4
John Alford	3
James Newton	3
John Baker	2
Peter Hellyer	3
Richard Browse	4
Elizabeth Holt	3
John Tubb	2
George Colly	4
William Wrayford	2
Richard Wood	3
Walter Strange	5
Bridgett Alford	4
John Reed	3
Widow Reev	4
Thomas Eastabrooke	3
Gilbert Leigh	7
Mr Kendall	1

Total 632

The poore of the parish of St. Mary the Moore

William Blake	1
John Munford	1
Widow Saunders	1
William Adams	1
George Moore	1
Robert Madocke	1
William Smyth	1
Widow Strashly	1
Widow Borough	1
Thomas Pedericke	1
Abell Ward	1
Widow Fish	2
Widow Cratchett	1
John Bowden	1
Roger Thomas	1
Widow Hearthman	2
Richard Moon	1
William Deane	1
Gilbert Filmore	1
Robert Upton	1
John Pope	1

John Triddle	1
John Harris	1
Robert Breakbacke	1
James Crocker	1
Amos Webber	1
Richard Collings	1
Sampson Collings	1
John Bowdon	1
Hugh Dyer	1
Richard Jones	1
Jonas Clerke	1
Widow Alebeare	1
Nicholas Jones	1
Anthony Herd	1
Robert Phillips	1
Thomas Hart	1
Zachary Ducke	1
Henry Davy	1
Richard Borough	1
Mathew Searle	1
Roger Bowman	1
Thomas Downinge	1
William Cornelius	1
Bartholomew Beckett	1
Nathaniell Jordan	1
George Denham	1
William Wynter	1
Widow Wilkins	1
Widow Pearse	1
Richard Chafe	1
Widow Stanly	1
Robert Younge	1
John Baker	1
Richard Sampson	1
Thomas Bawdon	1
Thomas Bury	1
Nicholas Angell	1
Jane Perkins	1
Edward Foxe	1
James Martin	1
John Bath	1
Widow Collings	1
Thomas Hawkins	2
John Burges	1
Gabriel Walch	1
William Allyn	1
Dorothy Lane	1
Thomas Kelly	1
Widow Hooper	1
John Bent	1
Morrish Casy	1
Roger Broadmead	1
Emanuel Luscombe	1
George Somerton	2
Francis Holmes	2
m.10d	
Widow Crocker	1
Widow Pluman	1
Widow Tayler	1
Nicholas Randle	1
Lancelot Thomas	1
Widow Foster	1
Bernard Foxe	1
Walter Trippett	1
Thomas Perry	1
John Hutchings	2
William Grenfield	1
William Perry	1
John Towills	1
William Stephens	1
Andrew Nicholls	1
Richard Rattenbury	1
Mary Burges	1
John Gillard	1
William Parker	1
Richard Harvy	2
Humfry Spencer	2
Mary Sowden	1
Jonas Sparke	1
John Symons	1
John Strannge	1
John Bowdon	1
Hannibal Ratcliffe	1
Rice Davy	1
Michael Yeabacombe	2
James Bale	2
Paul Bale	1
Henry Somerton	1
Nicholas Hellyer	1
John Chamberlayne	1
John Yeedy	1
Robert Carter	1
John Bremlecombe	1
Symon Chubb	1
Christofer Cocke	1
Edward Hooper	1
Thomas Lane	1
Thomas Jordan	1
Henry Lane	2
William Pearse	1
Richard Tucker	1
John Drew	1
William Goffe	1
Alexander Skinner	2
Thomas Bishopp	1
James Gale	1
Richard Kneebone	1
John Yeedy	1
George Hewett	1
Nicholas Bolte	1
John Gubb	1
Henry Magazine	1
Widow Lawder	1
John Luxon	1
Humfry Nordon	1
Richard Robinson	1
John Burkes	1
Widow Drummer	1
George Harris	1
Widow May	1
William Smallridge	1
Widow Hooper	2
Widow Halstaffe	1
William May	1

John Saunders	2
Philipp Bragg	2
Widow Stephens	1

Total [not given]

ST. LAWRANCE

John Savage	4
Widow Greedy	6
Thomas Quicke	10
Arthur Brocas	5
Bartholomew Poyton	2
Thomas Long	11
Robert Daw	3
Thomas Day	3
Christofer Wyatt	10
Henry Rogers	2
Thomas Willinge	1
Mrs Chappell	6
Henry Battiford	2
John Goodman	1
Roger Humphry	2
George Maisters	4
William Sydford	2
Griffen Lewes	2
Henry Hooper	4
William Hellyer	6
Thomas Facy	5
Edward Bradford	7
George Rogers	9
Josias Perry	2
Mrs Smyth	6
John Etheridge	5
Thomas Dowdall	2
Beniamin Risdon	4
Dorothy Bigglestone	3
Mr Woodyetts	2
John Comings	4
Robert Pafford	2
Edward Wood	10
Peter Risdon	9
Nicholas Evans	2
John Tayler	6
John Pope	2
Henry Humphry	2
Richard Hingston	2
John Baker	4
Edward Etheridge jun.	4
Doctor Thrustone	8
Peter Hagedot *esq.*	10
Thomas Bucland	6
Joseph Hellyar	3
Stephen Wilson	3
Peter Baker	2
Thomas Aysh	1
m.11.	
John Foxwell	1
Robert Soper	1
Hanniball Hayne	2
John Cheeke	2
Lawrence Wade	5
Joan Liddon	4
Christopher Mathew	4
Thomas Day	5
Stephen Bickford	2
Alexander Knight	1
Thomas Hall	1
Olliver Davy	8
Robert Soper	2
John Horrell	1
Peter Langsford	1
John Elsdon	1
Andrew Raddon	1
Widow Luscombe	3
Mr Gill	4

Total 261

The poore of St. Lawrance

Widow Mayne	2
John Torringe	2
Philipp Greedy	1
Elias Hill	1
Thomas Cheek	1
John Trott	1
Richard Warren	1
Andrew Stephens	1
Nicholas Slanninge	1
Jeffery Downinge	1
Ovid Glanvill	2
Widow Gribble	2
Widow Hall	2
William Wilson	2
Widow Pratt	2
James Paty	1
Widow Madder	1
John Smoot	1
Humfry Green	2
William Bonny	1
Thomas Gully	1
John Downe	1
Beniamyn Madder	1
John Foster	2
Robert Basse	1
Widow Hunt	1
Elizabeth Robinson	1
Julian Calender	1
Mary Smaldon	1
Christopher Pearse	1
Widow Pitman	1
Thomas Webber	1
John Heath	1
Widow Shapcott	1
Richard Pennyn	1
Andrew Stephens	1

Total [not given]

ST. STEPHENS PARISH

Richard Lunn	2
Richard Guswell	3
Richard Reynolds	11[1]
William Searle	1
John Trigges	5
Orlando Evans	13[2]
Christopher Coose	2
John Baker	22[3]
Widow Ledgingham	5
Thomas Tilly	2
Christopher Trehan	4
James Linington	2
Widow Hill	2
John Herman	2
John Pearse	6
John Leigh	4
William Bolithoe	8
Nicholas Wood	9
Widow Pitts	5
Thomas Savery	6
George Tompson	6
John Collings	7
Widow Parker	2
John Tredinnicke	3
Adam Pearse	6
James Rodd	9
Mr Steward	8
Mr Eveleigh	8
Samuel Pearse	4
John Bartlett	2
Philipp Pyne	2
Thomas Ware	7
Henry Close	1
Thomas Savage	1
Widow Moore	1
Francis Brady	6
Paul Martin	4
Thomas Jennings	3
Robert Reeve	5
John Kinge	10
James Searle	4
Thomas Ford	3
Edward Pyke	3
James Michell	5
Richard Reynolds	7
Thomas Savage sen.	4
Nicholas Joyce	3
Dorothy Jackson	4
Widow Salter	4
John Maber	6
Richard Freake	6
Widow Marsh	8
Elizabeth Shapcott	1
Widow Trosse	5
George Pitts	10
Richard Prowse	3
Elizabeth Salter	2
William Foxwell	3
Widow Mills	8
Jonathan Lange Castle (*sic*)	2

Total 300

m.11d.

ALLHALLOWS IN GOLDSMITH STREET

Richard Marsh	7
Widow Gould	9
William Michell	2
Walter Full	3
Richard Jackman	2
Walter Robins	1
Robert Pringe	2
Philipp Jerman	9
Thomas Guscott	2
William Younge	2
Edward Cockell	2
Symon Trobridge	10
Thomas Foxwell	2
Richard Morris	3
John Pym	6
Thomas Palmer	10
William Browne	2
Widow Tothill	3
Symon Bayly	14
Margaret Kinge	1
John Palmer	2
John Palmer sen.	5
Richard March	4
Daniell Gundry	4
Robert Eveleigh	4
Elizabeth Tucker	12
Richard Peryam	8
John Cholwell	9
Joseph Potter	2
James Rogers	3
Thomas Edmonds	7
James Trippett	2
Robert Edwards	2
Henry Floud	3
William Murch	3
William Ebdon	3
John Binham	2
George Tucker	4
Edward Bryant	5
Edward Hale	2
William Elsdon	3
Edward Hawkins	2
Mary Yarcombe	2

Total 185

[1] The Green Dragon Inn, which stood on High Street where Bedford Street now is.
[2] The Half Moon Inn, which stood on the corner of Bedford Street and High Street (W. side).
[3] The New Inn, held by John Baker on a lease from the city (E.C.M. Book 190, fo. 55).

The poore of Allhallows in Goldsmith Streete

Thomas Yarcombe	1
James Linnington	1
John Tuckett	1

Total [not given]

ST. MARTINS

William How	2
Robert Warren	11
John Hore	2
John Yeo	3
Joseph Pearce	1
Thomas Gilbert	2
Philipp Hooper	5
Edward Portbury	5
Thomas Collibear	3
Hugh Humphry	3
Thomas Gould	5
Joshua Raynolds	3
Nicholas Trype	6
George Saffin	11
Widow Prigg	6
Philipp Reep	3
Ezekiell Steed	3
Widow Moore	5
Daniell Tompson	1
Abisha Brocas	5
Richard Comings	3
Henry Foster	4
Roger Wood	4
John Brewer	5
Edward Portbury	3
Edward Painter	5
David Robinson	6
James Acland	5
John Barons	3
Robert Davy	6
John Butler *esq.*	10
John Parr	5

Total 144

ST. OLLAVES PARISH

John Mason	3
John Tony	2
Anthony Hacker	1
Anthony Wescott	1
William Pearse	6
John Ashley	1
Edward Richards	2
Nicholas Cosens	3
John Browne	2
Robert Paise	3
Thomas Castle	1
Widow Hawkins	1
William Roach	1
John Tayler	2
Joseph Clase	1
Nicholas Brokinge	10
Stephen Burton	4
Otho Bastard	6
Thomas Band	2
Widdow Fodder	3
John Acland	8
Agnis Hawkins	2

m.12

Thomas Dix	8
Richard Damerell	2
Robert Atkins	4
Mary Nicholls	3
William Ceely	6
John Pyke	4
Symon Ballamy	5
John Atwill	4
Richard Dewdney	4
Robert Pewtner	6
Jacob Stone	3
Joseph Wryford	1
Philipp Burgoyne	6
John Dagworthy	5
Joshua Branscombe	3
Henry Hernaman	2
Mrs Macy	7
Thomas Bale	5
Edward Tothill	2
Robert Vinicombe	2
William Copplestone	5
George Barons	2
Nicholas Kendall	6
William Bayliffe	3
William Cove	4
William Pyne	7
Nathaniell Madocke	4
John Beer	2
Widow Prigg	2
John Starr	7
Edward Ridge	4
Anthony Marly	4
Robert Elscombe	2
Alexander Bennett	2
Richard Hickes	3
John Made	6
Mary Coleman	5
Widow Hodge	3
Thomas Norris	1
George Roach	1
Jeffery Mounstephin	1
William Browne	2
Sivilla Soper	1
Ann Pope	1
Paschal Harris	1
Beniamyn Stanlake	1
Humfry Lake	1

Total 228

The poore of St. Ollaves parish

Anthony Dally	1
Widow Elwood	2
Widow Barker	1
Roger Willes	1
Widow Hawkins	1
Thomas Hacker	1
Henry Hamlyn	1
Richard Lucy	1
Cornelius Gyles	1
[Blank] Cocke	1
James S[blank]	1
George Mash	1
Jane Crosman	1
George Watts	1
Katharyne Pitcher	1
Margarett Tayler	1
Richard Palmer	1
William Mortymore	1
Thomas Curry	1
Thomas Wood	1
Richard Dare	1
Widow Hunt	1
John Frogpitt	1
Mary Kenn	1
Edward Boreman	1
John Sheres	1
Anthony Prin	2
Hugh Rowland	2
John Ford	1
John Warren	1
Francis Martin	1
John Etheridge	1
Henry Mounstephin	1
John Burt	2
Nicholas Mussell	2
Lawrence Striplinge	1
Rice Owen	1
Walter Harper	1
John Hawkes	1

Total [not given]

ST. PANCRAS PARISH

John Hayman	15
Robert Tayler	5
Thomas Hellyer	2
Leonard Treslow	2
Widow Beard	4
John Monngwell	2
John Robins	5
Thomas Atherton	6
George Tremlett	6
Humfry Leigh	3
Elizabeth Flaye	8
Edward Foxwell	6
The Guildhall	5
William Somerton	1
Peter Comings	1
Francis Galhampton	3
John Somers	5
William Brewen	7
Grace Parr	4
Peter Slade	2

Total 92

m.12d.

The poore of the parish of St. Pancras

George Atkin	2
John Messer	1
Robert Harris	1

Sum total of the aforesaid hearths paid 5041

William Sanford Mayor
Henry Gandy
John Butler
Nicholas Isacke
George Tothill

5. THE POOR RATE OF 1699.[1]

fo. 1r. col. i
Yeare [16]99

ST. STEPHENS

John Gandy
Peter Tucker *Wardens*

Jasper Jaine
James Norrington *Overseeres*

Peter Skynner ½d house 1¼d	1¾d
James Tredinnick ½d house 2d	2½d
Jasper Jaine 1d house 5½d	6½d[2]
Thomas Bennett 1d house 1¼d	2¼d
Samuel Jeffery 1½d house 6d	7½d
Charles Knowles 2d house 1s 3d	1s 5d[3]
Occupier of Mr Jeves house	7½d
John Beckett 1½d house 1s 10d	1s 11½d[4]
John Parsons	1d
The Citty of Exon for *the Shopps and Stables*	8½d[5]
Wm. Searle 1d house 4¼d	5¼d
Occupier of Hoopers house	2d
Occupier of *the New Stables* behinde Mr Hoopers house	2¼d
Occupier of Mrs Hestcotts house	1d
Humphry Norden	½d
Occupier of Mr Sanfords house	3d
John Burell *esq.* 2d house 4½d	6½d
Isarel Stafford 1½d house 4d	5½d
Peter Tooker 1½d house 3d	4½d
Joseph Trobridge 1d house 4½d	5½d
Anne Mills for her house	5d
Samuel Pope	1½d
John Viccary 1½d house 4d	5½d
David Binham 1d house 4d	5d
John Withers 1d house 3d	4d
Nicholas Purchass	½d
John Savory 1d house 3½d	4½d
John Medland ½d house 1½d	2d
Thomas Wheadon 1d house 4d	5d
Benjamin Beake 3d house 4d	7d

fo. 1r. col. ii

Occupier of Mr Rundles house	1½d
Mr Michell 3d house 8d	11d
William May & house	2d
Richard Attwill	2½d
George Gould 3d house 9d	1s 0d
John Lyford	2½d
Widdow Dancys 1d house 5d	6d
John Smyth	½d
John Pince 1d house 4d	5d
John Gandy 2½d house 6¼d	8¾d
John Rowe 2d house 4d	6d
Deliverance Larkcombe 1d house 2¼d	3¼d
Charles Challice 2½d house 5d	7½d
Mr Richard King for his severall tenements	1s 8d
James Norrington	1d
William Mahoone ½d & house 1d	1½d
Occupier of Mr Cudmores house	3d
Benjamin Hawkins 2½d house 5d	7½d
Thomas Ford	2½d
Edward Collings	2d
Occupier of Mr Horswells house	3d
William Southmeade for Mr Malacks house[6]	1s 2d
Samuell Butler or Occupiers	3½d

Total 23s 4d

To the Poor Weekley

Normans Bastard	3s
Hannah Hill	3s
Widdow Linnington	2s 6d
Grace Bennet	1s 6d
Richard Payne	2s
Isott Joyce	2s 4d
Prudence Small	4s 6d
Widdow Guswell	2s
Paul Martine	2s 6d

Total 23s 4d

[1] E.C.M., Misc. Books, 159B.
[2] The Green Dragon Inn
[3] The Half Moon Inn (see map at end) which stood on the west corner of Bedford Street and High Street.
[4] The New Inn, the largest and most important inn in Exeter, which stood immediately east of St. Stephen's Church (see map).
[5] These were "the shops of the New Inn", which belonged, like the inn, to the city.
[6] Mr. Mallack's house stood on the corner of Gandy Street and High Street (E. side), and ran back to a considerable depth along Gandy Street. In 1890 it was represented by No. 229 High Street; to-day by Messrs. J. Lyons's premises.

fo. 1v. col. i

ALHALLOWES IN GOULDSMYTH STREET

Mr George Stonening
Mr John Binham *Wardens*

Mr James Gould
Mr Thomas Wood *Overseers*

Mr Richard Crocker house in *Gandys Lane*[1]	1d
Mr William Moore & house	6d
Mrs Mary Pynes Sellers or occupier	3d
Mrs Elizabeth Rennols house or occupier	6d
Mr Nicholas Wood	2d
Mr William Bagwill	1d
Mr William Westcombe house or occupier	2d
Mr David Robertson	1d
Mrs Hutchings houses	1½d
Mr John Stephens	2½d
Mr William Pincombe	1½d
Mr John Bolt	2d
Mrs Mary Heskett & houses	1s
Mr Trobridge houses or occupiers	1s 3d
Mr Richard Briam	6d
Mr Thomas Foxwill	1½d
Mr Adam Peeare houses or occupier	8d
Mr Nicholas Cheeke	2d
Mr John Pym & houses	9d
Mrs Elizabeth & Mary Pearce	1½d
Mr George Tross house or occupier	5d
Mrs Elizabeth White house or occupier	8d
Mrs Udall	1½d
Mr John Harris	½d
Mr William Moores house that Mr Bucknall liveth in	2d

fo. 1v. col. ii

Mr John Palmer & house	4d
Mr James Gould & house	7d
Mr Symon Bayley houses or occupier	9d
Mr Thomas Tothill & house	3½d
Mr William Browne house or occupier	4d
Mr Aaron Tozer & house	8d
Mrs Mounstephen & houses	6d
Mr Thomas Wood	2d
Mr George Stoneing & house	5d
Mr Gilbert Davies house or occupier	4½d
Mr James Gould or occupier for *the Phenix*[2]	6d
Mrs Hester Mapowder or occupier	4d
Mrs Judith Tucker	1d
Mrs Archdeacon Drews house or occupier	3½d
Mr William Jope and house	9d
Madam Tuckfeild house or occupier	2½d
Mr Philip Jerman jun.	1d
Mrs Elizabeth Gandys house or occupier	3d
Mr Henery Harris	1½d
Mr Richard Stablie & house	1½d
Mr Edward Hayman for the house that Thomas Withicombe lives in & for the house Mrs Best lives in	2½d
Mr George Toms & house	1d
Mrs Edwards house or occupier	1½d
Mr Henery Edwards	½d
Mr John Bingham & houses	8d
Mr Thomas Walker	½d
Madam Tuckfeild for the house where Robert Foxwill lives	2d
Madam Tuckfeild for the house where Richard Turner lives	1½d

Sum 18s 4d

The widdow Trebret	11s
The widdow Jackman	4d
Hawkings Child	1d
The widdow Marker	1d
Rebekha Hill	4d

Total 18s 4d

fo. 2r. col. i

ST. EDMONDS PARISH

Philip Dart
John Shukburgh *Wardens*

Wm. Tudor and
Thomas Herring *Overseeres*

The Occupier of Cucking Stoole Mills & Racks in *the Bonhay*	4s
The occupier of the new erected Mills of Mr Foxwells	2s 6d
Mr Atkins & Mr Dart or occupier of *Bonhay Mills*	3s 2d
Mr Parr for the house Mr Rouse lives in	5d
Mrs Gubbs or occupier, of her other lands	2d
Mr Henry Dart for the house he lives in	10d

[1] The assessor evidently started at the large house (called "Mansion House" on the 1 : 500 plan of 1891) now occupied by Messrs. Timothy White and Taylors Ltd. (No. 228 High Street), and proceeded down the north-west side of the High Street (see the Phoenix Inn farther down the list).

[2] The Phoenix Inn stood on the High Street, a few yards east of Goldsmith Street, on the site now occupied by H. Samuel Ltd. A truncated portion of the inn (rebuilt) still survives under that name in Goldsmith Street to-day.

Widdow Pince 8d
Widdow Sanford or occupier of her houses 3d
Mr Roger Pyne & house 8d
Sir Thomas Jefford & house he lives in 8d
Mr William Morgan & house 4d
Mr William Morgan or occupier of *the Redlyon* 1½d
Mr Edgcombe & Mr Herring for there estate 5d
Mr Samuell Axe or occupier of his estate 4d
Mr Richard Mapowder or occupier of his estate 2d
Mr Christopher Mayne or occupier of his estate 6d
Mr Samuell Axe for Martayns lands 4d
Mr Pince for the estate late Mr Hills 3d
Mr William Rice or occupier of his estate 5d
Thomas Owen or occupier of his estate 1½d
John Pope or occupier of his estate 1d
fo. 2r. col. ii
Widdow Keen or occupier of her estate 3d
Benjamin Yelland or occupier of his estate 1½d
John Manly 1d
Widdow Pinsent or occupier of her houses 3d
Mr James Tucker or occupier of his estate 6d
William Mathews *esq.* or occupier of his estate 1d
Mr Peter Roberts & house 2d
Mr Philip Tamlyn or occupier of his house 3d
Mr Way or occupier of his estate 1d
Mr William Heard or occupier of his estate 1½d
Mr Christopher Bolt 1d
Widdow Anther or occupier of her houses 3d
Mr Joseph Hawkins 1d
The occupier of the estate late Burchess 5d
Mr William Jope or occupier of his house 1½d
Thomas Raphell & Joane Budd for there houses 2d
Mr Henry Dart or occupier of his house in *Bonhay Lane* 6d
Mr Richard Holder or occupier of his Estate 10d
Mr Pince for Mr Sanfords house 2d
James Keen for the house John Derry lives in 1d
Mr Peter Gunstone 2d
The occupier of the house late Chilcott 3d
Mr Henery Dashwood or occupier of his house 2d
Widdow Fox or occupier of her house 1d
The occupier of the old *Mault house* & dwelling house of the said City 5d

The occupier of the Mault house late *the City Brewhouse* 5d
The occupier of Mr Cornish house Widdow Cock lives in 4d
fo. 2v. col. i
Widow Cock 1d
Mr Jonas Bampfeild or occupier of his house 1d
Widow Mawry or occupier of her houses 2d
Mr Peter Battishill or occupier of his estate 1d
Mr John Stone for himself and house 3d
The occupier of Mrs Gubbs house which Leach lately lived in 6d
Mr Edgcombe for the estate in *the Iland* 3d
Mrs Margaret Mayne or occupier of her house 2d
John Huchens for himself & house 2d
William Tudder for Burchess mault house & his own house 6d
Widow Tudder 2d
Mr James Foot for Hecks house 1d
Mr Edward Bass 1d
Mr Pearse for the house Minson lives in 1d
Mr Joseph Rouse 2d
Mr John Winde 3d
Mr John Tudder 1d
Mr Peter Stephens 1d
Mr Henry Rooke 3d
The occupier of Mr Paul Drapers house 1d
Abraham Whiffell 1d
Mr Humphry Lee or occupier of his estate 7d
Mrs Rebeccha Leach or occupier of her estate ½d
Mr John Shugburdge 1d
Mr Philip Dart 1d
Mr Thomas Jefford for his new house 2d
fo. 2v. col. ii
Mr Peter Carter or occupier of his house 1½d
Mr William Haysombe 1d
Mr John Barons or occupier of his house 1½d
Mr Abraham Stone 1d
Mrs Beake or occupier of her house 1½d
Mr Abraham Cornish or occupier of his houses 3d
Mr James Clarke 1d
Mr Wannel or occupier of his house 1d
Mr Richard Ford and house 1½d
Mr Robert Elicombe for the house late Couches 1d
Mr Henery Hew 1d
Mr John Burch 1d
Mr Thomas Tucker 1d
Mr William Lobb 1d
Mr Richard or occupier of his house ½d
Mr Joseph Bethell ½d
Mr John Fryer 1d
Mr John Derry ½d

James Collens	$\frac{1}{2}$d
John Horsey	$\frac{1}{2}$d
Ezekiel Cooper	$\frac{1}{2}$d
Edward Foster	1d
Mr John Stone *fuller*	3d
Mr James Sparke	2d
William Pound	$\frac{1}{2}$d
Abell Catty	1d
John Mauris or occupier of *Cucking Stool Mills*	1d
Mr John West for the estate late Rogers	1d
Widow Lane for the estate late Rogers	$\frac{1}{2}$d
fo. 3r. col. i	
Daniell Chambers	$\frac{1}{2}$d
Richard Ford *fuller*	$\frac{1}{2}$d
Mr William Prouse	1d
Joseph Pitts	$\frac{1}{2}$d
Sarah Legg or occupier of her estate	$\frac{1}{2}$d
James Foot	1d
Robert Trewman	1d
Elizabeth Rogers	$\frac{1}{2}$d
Nathaniel Barons	1d

Total 31s 2d

To the Poor weekely

Edward Lee	1s 6d
Drews Children	1s 6d
Hoppins Child	1s 6d
Joane Tipper	2s
Widdow Casley	2s 6d
Isaac Edey	1s 6d
William Clogg	2s 6d
Elizabeth Heaward	1s
Margarett Mapis	1s
John Balch	3s
Susanah White	1s 6d
Margarett Heaward	1s
Widow Turpins Child	3s
Widow Hursk	1s
Widow Colderidge the elder	2s
William Wolland	1s 6d
Roger Ellery	1s 6d
Joane Tremlett	2s
Ann Gill	1s
Widow Colderige younger	1s 6d
Widow Page	1s
Widow Lashbrooke	8d
Widow Woodey	6d
Widow Daymond	1s 3d
Thomas Browne	6d

Total 38s

fo. 3r. col. ii

ST. JOHNS PARISH

Joseph Wood
Jacob Rowe *Wardens*

Thomas Templer
Thomas Bury *Overseeres*

William Atkins 2d his estate 9d	11d
Mr Gent *the Chirurgeon*	1$\frac{1}{2}$d
Symon Pincombe	1d
The Incorporation of Fullers their Hall	2$\frac{1}{2}$d
Robert Foster 1$\frac{1}{2}$d his house 3$\frac{1}{2}$d	5d
Richard Cornish 1d the house he lives in 4d	5d
Joseph Wood 1d the house he lives in 6$\frac{1}{2}$d	7$\frac{1}{2}$d
Thomas Baron 2d the house he lives in 5d	7d
Jacob Rowe 1$\frac{1}{2}$d the house he lives in 4d	5$\frac{1}{2}$d
John Bale 1d the house he lives in 2d	3d
John Canter[1] 1d the house he lives in 2$\frac{1}{2}$d	3$\frac{1}{2}$d
The Widow Honobrooke or occupiers of her estate	2$\frac{1}{2}$d
William Bice 1d the house he lives in 2$\frac{1}{2}$d	3$\frac{1}{2}$d
Anthony Hawkins 1d the house he lives in 5$\frac{1}{2}$d	6$\frac{1}{2}$d
Joseph Wood or occupiers of his estate	5d
The occupiers of the house Richard White now or lately lived in	3d
Nicholas Brooking or occupiers of his estate	6d
The occupiers of John Cann's estate	$\frac{1}{2}$d
fo. 3v. col. i	
Jeremiah Ward	$\frac{1}{2}$d
The occupiers of William Southmeads estate	4d
Thomas Templer 1d the house he lives in 5d	6d
Edward Baker 1d the house he lives in 6d	7d
The occupiers of the house John Turleing lately lived in	2d
The occupiers of John Turners estate	5d
Arthur Scholler	1d
Samuell Peters 1d the house he lives in 1$\frac{1}{2}$d	2$\frac{1}{2}$d
The occupiers of Mr Leachlands estate	11$\frac{1}{2}$d
Mary Skinner widdow	1d
Peter Powell	1$\frac{1}{2}$d
Thomas Basse	1d
The occupiers of William Williams estate	1d

[1] Initial letter altered from P to C.

Roger Hugins 1d
William Williams ½d
The occupiers of Binjamin Risdons[1] estate 2d
The occupiers of Mr Samuell Butlers estate 2d
The occupiers of William Hills estate 1½d
The occupiers of Philip Bennets house ½d
William Clarke 1d the house he lives [in] 1½d 2½d
John Lee or occupiers of his estate 1d
The occupiers of Mr Paynes estate 2d
Mathias Combe 1d his house 2d 3d
The Widow Mathews 1d her house 2d 3d
fo. 3v. col. ii
The occupiers of the house Edward Lemmett lately [lived] in 1d
Peter Prew 1½d the house he lives in 2½d 4d
John Macy or occupiers of his estate 1d
The occupiers of the house the Widdow Moore lately lived in ½d
Jaspar Radcliffe or occupiers of his estate 1½d
The occupiers of Thomas Bampfeilds estate 1½d
Thomas Hunt or occupiers of his estate 1d
Richard Bursey ½d
Edward Perkins 1d the house he lives in 3½d 4½d
The Widdow Cheeke or occupiers of her estate 1d
Nicholas Munklye[2] 2d the house he lives [in] 4d 6d
Samuell Munckley 2d the house he lives in 4d 6d
John Munckley 2d the house he lives in 4d 6d
William Rice or occupiers of his estate 4d
Nowell Pearse or occupiers of his estate 2d
Arthur Purchasse 1d
John Legg 1d the house he lives in 1½d 2½d
The occupiers of the Widdow Southards estate 2d
John Hornbrooke 2d the house he lives in 4d 6d
Thomas Bury 2d the house he lives in 4d 6d
The occupiers of Tristram Whiters estate 2d

fo. 4r. col. i
Samuell Glide 1½d the house he lives [in] 2d 3½d
William Elson 1d
The Widdow West 1d

Total 17s 4d

To the Poor Weekely

Joan Keele	1s
John Johnson	1s 6d
Richard Oake	2s 6d
Susanah Kent	2s 6d
Margery Ashleys children	4s 6d
Elianor Barber	1s
Roger Prower	1s 6d
David Tudor	1s
Widdow Moore	1s 6d
Widdow Paddon	2s
Jefferys child	1s 9d
Mary Dobles base child	2s 6d
Henry Minterne	1s 6d
Grace Brook	6d
Mary Walker	1s 6d
Susanah Egford	6d
Edith Cary	5d
Widdow Watts	6d
Stephen Parish	2s

Total 30s 2d

fo. 4r. col. ii

ST. GEORGES PARISH

James Berry
Thomas Tucker *Wardens*

Francis Bidwill
Joseph Gay *Overseeres*

King John Tavern & tenements belonging or occupiers[3] 8d
Caleb Palmer for himself and his house 6d
Nicholas Hatchfeild 1d his estate or occupiers 7d 7d (*sic*)
Jonas Pridham 1d Bayleys house 3d 4d
Joshua Gay & his house 3d
Nathaniel Lake 1d the house he lives in 3d 4d
The late Sainthills house or occupiers 2½d
The occupiers of Parson Birdalls house late in possession of John Deeble 1½d

[1] 'Risdons' altered from 'Riddons'.
[2] 'Cheek' crossed through and 'Munklye' inserted above.
[3] The assessor is starting at the parish boundary in Southgate Street (W. side) and proceeding down to Guinea Street, down which he turned to reach the *Royal Oak*, which stood on the North corner of Guinea Street and Milk Street. He then turned along Milk Street and so down Butcher Row and Smythen Street.

The occupier of Francis Pengellys house in possession of George Mason 2½d
Edward Pike 1d the house he lives in 2d 3d
William Mathew 1d for part of the *Royal Oake Inn* 2d 3d
George Mason 1d
Aaron Salter for the other part of the *Royal Oake Inn* 3d
Dudnyes house in possession of Bonney *the Glasier* 1d
Peter Gale 1d for the house he lives in 1½d 2½d
Tymothy Dart 1d for the house he lives in 1d 2d
John Oyens for Baylys house 1d
fo. 4v. col. i
Thomas Twiggs or occupiers of another of Bayleys houses 1d
John Chapling 1d & for another of Bayleys houses 1½d 2½d
Edward Worth 1d & for another of Bayleys houses 1½d 2d (*sic*)
Part of the house in possession of Joseph Helmor ½d
Charles Parker 1d
The occupiers of Edmond Richards & late Whites 1d
William Stone 1d & for the house he lives in 2d 3d
The occupier of the late Fryes house 1d
Anthony Oxenbeere 1d & for the house he lives in 1½d 2½d
Zachary Humphrey 1d & for the house he lives in 1d 2d
The occupiers of *the three Craines* Inn[1] 8d
Thomas Tucker 1d & for the house he lives in 2d 3d
The Widdow Penny for her estate 4d
The occupiers of part of *the Cornmarket* 4d
The occupiers of Christopher Paynes house 3d
Thomas Worth 1d
Peter Payne 1d & for the house he lives in 1½d 2½d
The occupiers of Worth houses, late Edward Foxwells 3½d
Tymothy Dart jun. 1d
Benjamin Stanley 1d & for part of *the Unicorn Inn*[2] 2d 3d
Nicholas Penney 1d & for his house 3d 4d
fo. 4v. col. ii
Richard Moggrage 1d
The occupiers of a house late Mrs Ann Cheeks of St Sidwills 1½d
Samuell Lory[3] 1d
Barnard Gale 1d for Griggs Lands 2d 3d
The occupier of late Margaret Pitts house, somtime Goulds *the Butcher* 6d
Richard Suter 1d
Henry Westcott 1d & for the house he lives in 1½d 2½d
John Legg 1d
Richard Takle 1d
The occupiers of Andrew Bagwells house & seller 3d
The occupiers of Charles Watts his house 4d
The occupiers of Alderman Yards houses 6d
John Cave 1d & for late John Toneys house 1½d 2½d
Francis Pengelly & the estate he lives in 6d
Jane Draper Widow & her house 3d
The occupiers of the late Christopher Mathews house 1½d
The occupiers of late Roger Cheekes houses, now Mr Gibbs his houses 3d
John Mason & his houses 6d
The occupiers of Barnard Watts his house 1½d
William Rice 1d for his house 1½d 2½d
Thomas Bass or occupiers of his tenement 1½d
John Walker ½d
fo. 5r. col. i
Henery Gidely ½d
The occupiers of the late Phipps his Lands 5d
The occupier of the late William Reepes house 3d
George White 1d
Barnard Sampson 1d
The occupiers of Elizabeth Hoppings house 2d
John Gouldsworthy ½d
Samuell Brimlecombe 1d
The occupiers of the late Walter Philips his houses 5d
Jonas Hawkridge 1d
Charles Gliston 1d
John Dix 1d & for Gouldsworthys houses 6d 7d
James Berry 1d & for Butlers houses or occupiers 6d 7d
The occupiers of Thomas Northmores Callender house 5d
Francis Bidwell 1d for late Hunts house 1½d 2½d

[1] The *Three Cranes* stood in Milk Street until 1835 when it was demolished for the making of the Lower Market.
[2] The *Unicorn Inn* stood on the East side of Butcher Row (at the top end of Smythen Street) but had disappeared before the 1891 plan of the city was made.
[3] 'Lorge' crossed through and 'Lory' substituted.

Elizabeth Southard for her house or occupiers	½d
The occupiers of John Hoopers houses, late the Widow Parrs	3d
The occupiers of the houses late in possession of Mr Thomas Barons	4d
Nathaniel Gist 2d for his house 4d	6d

Total 19s ½d

To the Poore weekley

The Widdow Lowton	2s
Grace Oxenbeere	2s
William Atkins	2s 6d
The Widdow Heaward	1s 6d
The Widdow Tribbet	10d
Thomas Gill	1s
Richard Wills	2s
The Widdow Boone	2s
fo. 5r. col. ii	
Christopher Hopkins	1s
The Widow Owens	1s 6d
William Row his wife & child	1s
George Vildue	2s
Sarah Koolcoot	1s 6d
For severall poor peoples rents	4s 6d

Total 25s 4d

ST. OLLIVES PARISH

Wm. Barter
Wm. Castle *Wardens*

Joseph King
Richard Tackle *Oversceres*

Nicholas Brooking & his estate	1s 2d
George Edwards 1½d for the house he lives in 4d	5½d
William Battishill & his estate	9d
John Salter 1½d for the house he lives in 3d	4½d
Joseph Potter & the house he lives in	4½d
John Browne 1½d for the house he lives in 3½d	5d
John Harris 1d for the house he lives [in] 8½d	9½d
John Prickham 1d for the house he lives in 3d	4d
Nicholas Cossens	1d
Nathaniel Dewdny 1½d for the house he lives in 6d	7½d
Philip Barons or occupiers of his estate	2d
Richard White or occupiers of his estate	2d
George Manning	½d
James Taylor 1½d for the house he lives in 6d	7½d
fo. 5v. col. i	
The occupiers of the Widdow Parkers estate	1½d
Richard Jennings	1d
The occupiers of Robert Vinicombes estate	1d
Mary Pease or occupiers of her estate	2½d
Tristram Whitter & his estate	10d
William Rice	1d
The occupiers of Andrew Glanvills estate	8d
Thomas Brace	1½d
John Snow	1d
The Widdow Glanvill	1d
Benjamin Atwill & his house	3d
Nicholas Rowe & the house he lives in	5d
The occupiers of Peter Colletons estate	7d
William Cassell	1d
William Barter	1d
Thomas Salter & his estate	8d
Joseph King 1d for the house he lives in 2½d	3½d
Thomas Harris & his estate	5½d
John Pike	1d
The occupiers of the Hospitall Lands	3d
The occupiers of *the Cornmarket*	5d
John Rowe & his estate	2½d
The occupiers of the house Benjamin Stanley lives in	1½d
Edmond Richards & his estate	2½d
Richard Taklle	1d
fo. 5v. col. ii	
John Wakeham	1d
The occupiers of the late *Flower de luce*	4d
John Strong	1d
Anthony Westcott & his house	2½d
Cornelius Mathew & his house	2½d
John Larramore occupier of the estate late John Tony	1½d
Charles Watts	1d
The occupiers of the back parte of the Widdow Anthonys house	2d
Nathaniel Salter 1½d for Roger Paynes estate 7½d	9d
John Lome[1] or occupiers of his house	1½d
The occupiers of John Canns estate	1s 3d
Alexander Sampson	1½d
James Bussell	1d
The occupiers of Richard Dewdnys Estate	1s 3d
William Drake	1½d
Christopher Taylor	2d
Bernard Cosserat & Company	6d
Samuell Atkins or occupiers of his estate	3½d
The occupiers of John Popes estate	½d
John Knight	½d

[1] 'Mr.' crossed through.

The occupiers of the estate late of Anthony Marly 2½d
The Widdow Collings or occupiers of her estate ½d
The occupiers of the estate late of Walter Collings 1d
The occupiers of Robert Ellacombes estate 2½d
fo. 6r. col. i
The occupiers of William Tudors estate 2d
The occupiers of William Chilcotts estate 1½d
The occupiers of George Cundys estate 2d
Richard Baker 1d for the house he lives in 2d 3d
William Mathews & his estate 3d
Mr Joshua Hickman[1] or occupiers of his estate 1s 2d
Richard Whitroe & his estate 3d
Ferdinando Ware ½d
Gabriel Heyward ½d
William Smyth & the house he lives in 4d
The occupiers of Samuell Sampsons estate 1d
James Atkins 1d for George Macys estate 5d 6d
James Birdall or occupiers of the estate late of Richard Gibbons 3d
The occupiers of the Widdow Gibbs estate 3d
The occupiers of William Sanfords estate 3d
Joshua Branscombe or occupiers of his estate 2d

Total 23s 9d

To the Poor weekly

The Widdow Shutt[2] 1s 7d
Henry Ford 4s
Thomas Holtons child 2s
The Widdow Cocke 6d
Anthony Pring 9d
The Widdow Lynn 1s 6d
fo. 6r. col. ii
The Widdow Hamlyn 4s
Grace Brabbin 1s
David Bake 1s 3d
Wayes Wife 1s 6d
Thomas Ashford 6d
The Widdow Huer 1s
John Barret 6d
Rices child 1s 7½d
Henry Pafford 8d
John Ford 1s
Robert Daniel 1s
Chideock Tutt 6d
James Shutt 6d

Total 26s ½d

ST. MARY STEPPS PARISH

Hugh Andrews
Wm Hart *Wardens*

Abraham North
Richard Mapowder *Overseeres*

Samuell Bidwill & houses 9d
Mr Broad & Mr Jordon for there houses 3d
John Ball *Maulster* 3½d
Edward Hill 1½d
William Bingham for the estate late Mr Hills 1d
William Bingham for the estate late Mr Tremans 5d
Henery Rooke or occupier of his estate 5d
Hugh Andrews 1d
Mrs Turner or occupier of her estate & Horrells 9d
The occupier of the house Edward Penny lately lived in 2½d
fo. 6v. col. i
The occupier of the house Edward King lives in 4d
The occupier of the house Gill & Loynes lives in 5d
Nicholas Carwithen or occupier of his estate 6d
Joseph Bass 4d
Mr Pengelly or occupier of his estate 8d
John Ball 3d
Mr Trewman for the house Mr Pearse lives in 4d
Richard Ford & houses 3½d
Widdow Sanford or occupier of her houses 2d
The occupier of Mr Butlers house 1½d
John Hawker for himself & house 3d
Peter Carter or occupier of his houses 3d
Mr Cursons for Gale & Mauris houses 2½d
John Silly or occupier of his house 1½d
Charles Bennet 1d
Mr Holder for the house Charles Bennet lives in 1½d
Mr Holder for the house Mr Heard lives in 2½d
William Heard 1d
Mrs Renolds or occupier of her house 2½d

[1] Altered from 'Hickmore'.
[2] Altered from 'Shute'.

Hugh Bidwills for Cowards house	1d
Abraham Stone	3d
Widow Squire or occupier of her house	3d
Mr March or occupier of his house	2½d
fo. 6v. col. ii	
Francis Haysie or occupier of his estate	3½d
The occupier of the house Widow Dawkins lives in	2d
The occupier of *the shilly*	6d
The occupier of *the new Key*	6d
The occupier of Mr Bakers house on the hill	1d
Philip Andrews *esq.* for the house Soaper lives in	4d
The same for tenements in possession of Pearse	3d
Humphry Lee or occupier of his estate	2d
Edmond Starr or occupier of his estate	4½d
John Gale	1d
Richard Dewdney or occupier of his estate	1½d
Mary Collens or occupier of her estate	1d
Thomas Avery or occupier of his estate	1½d
Widdow Rich or occupier of her estate	1½d
Mr Beavis or occupier of his estate	5d
The occupier of the house Thomas Mugford lives in	1½d
The occupier of the house late Potburyes	½d
Mr Taylor or occupier of his house	1d
Mrs Leach or occupier of her house	3d
Mrs Pease for her house	1½d
The occupier of Mr Sanfords house	3d
The occupier of Mr Gandyes estate	1d
The occupier of the house late Fosters	2d
Widow Legg	1d
Richard Mapowder & houses	6d
f. 7r. col. i	
Richard Gilbert & house	3d
John Stile	1d
William Cleake	1d
James Keen	1d
John Pearse	1d
Thomas Michell & house	1½d
Thomas Jones	1d
John Manly	½d
William Hart	1d
John Turner	1d
Joseph Comings	½d
Abraham North	1d
Nicholas Lobb & house	1d
William Pearse	1d
Jasper Pascho	1d
The occupier of Doctor Waterhouse estate	2d
Dabynott Chilcott	2d
Richard Clarke	1d
John Hooker	½d
Francis Basse & his house	2d
George Hockeridge	1d
Soloman Bowden	½d
Mr Canniton	1d
Nicholas Morlis	½d

The Mills

Mr Weeks & Mr Adams	8d
Mr Hicks mills	2s 6d
The Mills late Mr Crispins	8d
Thomas Summers	8d
Joseph Wood for Mr Brookings Mills	1s 4d
Thomas Barons for his Moyety of *Crickle Pitt Mills* & house	1s 8d
Thomas Birdall for his moyety of *Crickle Pitt Mills* & house	1s 8d
Mr Weeks & Mr Adams for their new Wheel	8d

fo. 7r. col. ii

Total 26s 8½d

To the Poor Weekley

John Walker	1s 3d
Elizabeth Hooper	2s
Widdow Holman	1s
Markes Reeve	3s 6d
Widdow Bolt	4s
Widdow Warren	1s 6d
John Leniton	2s 6d
Thomas Cockram	1s
William Nickolls	2s
Widdow Fook	1s 6d
Widdow Bragg	9d
Widdow Tincombe	1s 6d
Hosgoods child	1s 9d
Widdow Burges	9d
Widdow Knight	1s 3d
Symins child	2s
Widdow Leniton	1s 6d
Widow Stickland	2s 6d

Total 32s 3d

ST. PAULS PARISH

Wm. Combes
Benjamine Bradshaw *Wardens*

Wm. Gandy
John Combes *Oversecres*

Elizabeth Gandy sen.	4d
Nicholas Wood *marchant*	4d
William Gandy	6d
Mary Pyne jun.	2s
Mr John Turner *merchant*	4d
Occupier of Arch Deacon Drews estate	4d
John Norman	2d
Mr Bowdage for Mr Prouse estate	2d

f. 7v. col. i

Courteny Crocker Esquire for late Butlers	9d
Hugh Palmer *merchant*	2d
Sarah Tucker for *Northgate* house	4d
John Hill for his estate	4d
Andrew Bowman	2d
Occupiers Mrs Michills estate	3½d
Sir Edward Seaward his estate	2d
Occupiers Elizabeth Paynes house	1d
Occupier of Mayes house	1d
Occupiers Mr Samuell Butlers two houses	3½d
Abraham Troute	4d
James Pope houses & gardens	2½d
Jone Dight	2d
Thomas Bisfehaham	1d
Tristram Bowdage	5d
Thomas Baumfeild	3d
Robert Davies estate	3d
Occupiers Thomas Penningtons estate	3d
Occupiers Hugh Butlers estate	2d
Thomas Turner *merchant*	4d
John Elston for his estate	5d
John Burell *esq.* for *the Bull*	7d
Daniel Gifford	2d
Benjamin Bradshaw	1d
Stephen Love	½d
Occupiers Mr Leachbridges house	1½d
Occupiers Mr Dudneys houses	2d
The Corporation of Taylors	2d
The Chamber for *the Bridewill*	2d
Occupiers[1] Simon Bayleys Lands	2d
Robert Force & estate	3d
Robert Foxwill	2d

fo. 7v. col. ii

Occupiers Thomas Webbers estate	2½d
Philip Bastard & John Boyland	3d
John Bunce	3d
Occupiers Mrs Prouse estate	4d
Occupier Mr Braggs estate	6d
Richard Laness [Lanes's]	1d
Occupier Mr Risdons estate	2d
Occupiers Edward Potbury estate	½d
Occupiers Edward Bakers estate	2d
Occupiers Mr Jona[than] Ivie estate	8d
Gilbert Grenslade	2½d
James Tuckers garden	½d
John Vigors	3d
Occupiers John Palmers estate	4d
Mr Cudmore for Westcombes estate	5d
Richard Hacker for his houses	2½d
Mr Kings & Alfords estate	8d
John Pratt	½d
Henry Doughton	½d
Samuell Braund	½d
Occupiers Robert Glanfill estate	1½d
Mr Sommers & estate	2d
Daniel Sommerton	½d
John Doughtons estate	2d
Mrs Liscombes estate	2d
William Coombe & estate	4d
John Hooper for late Mr Parrs estate	4d
Mr Dinnis for Worpools estate	1d
him for Blackingstones estate	2d
Occupiers Richard Paynes house	1d
Widdow Williams house	1d
Binjamin (Binja:) Ivies estate	12d

fo. 8r. col. i

John Yeo	3d
Charles Preist	1d
George Roach	3d
Occupiers John Silicks house	1d
Thomas Bowdon	3½d
Bartholomew Whites stable	½d
John Thomas	½d
Julian French *merchant*	2d
Mr Samson for Grace Barons	2d
John Gale	1½d
Mr Battishill for *the Fleece*[2]	5d
Charles Boules	½d
John Saunders	1d
Aaron Burne	½d
George Hodge	½d
Widdow Emmett	½d
Mr Eldridg	½d
Thomas Floyd	½d
Francis Craduck	1d
John Cumbes	1d
Charles Hollet	½d
John Tapper	½d
David Loosemore	½d

Total 22s

To the Poor Weekly

Grigory Ball	2s 6d
Jone Chubb	1s
James Cox	2s 6d
Michall Hudge	1s 8d
Alice James	1s 6d
Widdow Lavers	1s 10d
Widdow Morgan	1s 10d
Jone Budd	1s 6d

fo. 8r. col. ii

Hanah Couse	2s
Charles Potter	1s
Widdow Tymothy	1s 6d
Widdow Baker	1s 4d
Catherine Saunders and children	2s
Thomas Herring	1s 6d
Richard Berry & children	2s 6d
Elizabeth Wall	1s
Pikes child	2s
A base child att Milton	2s

[1] 'Mr.' crossed out.

[2] *The Fleece* stood on the West side of Northgate Street a few yards up from Bartholomew Street. Its site is now represented by No. 25 North Street (the Devon & Somerset Stores in 1955).

Joseph Johnsons children 0 0 (*sic*)
Ann Gibson 1s 4d
Margery Jones 1s 6d
Mary Pafford 2s 6d
Mary Keene 1s 6d
Widdow Hurly 1s
Sarah Thomas 9d
Widdow Irish 1s 6d
Lenions Widdow 1s 6d
Clemmett Colwill 2s
William Powill 1s
Robert Sommerton 1s 8d
Thomas Manly 9d
Charles Norrish 6d

Total 48s 2d

ALHALLOWES UPON THE WALLS

George Knowling
Richard Veale *Wardens*

John Southard
Samuel Vann *Overseeres*

George Knowleing 8d his house 7d 15d
Mrs Knowleing for her house 3d
The occupiers of Mr John Starrs house 5d
Francis Ludstone 6d his house 4d 10d
fo. 8v. col. i
Mr Limbery 3d
The occupiers of Mr Newcombes house 5d
Thomas Townsend for himself & house 8d
John Southard 1d the occupier of Mrs Pitchers house 1½d 2½d
Thomas Sommers or the occupiers of his house 3½d
The occupiers of Edward Balls houses 5d
John Woodwalls 1d the occupier of Mr Cheekes house 3d 4d
Nowell Pearse for himselfe & house 7d
Mrs Keffe Widdow for the house she liveth in 4d
The occupiers of the house lately John Keffe lived in 3d
Mr John Keffe 2d
Terrill Ares or occupiers of his house 1d
Richard Vale 4d the occupiers of Mrs Boylands house 10d 14d
The occupier of John Hawkers house 2d
William Bingham 2d
The Widdow Pinsent or the occupiers of her house 2d
The occupiers of Mr Pim his house 1d
The occupiers of George Brients house ½d
The occupiers of Philip Tamlins house 1d
The occupiers of Joshua Branscombes house ½d

fo. 8v. col. ii
John Gilbert or the occupiers of his house 1d
James Clarke or the occupiers of his house 3d
The occupiers of Edeth Stephens house 2d
Samuell Wardoll 1d
Henry Hugh or the occupier of his house 2d
The Widdow Heard 1d her house 1½d 2½d
Joesph Maudit or the occupiers of his house & garden 2d
Mr Wood or the occupiers of his house 1½d
Sir William Davyes or the occupiers of his Lands 7d
William Burges 1d the occupiers of Joseph Stones house 2d 3d
Richard Dudney or the occupiers of his house 2d
Robert Elicombe or the occupier of his house 1½d
Mrs Gilbert or the occupier of her house ½d
James Baker or the occupier of his house 2d
Richard Mapowder or the occupier of his house 1½d
Richard Payne or the occupiers of his house 1½d
The Widdow Bone or occupier of her house 2d
John Cann[1] or the occupier of his houses 4d
The Widdow Arthur or the occupiers of her houses 4d
Nicholas Row for his Garden ½d
fo. 9r. col. i
Mrs Arundle for her Garden ½d
Samuell Axe or the occupiers of his house & Garden 2d
Mrs Bradrige for her Garden ½d
Sir John Elwill or the occupier of his houses which Bowden & Hellyar liveth in 4d
Thomas Parminter 1d his house 3d 4d
Alderman Bale or the occupier of his house 1½d
Mrs West for her Garden ½d
Thomas Baron or the occupiers of his houses 2d
Caleb Hudg 1d his house 1d 2d
Bernard Watts 1d his house 1d 2d
The occupiers of the Cordwinders house 1d
Aaron Atkins 1½d
William Pool or the occupier of his houses 2d
John Hamley 1d

[1] Altered from 'Cane'.

Mrs Cross for her Garden	½d
Alderman Yard for his Garden	½d
Christopher Bolt or the occupiers of his house	1d
Samuel Van	1d
Thomas Hutchins	1d
Joseph Pike	1d
Samuell Bidwill for his stable	½d
Binjamin Rice	1d

Total 14s 11½d

fo. 9r. col. ii

To the Poor Weekly

Thomas May sen.	4s 9d
The Widdow Clarke	1s 6d
The Widdow Bamlett	2s
Robert Leight	2s
Luxtons daughter	1s
Roles child	2s
Nicholas Barons wife	2s
Roger Squibbs wife	3s
Thomas Cremer	3s 3d
The Widdow Gold	1s 6d
Denfords children	4s 6d
James Blanchford	2s 6d
The Widdow Baker	15d
Roger Leight	1s
Mathew Minson	6d
The Widdow Buney	1s
Thomas Macy jun.	1s
Mary Rayder	6d
George Gibson	1s 3d
Mathew Leonard	1s 3d
The Widdow Mortimore	6d
The Widdow Jacob	1s

Total 39s 9d

ST. MARTINS PARISH

Mr George Yard
John Avery *Wardens*

Thomas Saffin
Thomas Tilly *Overseeres*

Mrs Rouse or occupiers	4d
Jerom Kings house & person	7½d
John Warrens house	1½d
Humphry Evans & house	3d
John Colsworthy for Mr King his house	3d
fo. 9v. col. i	
John Colsworthy for himself	1½d
James Tuckers house	1½d
Mr Renols House Mr Gabriilt (*sic*) Mayne occupiers	3d
Mr Mayne for himself	1d
Mrs Isacks house Mr Yard occupiers	4½d
George Yard	2d
Francis Cooke & house	4½d
Joseph Quashs house	4½d
Joseph Quash	2d
Richard Crockers shop & house	2d
Francis Crossing	1d
Spicers House or occupier	2¼d
Christopher Spicer house or occupier	3½d
Edward Spicer	2d
John Yeoatts house	2d
Binjamin Brimley	2d
Jespar Rattclíftes house	4½d
Mr Saffin	1½d
Hugh Butlers house or occupier	6d
Thomas (Tho.) Smyths house Mr Wiggington occupiers	2d
Mr Wiggington	1½d
Binjamin Risdons house Mr Pear occupiers	2½d
Philip Peare	1½d
Mrs Vinicombes [house] Mr Avery occupiers	2d
John Avery	1d
Richard Crockers house	1½d
Thomas Sampson & house	6d
Mrs Ledginghams house Mr Thomas Collibeer occupiers	1d
Mr Collibeer	1d
Philip Bishop & house	3d
Mrs Halls[1] house or occupiers	2½d
Thomas Tilly	1d
fo. 9v. col. ii	
Thomas Smyths house or occupiers	1½d
Nicholas Wood	1d
James Ross & house	3d
John Cove	1d
Mrs Casses house Mr Hill occupies	1½d
Mr Hill	1d
Mrs Jane Tripe & house	3½d
Thomas Clarke & house	3d
Samuell Butlers house Mr Horswell occupies	2d
James Horswell	1d
Charles Yeo & house	2½d
Samuell Sampson and house	4d
Daniel Slade & house	3½d
John Longs [house] Mr March occupies	2½d
Richard March	1d
Joesph March	½d
Mr Thomas & Kings house Mr Hoppin occupies	1d
Mr Hoppin	½d
Mr Owen	1d
Mr Henry Arthur	2d
Thomas Richards house	1d
Mr Mudge	1d
Thomas Smyth house Mr Mudge occupies	2d

Total 11s 6d 1¼ (*sic*)

[1] Altered from 'Halts'.

To the poor weekly

George Score 2s
Frances Score 1s 6d
Widdow Acland 2s
Widdow Ashtons sonn 3s
Martin Weeks 3s

Total 11s 6d

fo. 10r. col. i

TRINITY PARISH

Clement Weekes
John Adams *Wardens*

Abraham Guswell
John Glanvill *Overseeres*

Alderman Snell or occupier 10d
William Pool & sonn 6d late
Thomas estate 6d 1s
John Pool for Ganthonys house 2d
John Boucher 2d
Joseph Merson 1d
Joseph Cheeke or occupier 1s
Thomas Clutturbrooke 1d
Iles Pearce 2d
John Wills for late Potters house in
Southenhay 1d
Mary Saunders or occupier 4¼d
Widdow Channon or occupiers of
Madam Travills Estate 2½d
James Moore or occupier of Madam
Trevills Estate 1¼d
James Moor or occupier 1½d
John Penwell or occupier of
late Ford Tenement 1d
George Barons or occupier ½d
John Autherton or occupier 3d
Occupiers of Madam Walkers estate 4½d
Occupiers of the new erected house
on Madam Walkers estate 1½d
Clement Weeks 4d
John Adams 4d
Samuell Sparke or occupier 1½d
fo. 10r. col. ii
William Bincombe or occupier 2d
John Palmer *painter* or occupier 1d
Edward Dally or occupier 4d
himself 1d 5d
William Swaine or occupier 3d
William Baker or occupier 6d
Philip Lightfoot or occupier 1d
John Bond or occupier 1d
Joseph Hallet or occupier 1d
Madam Trevill or occupier where
William Butler live 4d
William Butler 1d

Nicholas Williams *the joyner* ½d
Widdow Abbott or occupier 1½d
Timothy Abbot ½d
Late Widdow Bawdon or occupier of
the house near *southgate* 6d
Abraham Guswill 2½d
Late Strang for *Key Lane Tenement* or
occupier ½d
Charles Lysson or occupier ½d
Mathew Purkins or occupier ½d
Widdow Yeo or occupier 2d
Thomas Britland sen. 1d
Thomas Banfill or occupier where
Walter Cawly live 1½d
Walter Cawly ½d
Thomas Richards or occupier 1½d
& for his Garden ½d 2d
Thomas Glanvills house by *Key gate* or
occupier 1d
Michah Ching or occupier 2d
Occupiers of *the Key house Wharfage
& Custome house*[1] 1s
Receiver Generall for part of *the
Cloath Market* 3d
Stephen Tothill ½d
Thomas Townsing *Smith* ½d
William Thomas or occupier 6d
fo. 10v. col. i
Thomas Jennings or occupier 9d
George Bingham 1d
Mrs. Bawdon or occupier where
Mr Jeffery did live 7d
William Marker 2d
Mrs Bawdon or occupier where
Mr Malachy Bidwill did live 4d
James Fortescue 2d
Mr Spurway 2d
Mrs Bawdon or occupier where Mr
Hugh Bidwill did live 5d
Edward Mann 1d
Mrs Bawdon or occupier of *the
Kallendar house* 5d
Widdow Hopkins or occupier 3d
Occupiers of Nicholas Saunders house
in the Fryers 3d
Henery Hawckins ½d
Simon Stanaway or occupier 1d
John Kennick or occupier ½d
William Tedder or occupier 2d
Robert Soper or occupier ½d
John Banfill or occupier 1½d
Widdow Wheeler or occupier ½d
Widdow Hall or occupier 2d
Edmond Cock or occupier 6d
Etheldred Thuell or occupier 2½d
John Gouge 1d
Mr Heart or occupier 2½d
Mrs Lavington for *Larkbeer Garden* or
occupier 1d
Alderman Dabynot or occupier 1s

[1] The Custom House had been built on the Quay in 1681.

Andrew Jeffery for late Harvys estate 6d `Squire (Sqr.) Speak plot ¼d	6¼d
Andrew Jeffery for his dryhouse & late Banfilds	7d
Thomas Jeffery & house or occupier	1s
George Powle (or Poule)	1d
Peter Ganthony or occupier	3d
fo. 10v. col. ii	
Thomas Welch or occupier	2½d
Robert Heath	1d
Widdow Rich or occupier	2½d
Sir John Colliton or occupiers	2s 6d
John Morish or occupier late Mr Mannington 3d	4d
Mr Pittman for his part of *the Valiant soldier*[1]	4d
John Gilbert or occupier	3d
Mrs Wise widdow or occupier	7d
Julius Deeds	4d
Nicholas Carwithen & for late Fitzwilliam estate	10d
Mr Lowdham or occupier	10d
Caleb Lowdham jun.	2d
Thomas Facy or occupier	2d
Nicholas Barry or occupier	3½d
John Coker or occupier	3d
William Bowdon or occupier	2½d
Peter Gunstone or occupier	4d
Francis Collings 1d for late Tollers estate 3d	4d
Late Bartholomew Potberry or occupier	2d
Emanuell Munjoy or occupier	2d
Late Roger Mallet or occupier	2d
William Morrice	3d
James Sparke or occupier	1d
Charles Watts or occupier	2d
Elias Offe or occupier	½d
Sarah Williams late Mrs Bake or occupier	2d
George Gibbs or occupier	1d
John Tucker or occupier	½d
Widdow Wills or occupier	1d
William Clarke or occupier	1d
Mr Hull or occupier of late John Tucker estate	2d
fo. 11r. col. i	
Widdow Bradford or occupier	2d
Widdow Munday or occupier	¼d
John Coombe or occupier	1d
Luke Lee or occupier	½d
John Fry or occupier	½d
The Quakers house & garden	2d
William Cape & house or occupier	1d
William Cape or occupier of Warren estate	2d
Thomas Morrice sen.	6d
Occupiers of Thomas Morrice jun. estate	4d
Edward Collings or occupier	5d
Widdow Lock or occupiers	6½d
Ann Case for *the Redlyon* that was	2d
Ann Case for late Mrs Isacks or occupier	3d
John Hamlyn	½d
Robert Coker or occupier	1½d
John Palmer *maltmaker*	1d
Hugh Peyne	1d
Thomas Weeks or occupier	2d
John Rude or occupiers	2½d
Hugh Flowers or occupier	2d
Daniel Ivy or occupier	1½d
Joseph Turpenny or occupier	1d
Richard Hook or occupier	2d
Thomas Huett or occupier 1½d for *Winards Close* ½d	2d
Mr Etheridge for late Cunningham garden & stable or occupier	1d
Mrs Isaacks Garden in *Southenay*	½d
Elizabeth May or occupier	1d
Late Nicholas Palmer or occupier where George Britland live	3d
fo. 11r. col. ii	
George Britland	1d
George Browing or occupier	1d
Samuell Searle or occupier	1d
John Dawton or occupier	½d
John Glanvill	1½d
Daniel Gifford or occupier	½d
Gilbert Grenslade or occupier	½d
Andrew Lyscombe or occupier	½d
Shadrack Piprell or occupier	4d
William Mathew or occupier	8d
Henery Wotten	½d
Abraham Audery	½d
Hugh Bidwill jun. & *Blackhorse* house	8d
John Hayman or occupier where the Widdow Dagworthy live	2½d
Widdow Dagworthy	½d
Hugh Bidwill sen. or occupier where the Widdow Glanvill live	3d
Widdow Glanvill	1d
William Yeo or occupier	1½d
Abraham Downe	½d
William Laskey *barbor*	½d
John Norton for *the Prison*	3d
Robert Bass or occupier	2d
Peter Tross or occupier	3d
Thomas Britland jun.	1d
Robert Sholders or occupier late Thomas (Tho.) estate	4d
Robert Sholders	1½d
John Dart	1d
Richard Hornebrooke or occupier	4d
Widdow Farrent or occupier	1½d
George Croker or occupier late Norsworthy estate	3d
Mr Holdrich	1d

[1] The *Valiant Soldier* still stands on the corner of Magdalen Street and Holloway Street.

fo. 11v. col. i
John Saunders or occupier late Joseph Pinces estate 4½d
John Hawk's ½d
Mr West or occupier 2d
Josias Burgess or occupiers 10d
George Dennis 1d
Mrs Tozer or occupier 3d
Mr Berry at *the Lambe* 1d
Thomas Birdall or occupier 9d & the adjoyning estate 6d 1s 3d
Widdow Kingdom or occupier 1d
John Heydon ½d
John Carell or occupier 3d
Mr Evans *the Sadler* 1d
Mr John Cursons or occupier 6d
Abraham Jennings 2d
John Allford 1d
Mr Hubert 1d
Ambrose Shepherd ½d
Edward Gladwen ½d
Mr Butson or occupier for the garden behind *the Winnards*[1] ½d
Richard Jackson 1d

Total £2 6s 5d

To the Poor Weekley

Thomas Are & wife 2s for Rent 1s 3s
Nicholas Bickley 1s 3d
Gilbert Comeings 1s
Anthony Comps son 2s
John Crossman 1s for Rent 6d 1s 6d
John Drake 1s 6d
Elinor Grinding 2s 6d
Caleb Johnson 6d
fo. 11v. col. ii
Thomasin Massey 2s
Waldron son 2s 3d
Margery Gendle 2s
John Perriman 9d
Anthony Richardsdon 8d for Rent 7d 1s 3d
Widdow Stile 1s 3d
Grace Saunders two children 1s 6d
Joane Deane 9d
Margarett Tanner in & (*sic*) Almhouse 2s
Honor Trehan[2] 1s 6d
Widdow Taylor 1s 9d
Widdow Tanner her two daughters 1s 6d
Samuell Angell & wife 6d
Samuell Wilks 2s
Thomas Crisping 1s 3d
Widdow Chard 2s 6d
Grace Trump for Rent 6d
Dinah Masey 2s
Widdow Searle 1s 6d for Rent 6d 2s
John Browne child 2s
Bartholomew Kennick for Rent & wife 1s
Rebeccha Mathew 2s
Marin Barns two children 1s 5d for Rent 7d 2s
Joan Crosman 9d for Rent 6d 1s 3d
Mogridge wife & Ching child 2s
Widdow Russell & three children 2s
Widdow Court & her three children 2s for Rent 6d 3s
Widdow Hooper 2s
Katherine Bamlett for Rent 6d
fo. 12r. col. i
Widdow Drake for her self 1s for Rent 6d 1s 1d (*sic*)
Widdow Bull & her two Children 1s 6d
Widdow Atkins 1s
Widdow Bowden & Children 2s 6d
Margrett Gove 1s 3d
Nicholas Lee 1s 9d
Widdow Clark 2s
John Ozborne wife & Children 2s 6d
William Edwards & two Child[ren] 3s for Rent 6d 3s 6d
Siah Peddrick & sonn 9d
Charles Toms Child 2s
Ann Wotten 6d for Rent 6d 1s 3d (*sic*)
Esther the Child found in the Entrey 2s 6d
John Lee 1s
Widdow Prigg for her selfe 1s for Rent 6d 1s 6d
Walter Horwood 1s 6d
John Smyth for Rent 6d for himself 3d 9d
Robert Edwards 6d for Rent 6d 1s
Peter Ozbournes wife & Children 2s
Richardsdon two daughters for Rent 6d
Joane Philip Childe 6d
Joane Linnington 1s
Joane Cattford 6d
Widdow Moor 6d
William Honywill and wife 1s 6d
Richard Roberts & wife 1s 6d
fo. 12r. col. ii
David Segar 6d
Mary Madder sonn 1s
Thomas Lovelyes for Rent 6d
Thomas Greedy 8d
Widdow Huesy & Children 2s
Joseph Gittsum for Rent 6d
Widdow Tucker 6d

Total £5 3s 8d

ST. DAVIDS PARISH

Robert Tristram
Wm. Tudor jun. *Wardens*

Wm. Adams
Samuell Bidwill *Overseeres*

[1] Wynard's Hospital in Magdalen Street.
[2] Final 'e' blotted out.

Sir Thomas Jefford for his estate[1]	1s
William Adams for his estate	9d
The occupiers of Alderman Tuthills estate	9d
Mrs Gandy for Bistol jun. or occupier	5d
Mrs Gandy for part of Mr Henry Gandyes estate	6d
Mrs Gandy for *Hooperne* or occupier	10d
Mr Beckett for Sir John Malletts estate	1s
Mrs Moore for the house & Ground	3d
Mr James Jenkinson for his estate or occupier	1s 6d
Mr Elston for Mrs Goulds Marsch or occupier	4d
Mr Samuell Bidwill for his estate	6d
The occupiers of Mrs Goulds ground Peter Payne	6d
The occupiers of Mr Foxwells Mills & ground	1s 4d
fo. 12v. col. i	
The Widdow Gay for her estate	5½d
Joseph Gay for his estate	3½d
The occupier of the Widdow Tremletts estate	5½d
Edward Dally for his estate or occupier	6d
The occupier of Edward Edgcombes estate	4d
The occupier of the Widdow Davys estate	2d
John Jorden for his estate or occupiers	3d
The occupier of John Freaks estate	3½d
The occupier of Mr Richards ground	1½d
Robert Clarke for his estate	3d
Henry Berry for his Feild on *Northenhay*	1d
Peter Parr for his ground	1d
Mr Elson for Mr Nicholas Kennicotts feild called *the Fower Acres*	1½d
Nicholas Kennicott for his estate	3½d
Mr Quick for his Ground	1½d
The occupier of Mr Anthonyes houses	2d
Mr Burell for his Ground or occupier	3d
Mr Burell for his Ground or occupier	1d
Elizabeth Gird for her house or occupier	1d
Henery Adams for his estate	1d
fo. 12v. col. ii	
Mrs Cornish for her house	1d
Abraham Cornish for his estate	1½d
Charles Bartlett for his house	½d
William Townsend for his estate or occupier	3d
The Widdow Hore for *Oxford Inn*[2]	10d
Thomas Banfeild for *the Red Cow*[3]	1½d
Mathew Wyatt for his estate	3d
Thomas Edmonds estate	3d
The Widdow Rooper for her house	1d
Jacob Ceely for his houses	1d
Martyn Hill for his houses	2d
Thomas England for his estate	5d
Mr Bagwill for his house	2d
John Dowdall for his estate	4d
The occupiers of the Widdow Broads estate	1d
William Mahoone for his house	1d
Robert Elicombe for his estate	2d
William Dony	1½d
Mr Beckett for *Longpath Close* & the Ground Mrs Warren had formerly	6d
John Viccary for *Chapple Meadow*	1d
Robert Stutson for his house & ground	1½d
fo. 13r. col. i	
James Knowlton for his estate	1½d
Mrs Knowlton for her estate	1½d
Mr Morgan for his estate	2½d
Mrs Gandy for her house in *Exlane*	½d
Thomas Rice	1d
John Hill	1d
The Widdow Jewell for her selfe & house	2½d
Alderman Smyth for his house or occupier	½d
Mr Facy for his Ground or occupier	3d
Christopher Gird jun.	1d
Alderman Bale for *the Sheefe*	8d
Esquire Anthony for his estate	6½d
William Mathew for his estates[4]	1s 1d
Christopher Gird sen. for his estate[5]	11d
Mr Bingham for *Starcombe*	5d
Mr Bingham for parte of Mrs Crossings ground	2d
Mr John Mathew for his house & Ground	1d
Peter Risdon for his estate or occupier	7d
Joseph Shepcotts *Rack Close* or occupier	3d
Madam Roads for parte of *Great Hoopern* or occupier	1s 6d

[1] This is *Great Duryard*, where Sir Thomas Jefford, who made a fortune in the Exeter cloth trade, built himself a handsome mansion (which still stands) between 1686 and 1691. He took a lease of a tenement and 55 acres of land from the Chamber, for two lives, on 1st June, 1686. He was rated on the property in 1691 (poor rate book), when he was one of the overseers for St. David's parish and therefore presumably resident in the parish.

[2] The *Oxford Inn* was later rebuilt as the *New London Inn* (in 1794) facing London Inn Square. The site is now occupied by the Savoy cinema.

[3] Jonas Banfield, mason, held the *Red Cow* on a lease for three lives from the Chamber dated 22nd August, 1693 (E.C.M. Book 192, Rental of city property).

[4] This was *North Duryard*, a 200-acre tenement held by William Mathew, gent. on a lease for two lives dated 22nd July, 1690 (E.C.M. Book 192).

[5] This may be identified from various rentals of city property as the present 26–28 St. David's Hill. Christopher Gird, fuller, had a lease for three lives from the Chamber dated 3rd March, 1695 (City rental, 1700).

Madam Roads for parte of *Great Hoopern ground* or occupier 10d
Abraham Payne for parte of *Great Hoopern ground* 4d
fo. 13r. col. ii
The occupier of Mr Gills Cosyes ground 2d
Mr Payne for his Marsh att *Cowly Bridge* or occupier 3d
The occupiers of Mr Turlings estate 2d
Mr Ridler for his Ground 2d
Robert Tristram for St Petrocks Land 3d
Robert Tristram for Mrs Estcotts Ground ½d
The occupier of Mr Atkins feild 4d
Esquire Andrewes for parte of *Great Hooperne* and *Pessell Downs* 10d
Mr Fryer for his estate 3d
Thomas Long for his estate or occupier 4d
Mr Pym for his houses 1d
Mr Heron for his Ground 2d
Christopher Hunt for his house or occupier ½d
John Weekes for his house 2½d
Henry Bonnaday (or Bounaday) for his house 1d
The occupier of Mr Jonathan Carters houses 3d
The occupier of Conawayes houses 1d
Robert Lidstones house & garden 1d
William Bayleyes houses 2d
William Browne for his house 1d
The Widdow Abbott for her house 1d
William Plyman for his house occupier poor [blank]
Northernhay or occupier 1d
Mr Drew for his house, called the *Fa[l]con* or occupier[1] 4d
Samuell Jeffery for his estate or occupier 1½d
Mr Mahoones house or occupier 4d
Mr Ridler for *Deanes Cassell*[2] 2d
John Palmer *cutler* 1½d
fo. 13v. col. i
Tristram Squier for his house 1½d
Daniell Bartlett or occupier 1d
Abraham Harris for his houses 1½d
The occupier of Backers house 1d
Widdow Towills for her houses ½d
Margarett Poe for her house 1d
Anthony Poe for his house ½d
The occupier of *the Tuckers feild* ½d
Samuell Hartfords house poor [blank]
John Loveles ½d
Peter Tucker for his house 1½d
Peter Edwards 1d
The occupier of George Feays house & Garden 1d
Thomas Downing poor [blank]
John Johnson 1d
Widdow Woolman poor [blank]
Nathaniel Ford ½d
George Saunders ½d
Oliver Vile 1d
The occupier of late John Ellets house 1d
John Lory ½d
John Lugg 1d
Henry Boult 1d
Henry Berry 1d
Henry Berry for the house he lives in 3d
Widdow Midyett for her house 1d
John Stutson 1d
John Lane 1d
Widdow Slade for her estate 2d
The occupier of Mr Robert Skinners house 1½d
fo. 13v. col. ii
Robert Upcott ½d
Mr Northmore for his feild 2d
Benjamin Pitts ½d
Edward Rice 1d
Robert Skynner 1d
Robert Dacy 1d
John Truman ½d
Robert Adams 1d
Johan Hole ½d
Mr Clement for Michells Ground ½d
John Kingdome for his estate 1d
The Widdow Penny for her estate 1½d
James Johnson 1d
The Water house or occupiers 6d
Richard Chryston *hellyer* 1d
Edward Dally att *Hooperne* 1d
John Dedly 1d
Charles Skelton 1d
Michaell Babbidge 1d
Joseph Garman ½d
William Tremayne ½d
Widdow Morrie [blank]

Total 33s 3½d

To the Poor Weekly

Johan Tremlett with her house Rent 2s
Wilmet Carpenter 1s
William Crispen 2s 3d
Nicholas Turner 1s
Robert Venners wife & Family 1s 6d
Willmett Bagwill 1s 2d
Margarett Pitts 2s 4d
Thomas Channing 1s
Mary Hore for her two Children 1s
Thomas Wilky 6d
Johan Ford 9d
Richard Dart 2s

[1] The *Falcon* is marked on a map of 1818–19 (E.C.M.) as exactly opposite the present *Crown and Sceptre*, and abutting on the city wall (W. side).
[2] The earliest record of the misnomer Danes' Castle, on the North side of Howell Road.

fo. 14r. col. i

Elizabeth Davies	2s
William Risdon	2s 4d
Mary Gosnett with 6d for her house Rent	1s 6d
Rebecca Mortimore	1s
Darothy Johnson	9d
Elizabeth Hobbs	1s
Bersheba Jenkins	2s
Mary Lyle	4s
John Chapell	9d
Honor Leamon	1s 6d
Ursula Hunt	1s 6d
John Saunders	1s 4d
Urah Busturgus	2s
Joane Black	9d
Hanah Wadlen	1s
John Tagford & wife	2s 8d
Agnes Bidwill	2s 6d
Richard Battens family for house Rent	7d
Thomas Barletts childe att Nurse	2s 6d
Elizabeth Barrett	1s
Edward Job with house Rent in all	1s
Wilmot Bennett	1s

Total 51s 2d

ST. MARY THE MOOR

Wm. Wrayford
Daniel Clutterbuck *Wardens*

Marke Burrage
George Hoe
Jonathan Carter jun.
James Foster *Overseeres*

John Pyle or occupiers	9d
Edward Ball or occupier	5d
William Browne *the shoemakers* houses or occupiers	6d
fo. 14r. col. ii	
The Dolphing Inn[1] & other Tenements of Francis Pengelly or occupiers	1s
Thomas Barons or occupiers of his house	3d
Arch Deacon Drews house by Pallace Gate or occupiers	4d
John Holditch or occupiers of late John Butsons estate	11d
The Bare Tavern[2] & Tenements belonging or occupiers	1s 8d
The Myter Tavern[3] & Tenements belonging or occupiers	1s
Joseph Willis or occupiers of *the Maremaid Inn*[4]	10d
Esquire Yards house late John Sparkes or occupiers	6d
Edward Allen	2d
Mathew Purkis his houses or occupiers	4d
Doctor Thomas Waterhouse 5d & for the house he lives in 4d	9d
The Widdow Hornobrooke houses or occupiers	4d
Moses Deeble	1d
Charles Stanway	1½d
The Widdow Warren & her sonn William *The Cooke* or occupiers	4d
Robert Carells houses or occupiers	1s 2d
The Widdow Barrett or occupiers of her houses	8d
John Gilbert or occupiers	6d
Nathaniel Beard for his Two houses or occupiers 5d & for Palmers house 3d	8d
fo. 14v. col. i	
Jacob Prideaux	1½d
The Widdow Trowts house or occupiers	5d
Marke Burridge	2d
Robert Ridlers house or occupiers	3d
Daniel Clutturbucke or occupiers	4d
Philip Hooper *marchant*	5d
Abraham Heard or Samuell Huett	1d
John Lobb or occupiers of his two houses	3d
William Wakham or [occupiers] of his houses	3d
Joseph Saunders	1d
James Kingwell 2½d for Benjamin Bakes house 6d	8½d
Thomas Foote 1d for the house he lives in 3d	4d
The occupiers of Hookers houses	3d
James Strangs houses & others in partnership in *Rockes Lane*[5] or occupiers & himself	4½d
The Widdow Brinly	1d
Thomas Floud or occupiers of the late Macartys houses	4d
Jonathan Lavington or occupiers	5d
William Sprey or occupiers	8d
The Widdow Parr or occupiers	3d

[1] The *Dolphin Inn* stood at the top of Preston Street (W. side), near the junction with Market Street.
[2] The *Bear Inn*, which had been the Abbot of Tavistock's town house down to 1539, stood in Southgate Street, on the South side of Bear Street. The site is now occupied by the Roman Catholic church.
[3] The *Mitre Inn* stood in Southgate Street (later Nos. 87–88) on the West side.
[4] The *Mermaid Inn* stood at the top of Rack Street, the site being commemorated in the Mermaid Buildings.
[5] Rock Lane or Rocks Lane was an alternative name for Coombe Street.

George Major 1d & for Hutchings his house 2d — 3d
William Farewells house or occupiers — 2d
The house late in possession of James Gould *fuller* or occupiers now Thomas Woods — 2d
fo. 14v. col. ii
John Wills his houses or occupiers — 4d
John Willes or occupiers of William Ekings his house late Hannah Seamans — 2d
Nathaniel Seamans three houses or occupiers — 3d
Nicholas Glanvill or occupier — 3d
Christopher Kennick 1½d & for Butlers Tenement in his possession 3d — 4½d
The Widdow Foxwell & her sonn Thomas or occupiers — 7d
The late Bawdon & Harris houses now Worthes houses or occupiers — 4d
George Poe — 2d
Sir William Davies houses or occupiers — 7d
John Gifford — 1d
The occupiers of Thomas Butlers Tenements late Strangs — 1½d
The Widdow Linscotts house or occupiers — 3½d
Gideon Stafford — 2d
John Bingham or occupiers of late the Widdow Sparkes houses & for the house he lives in — 6d
The Widdow Bawdons house late Quickes or occupiers — 1d
The late John Bawdons houses now Worths in *Billeter Lane* or occupiers — 1½d
John Kempthorn or occupiers of the *Sunn Inn*[1] — 3d
Richard Gilbert — 1d
fo. 15r. col. i
Joseph Cheekes house by the *Sun Inn* foredore or occupiers — 2½d
Joseph Cheekes houses by the *Sun Inn* backdore or occupiers — 5d
Joseph Cheeke for the *White Hart Inn* or occupiers[2] — 9d
Parsons *the Apothecary* his houses or occupiers — 1½d
The late Darkes houses or occupiers — 6d
The Widdow Hellyar or occupiers — 1½d
Digory Sparkes grand childes houses or occupiers — 4d
Zachary Hatchfeild att *the stone Stepps* — ½d
William King 2d for the house he lives in 2d — 4d
Edward Barber — 1d
John Harris *the School Master* — 1d
The Globe Tavern[3] & Tenements adjacent or occupiers of Mr Northmores tenements — 2s
The late Savages house now Mr Thomas Northmores house or occupiers — 2d
Thomas Robinson — 4d
Poole & Hawkings house late Alderman Smyths house or occupiers — 5d
Thomas Boyings — 1d
The Widdow Southcombe — 2d
John Harris *the taylor* or occupiers — 3½d
Kerslakes houses or occupiers — 1½d
Robert Irish ½d & for Ollivers house 1d — 1½d
fo. 15r. col. ii
Dawsons house or occupiers — 1d
John Quick 1d & for his two houses in *Billeter Lane* or occupiers 1d — 2d
Digory Sparke or occupiers — 2d
The late Widdow Reeds house or occupiers — 2½d
Joseph Mawry — 2d
The Widdow Chilcotts house or occupiers — 2d
John Tuckett — 1d
The late Whites houses or occupiers — 6d
Andrew Periams houses late Thomas Crosses or occupiers — 2d
Richard Periams late Bucknolls *the taylor* house or occupiers — 1d
The late William Bruens house now William Bakers house or occupiers — 2d
Richard Symons — 1d
The Receiver of Exon for *the Shambles & other Marketts* — 1s 6d
John Salter or occupiers of his house — 1½d
William Wreford or occupiers — 8½d
Philip Bennet — 1½d
The late Francis Fryers house or occupiers — 2d
William Browne *the smyth* — 1d
The houses late Henry Darts or occupiers now James Goulds Demolished — 3½d
The Black Lyons Inn[4] or occupiers — 6d
Nicholas Webber — 1d
George Browning Wilmott Crootes or George Clares houses or occupiers — 5d
Samuell Baldwine *founder* — 1d
William Mawry — 1d
Josiah Seily & the house that late John *the Attorney* lived in — 4d

[1] The *Sun Inn* gave its name to Sun Street, which was formerly known as Billiter Lane.
[2] The *White Hart* still stands on the South-west side of South Street. It had belonged to the Cheekes as far back as the 1640's (see Izacke, *Remarkable Antiquities of the City of Exeter* (1724 edn.), p. 161).
[3] The *Globe* stood in the far corner of Cathedral Yard, not far from St. Petrock's Church. It was in existence in 1690, and was destroyed in May, 1942.
[4] The *Black Lions Inn* stood on the West side of South Street. Its site was represented in the late nineteenth century by No. 78. It had a large yard opening out into Sun Street.

fo. 15v. col. i

The occupiers of two small tenements late George Clares now Hawkins & Pooles 2d
Edward Row 1½d & for *Alderman* Smyths house 3d 4½d
William Holmes & late Jordains house 3d
The Widdow Pope or occupiers 7d
John Hornabrookes house or occupiers 2d
Trobridges house & seller or occupiers 2½d
John Steevings his house or occupiers 1d
William Knight & house part of Steevings 1d
Christopher Paynes houses & *Slaughter house* or occupiers 5d
John Hyndes house or occupiers 2½d
William Slafter *cordwinder* ½d
William Morgans house ½d
John Freake ½d
The occupiers of Samuell Sampson houses 3d
The Widdow Glanvill 1½d
William Dambrells house or occupiers 1½d
Hugh Dennis 1½d
Tapperills houses or occupiers 3d
Birchess houses or occupiers 5d
Wilcox house or occupiers 2d
Zephaniah Holwell 2d
Francis Jewell or occupiers 3d
Charles Heron or occupiers 2d
Mathew Frost or occupiers 4d
William John 1½d & for the house he lives in 2½d 4d

fo. 15v. col. ii

Richard Score or occupiers 5d
Peter Menheire 5d & for the house he lives in 3d 8d
Christopher Slade or occupiers 5d
Worths houses in *Rack lane* or occupiers 4d
Part of *the late Unicorn Inn* or occupiers now Cheeks 1d
William Martyns house or occupiers 1d
John Dowdall houses or occupiers 2½d
George Blatchford or occupiers 3d
Thomas Sommers or occupiers 6d
Parson Lombs (Lambs ?) house in *Rocks Lane* or occupiers 3½d
James Gould 1½d
Richard Mahoones Tenements or occupiers 1½d
The Widdow Coliberts houses or occupiers 5d
Thomas Facyes late houses or occupiers now James Goulds 4d
John Clace 1½d
Arch Deacon Drews house & *Slaughter house* late Mallacks or occupiers 2½d
Thomas Salter 1d
Daniel Searle 1½d
George Norton 1d
Benjamin Chappel ½d
John Hardey 2d
Constantine Hart 1d & for the late William Pranketts house 2d 3d
The Widdow Paddon & the Widow Jenkins 1d

fo. 16r. col. i

Potburies houses or occupiers 3d
The late Widdow Brocas her house or occupiers 3d
Thomas Woods house late the Widdow Pennyes in possession of Marting Harris 3d
Marting Harris 1½d
Peter Commings or occupiers of the house he now lives in now Worths 1d
Thomas Potters houses or occupiers 4d
Richard Cooper 2d
Nicholas Elwills houses & Garden & for Alfords house next his Garden or occupiers 4d
Simon Mayo 1d
The late Alderman Gandeys house or occupiers 1½d
George Follett or occupiers 3d
John Birdalls house in *Billeters Lane* or occupiers 1d
Angell Sparkes house or occupiers 2½d
Richard Head 1d
James Tuckers houses or occupiers 3d
Gunstones houses or occupiers 2½d
The Widdow Westcott or occupiers 2½d
Samuell Axe his houses or occupiers 2d
Elcanah Hus 1d
Thomas Dowdalls house or occupiers 2d
Anthony Keefe & late Pitts his house or occupiers 2½d
The late Young Walter Strangs house now John Boylands house or occupiers 1½d

fo. 16r. col. ii

John Heard 2½d
Jonathan Carter jun. & his house 3d
The late Katherine Goulds *seller* now Slades *the gouldsmyth* or occupiers ½d
Paynes house late Holwells or occupiers 2d
William Burges his house or occupiers ½d
The Widdow Pince or her daughters house or occupiers ½d
Sir John Elwill for late John Basterds house & two other new houses in *Rockes Lane* or occupiers 9d
Edward Clode 1d & the house or occupiers 2½d 3½d
Alderman Bales houses & Garden in *Billeter Lane* & *Rack lane* or occupiers 4d
Joseph Purchase 1d
Thomas Hutch 1d
William Goswell & his house 6d
Robert Tozer *the taylors* house or occupiers 2½d
Joshua Maycho 2d

Thomas Eliot *vinctner* 1½d
John Cowse 1d & for the house he lives [in] 4d 5d
John Halstaffe 1d
The occupiers of Edward Cheekes houses where late William Gale lived 1d
Ezekiel Steevings or occupiers 2½d
fo. 16v. col. i
Esquire Beavis his house late James Elliotts or occupiers 2½d
Mr Kings house late Bridget Alfords or occupiers paid now by Mr Samuell Butler 2d
William Bartlett 1d
Richard Hooke sen., or occupiers of his house 5d
Abraham Harris *the Hellyars* house or occupiers ½d
Nicholas James ½d
Nathaniel Reeve or occupiers ½d
William Whiteway 1d
Henry Tombs 1½d
Thomas Moore 2½d & for Two Gardens in his possession in *Rack Lane* ½d 3d
James Bolt 1d
James Foster 1½d
John Adams 1d
Nicholas Cholwell 1½d
Thomas Glanvill 1½d
Elizabeth Rookes houses or occupiers 7d
Samuell Palmer 1½d
Peter Townsend 1d
Charles Curtis *taylor* ½d
William Burgoyne or occupiers 2d
Richard Halce 1d
Thomas Sanford 1d
James Warren 1d
Late John Palmer *the Cutlers* house now James Goulds or occupiers 2d
fo. 16v. col. ii
Robert Bampfeild 1d
John Haynes or occupiers 3d
James Penney 1d
Philip Mahoone ½d
The Widdow Hart or occupiers of her Seller ½d
The occupiers of a Garden & seller late George Greenwayes now two built houses thereon now Gideon Wares 4d
Edward Dally for late George Greenwayes house or occupiers 2½d
Roger Mathew ½d
Thomas Whitehare *grocer* 1d
Francis Dunning 1d
Henry Michell or occupiers of the third part of the late Henry Flouds houses 2½d
William Floud or occupiers of another third part 2d
John Floud or occupiers of the other part Paid by Mr Henry Harris *glover* 2d
John Barons *the Bakers* house or occupiers 1d
Robert Upward & his house or occupiers 2½d
Henry Combe 1d
The occupiers [of] Alfords houses late Strangs 4d
Christopher Stutt ½d
Gideon Ware 1d
Arthur Dodge ½d
Thomas Marting ½d
fo. 17r. col. i
Richard Prin *fuller* 1d
Strong *a mason* 1d
Abraham Page 1d
William Dannel or occupiers ½d
John Males 1d
Thomas Ching jun. ½d
Henry How ½d

Total £3 3s 4d

To the poor Weekely

John Allens Childe 2s 6d
John Bath 3s
Late Widdow Bowdons Childe 2s 6d
Roger Bowman 1s 6d & for the Almeshouse pay 9d 2s 3d
Margarett Bowdon 6d
Breakebacks Childe 6d
Widdow Barber & her Children 1s 6d
Christopher Beale & Joane his daughter 3s 6d
Widdow Broad 1s 6d
Sarah Breakback 6d
Alice Bicknall her two Children 3s
Widdow Binmore 2s
Bonds wife 6d
Thomas Bishop 1s 6d
Late Cheaney *the Clerkes* Child 2s
Alice Carter 2s 6d
William Chilcott sen. 1s 6d
fo. 17r. col. ii
Mary Crossing 1s 6d
Widdow Clapp 1s
Henry Colburne 2s
A base Child found upon a Hoggshead in the Widdow Clarkes Entry & Cornish 2s
Clutturbrookes Servants base Child 2s 6d
Thomas Drake 6d & for the Almshouse pay 9d 1s 3d
Maurice Causey & his wife 3s
Samuel Darte & his wife & for the Tender 4s
Catherine Dumbe 1s
Owen Davey 1s & for the Almeshouse pay 9d 1s 9d
Barnard Fox 1s 6d & for the Almeshouse pay 9d 2s 3d
Late Margarett Guiles base Childe 2s

Widdow Gilbert	1s
Priscilla Gubbs & her three Children	3s
John Harris & his wife	2s
Abraham Hacker	1s
Widdow Pasmore	2s
Joseph Hight	1s
Heaths Childe	2s
Widdow Hellyar & her two Grand Children	4s
Grace Hutchings	2s
Elizabeth Hawkings	2s 6d
fol 17v. col. i	
Widdow Hinskon sen.	2s 6d
Robert Hyscombe	6d
Rose Collings	1s
Widdow Huett	1s
John Slow *pipemaker*	1s
Nathaniel Jordaine & his wife 2s & for an Almshouse pay 9d	2s 9d
Dorothy Irish	2s
Widdow Jordaine	1s 6d
John Jarman	1s
Widdow Knight	1s 6d
Thomas Carter 1s & for the Almshouse pay 9d	1s 9d
Agnes Kelland	1s
Gabrill Lambole his Widdow	1s 6d
Thomas Lane & his wife	2s
Langdons Children	3s
Widdow Johns	1s 6d
Peter Miller	3s
Widdow Minson	1s
Mary Parker Widdow	2s
Widdow Rigg	6d
Widdow Radchliffe	2s 6d
Robins his wife he being at Sea in Service	1s 6d
Elizabeth Sherrum	9d
Jonathan Ramster	1s 3d
Widdow Steevings	6d
George Sparke & his wife	1s 6d
John Towill & his wife	1s 6d
Elizabeth Price	6d
fo. 17v. col. ii	
John Purchase 1s for the Almshouse pay 9d	1s 9d
Thomasine Sowdon	1s
Strangs Maid	1s 3d
Widdow Truman	1s 9d
Widdow Tutson 9d for the soldiers Childe 2s	2s 9d
Late Widdow Trenemans Childe	2s
Late Humphrey Thomas his Childe	2s
Widdow Tucker	1s
Late George Thomas his Childe	9d
Ventons Sister	2s
Widdow Winneard	1s
Wiles Daughter	1s 6d
Thomasine Webber	1s 6d
Widdow Weekes	1s 6d
Widdow White	2s 6d
Robert Wilde	6d
Michaell Yeos Widdow	2s
James Marting 6d & for the Almshouse 9d	1s 3d
Argentum Wescotts wife & 3 Children	1s
Robert Brimely	6d
William Adams his wife	1s
Elizabeth Parsons	1s
Roger Bowmans Grand daughter	2s
for divers poor peoples Rents	7s 6d
John Bicley for the Almeshouse pay	9d
fo. 18r. col. i	
Charles Weekes for the Almshouse pay	9d

Boyes & Maids to be bound out

Late Chayney *the Clarkes* boy	2s
The late Widdow Trewmans boy	2s
Bicknalls boy	2s
Londons daughter	2s
Late Margaret Guiles base child	2s
Roger Bowmans grand childe	2s
Bowdons boy	2s

Total £8 12s 6d

ST. LAWRENCE PARISH

John Bagwell
John Rhood *Churchwardens*

Wm. Wilson
Timothy Terry *Overseeres*

Doctor (Doco') Northleigh or occupiers	1s
Madam Cary or occupiers	9d
Doctor Musgrove	1s
William Reynell for his two houses or occupiers	4d
Timothy Terry 1½d house 2½d	4d
John Baker or occupiers	3d
William Bryan	1½d
George Masters or occupiers	3d
Joseph Wood	1d
Edward Bampfeild 1d & house 1d	2d
fo. 18r. col. ii	
Stephen Thorpe or occupiers	4½d
William Seager or occupiers	2d
Jeremiah John or occupiers	2d
Occupiers of Orchards house over *Eastgate*	3½d
Occupiers Orchards house next *Eastgate*	2d
Walter Sparke or occupiers of Orchards house	3½d
John Ordway	1d
John Etheridge or occupiers	5½d
Thomas Dowdall or occupiers of his two houses	2d
Widdow Trosse or occupiers	4d
Walter Farthing	2d

Ditto Trosse or occupiers of Davys & Mannigs (*sic*) (Mannings ?) house	3d
Ditto Trose or occupiers of *the Brewhouse*	5d
Edward Clement	1½d
William Farewell or occupiers	4d
John Bagwell or occupiers	2d
William Farewell or occupiers	2d
Rose & Crowne 6d[1] occupiers 1d	7d
Peter Risdon or occupiers	8d
Occupiers of Purkins house	1d
Occupiers [of] Roger Cheekes house	1d
John Rhood or occupiers	1d
John Bant or occupiers	2d
Goale Celler	1d
John Bant or occupiers of his two houses	2d
Ditto Bant or occupiers	3d
Benjamin Risdon or occupiers	1d
Spred Eagle or occupiers	2d
fo. 18v. col. i	
Roger Cheeke or occupiers	4d
John Curtis	1½d
William Morgan or occupiers	½d
Occupiers of the Widdow Humphreys house	½d
Stephen Betty	1d
Mr Long for his house & stable	2½d
John Pope	1d
John Taylor or occupiers	6d
John Rhood	1d
William Wilson	1d
John Palmer or occupiers	1d
Charles Brimlecombe	2½d
Occupiers of Hoopers house	1d
Henry Rogers or occupiers	5½d
Samuell Darke	1½d
Redlyon or occupiers	10½d
Robert Dawe or occupiers	5½d
Robert Skinner	1½d
John Bovett	1½d
Mr Long for his dwelling house	10d
Joseph Long	1½d
Richard Stone	1½d
Occupiers of Mrs Cases two houses	1s
Occupiers of *the High Schoole*	5d
Occupiers of Robert Ash's house	5d
Widdow Dowrish or occupiers	3d
Widdow Cheeke or occupiers	3d
Samuell Mathew	1½d
John Herbert	½d
Thomas Worth	1½d
Roger Cheek sen. or occupiers	2d
Christopher Pike	½d
fo. 18v. col. ii	
Roger Cheeke jun. or occupier	2d
Ditto Cheek or occupiers of *Black Dog*	6½d
Richard Perriam or occupiers	1½d
Richard Gill	1d
Benjamin Steed or occupiers	6d
Hanah Steed or occupiers	2½d
William Yeo	1½d
William Taylor	1½d
John Gaff	1d
Mr Tuthill or occupiers	4d
Mr Long or occupiers	1½d
Mr Ekins or occupiers of Celler under *Free Schoole*	2d
City houses behinde George Masters or occupiers	2d
Gilbert Halse	½d
Robert Ash	½d
Charles Manning	½d
Widdow Southmeade	1d
Isaac Rowse	1d
Leonard Rogers	½d

Total 21s 11½d

To the Poor Weekly

Widdow Perryman	1s 6d
Widdow Foster	1s 4d
Hanabel Hayne	2s 4d
Buclands childe	1s 9d
Widdow Pearse	1s
Widdow Pawford	1s 6d
Mary Otton	2s
Widdow Steevens	1s 4d
Widdow Patch	6d
Widdow Randells child	2s
Richard Martin	3s
fo. 19r. col. i	
Alice Pulmans base child	2s
Edward Green & childe	1s 8d

Total 21s 11d

ST. MARY ARCHES

Thomas Mill
Richard Warren *Wardens*

Dame Mary Walkers house or occupiers	4d
Richard Warren	1d
Thomas Whitehares house or occupiers	10d
William Staplehill	2d
Jonathan Came	1½d
Elizabeth Walkers house or occupiers	5d
Thomas Copplestone	2d
Sir William Davyes house or occupiers	6d
Madam Davyes house or occupiers	4d
Joshua Hickman	3d
Joshua Hickman for his house	9d

[1] The *Rose and Crown* stood in High Street, opposite St. John's Hospital, and was pulled down in 1834.

Madam Tucker for her houses 1s 1d
Charles Alden 3d
Thomas Mill & house 4d
Philip Andrew *esq.* for his houses or occupiers 1s 8d
Frances Bere 2d
John Bankes *esq.* 2s 4d
Robert Pearce 2d
fo. 19r. col. ii
Walter Ralph 1d
Mary Cross for her house 1s
Mrs Crosse 4d
Binjamin Pearce for the house he lives in 6d
Binjamin Pearce 2d
Mrs Wottons house or occupiers 7d
John Ridler 3d
Sarah Arrundle & house 6d
William Maudit for the house he lives in 6d
Mr Maudit 1d
Mr Hardy for his house or occupiers 6d
Binjamin Connaway for the house he lives in 5d
Mr Connaway 1½d
Henry Harris 1d
John Tapley ½d
Robert Newcombe 2d
Isacc Gibbs for his house & self 1s 3d
James Salter for the house he lives in 3d
Mr Salter 1d
John Newcombe for the house he lives in 6d
John Newcombe 3d
Widdow Norris for her houses 1s 2d
Thomas Atkey 2d
Richard Langman for his houses & self 3d
fo. 19v. col. i
James Tucker for his houses or occupiers 8d
Peter Parr for his house 2½d
Robert Newcombe for the parish house 1d
William Ekins for his Stable & Court or occupiers 1d
John Dennys for his house or occupiers 1½d
Sir John Elwill for his house or occupier 1d
Widdow Coombe for her house or occupier 5d
Mr Herons house or occupier 2d
Esquire Chafes houses or occupiers 3d
Mrs Tucker for her garden or occupiers 1½d
Samuell Fords house 2d
William Harris house or occupiers 2d
The late Mr Showers house or occupiers 2d
John Crosse 1d
John Luccombes house or occupiers 1d
Mrs Tucker for her house & selfe 4d
Abraham Guswell for his house or occupier 3½d
Edward Cross house or occupier 2½d
Mr Dewdneys house or occupier 1½d
fo. 19v. col. ii
Thomas Northmore esquires house or occupier 1d
Clarkes houses or occupiers 4d
Joseph Miller 1d
Mr Fowler 1d
Samuell Sparke for his house ½d

Total 23s 10d

[*To the poor weekly*]

The Widdow Delve 2s
Widdow Blackdon 2s 6d
Widdow Gill 1s
Widdow Lawrence 1s 9d
Widdow Philips 2s 9d
Widdow Bidwill 2s 6d
Nathaniel Burt 2s 6d
Thomazine Gasick 1s 6d
Parrish child 3s 6d
Livermores child 3s 6d
Whiterowe 3s 6d
Thomazin Comer 2s
Philip Gaydon 5s
Emanuel Binne wife 2s 6d
Mathew Harris 1s

Total 37s 10d

ST SIDWELLS PARISH

John Moffatt
Thomas Dennis *Churchwardens*

John Carne jun.
Roger Follett
John Peryman
Samuel Sparke *Overseeres*

fo. 20r. col. i
Edward Rice occupier of a feild behind the Church 1½d
Occupier of Mrs Hesketts house behind the Church 1½d
William Weeks or occupier 1½d
Isacc Weeks ½d
Occupier late Londons house
Occupier of Mahoones house 1½d
Occupier of Mr Claps house, Mr Bussell 2½d
Robert Shipcott 1d
Joseph Harris ½d
Occupier of Mrs Lakes house 2d
Occupier of late Jeptha Moryes house 1½d
Occupier of Mrs Tuckers house 1d

Occupier of Mr Dowdalls house	2d
Occupier of Mrs Tuckers house and Feild	4d
Binjamin Rochester	1d
Mr Carne & houses	4½d
Occupier of Mrs Bones house, May	1½d
Occupier of Mrs Bones house, Widdow Jenkins	1½d
Widdow Jenkins	½d
Mr John Weeks or occupier of his house	1½d
Occupier of Mr Raynalls house, John Flood	3d
Occupier of Thomas Skinlys house	1½d
Mrs Saunders	1d
Widdow Kinsman	1d
Occupier of Holls house	1d
Mrs Bussell & house	3d
Robert Dann	[blank]
fo. 20r. col. ii	
Occupier late John Moores house	1d
Occupier Edward Markers house	1½d
Henry Hooper or occupier	½d
Mr Eustace	1d
Occupier of Mr Daws house	1½d
Occupier of late John Webbers house in *Pallisstreet*	1d
Occupier of Mrs Hills house	1d
Occupier late Nathan Bakers house	½d
John Raddon & Tristrem Hare or occupier	1½d
Occupier of Hugh Flowers houses	½d
Widdow Stanaway or occupier of her houses	1d
John Grinter	1d
John Callaway or occupier	1½d
Occupier of Mrs Tuckers house	½d
Occupier of William Rices house	1d
Jeremy Browne	½d
Occupier [of] John Goves houses now Francis Hopping	½d
Peter Clapp or occupier	1s 6d
Occupier of Mr Dewdneys houses	½d
Occupier of Mr Horswells house	1½d
Occupier of Samuell Darts house	1½d
fo. 20v. col. i	
Occupier late Purkins house now Mrs Pasmores	1d
Richard Langbridge or occupier of his house	½d
Occupier of Holls house	1½d
Philip Burges or occupier	[blank]
William Newton or occupier	1½d
Occupier Secoms house, Alis Pudington	½d
Richard Filmore or occupier now Mrs Pasmore	½d
Occupier Mr Barletts house in *little Silver* & on *the Cassway*	1d
John Tuckfeild or occupier	3½d
Occupier of Mr Isackes house & garden	2d
Mr Ashwood or occupier	1½d
Thomas Barret or occupier	½d
Occupier of Doctor Jents house	1d
Occupier late Goyne Mathews houses	1d
Occupier late William Sweetlands house	1½d
Mr Ewins	1d
Occupier of Mr Dewdneys house	3d
Mr Bryant or occupier	3d
Nicholas Stroud	½d
Anthony Poe	½d
Richard Weeks or occupier	3½d
Joseph Carter or occupier	½d
Barnard Hatherly or occupier	½d
James Osmon or occupier	½d
fo. 20v. col. ii	
Occupier late John Smyths house	½d
John Hooper or occupier of two tenements late Smaldriges	2½d
Christopher Ellett or occupier	1d
Richard Ellett or occupier	½d
Joseph Gibbons or occupier	½d
James Jenkins	1d
John Row or occupier	1½d
Occupier of late Andrews Tenement	[blank]
Thomas Smaldridge or occupier of his tenement	4½d
John Yovatt jun.	4d
Occupier of Mrs Hellyars house	1½d
John Carne jun.	1d
Occupier of late Jeptha Moryes house	1d
Occupier late George Smyths tenements	4d
William Strong or occupier	1d
Occupier late Bennets house	1d
Ismaell Chaple or occupier of severall tenements	3d
Amos Boutcher	½d
Peter Coffin	[blank]
David Jones	1d
Edward Cheeke or occupier of *Rose*[1] & other tenements	1s 2d
Occupier of Mr Deanes house	2d
fo. 21r. col. i	
John Hill	1d
Occupier late Ellets house	1d
William Heyward	½d
Nathaniel Horsey or occupier	3d
Occupier of Woods house	1d
William Bidgood	1½d
Occupier of Mrs Foxwells house	1d
Thomas Dennis	½d
Occupier late Cases house	2d
Occupier [of] Mr Cheekes house, Mr Withers	1d
Mr Sealley or occupier	2½d
John Kingdom or occupier	3d

[1] The Cheekes were big brewers in seventeenth-century Exeter and owned a number of inns.

John Moffatt	3d
Occupier late Mayows house	4d
James Sheares	[blank]
Robert Thomas or occupier of his house	1d
John Piriman	1d
Occupier late Richard Mathews house	1½d
Henry Osmond	½d
George Wey	½d
Occupier of Townsons house	3½d
John Heyman	½d
Occupier of Thomas Whiteings house	½d
Occupier of Widdow Hoopers house	1d
Thomas Hooper	1d
Roger Cheeke or occupier	1s
Abraham Gess	½d
Occupier of Mr Battershills garden	½d
fo. 21r. col. ii	
Occupier of Mr Thomas Smyths house	½d
Occupier of Mr Mitchells house	½d
Henry Thomas or occupier	½d
Francis Ware or occupier of his house	1½d
John Rendall or occupier	1½d
Joseph Mountstephen or occupier	1d
Occupier John Tuckers house, barn & orchard	2d
Samuell Sparke or occupier	3d
Occupier late Slocoms houses	1½d
Occupier of Thomas Ledgers tenements	1½d
John Willis	1d
Occupier of John Bants tenements	4d
Occupier of Widdow Bicknell house	[blank]
Occupier of Mrs Traverse house	1½d
Ambrass Clogg or occupier	1d
Edward Leamem	½d
Ezekiel Gribble & tenements	2½d
John Sherman or occupier	1d
Roger Follett	1d
John Sones or occupier	4d
Occupier of Madam Drews house	1½d
Roger Bent or occupier	½d
Occupier of Cokers houses	1d
Occupier of late Pikes house	2d
John Coates or occupier	1d
Occupier John Claces house	1½d
Thomas Bunts	½d
Occupier of James Goles house	2d
Occupier late Mr Powels house	2d
fo. 21v. col. i	
Occupier of Thomas Hooper late Williams tenements	1½d
Occupier of Thomas Richards house	1½d
John Barnes	½d
Occupier *London Inn*[1]	9d
Moses Marning	1d
Occupier *London Tenements*	4½d
Occupier of *Mews Gardens*	1d
Occupier late Mr Facies tenements	1d
James Lee or occupier	4d
Occupier of Mrs Anthonys tenements	2d
John Bowden	[blank]
Occupier late Gravets garden	1d
Occupier late Fitts Williams house & feild	5d
Occupier Tho[mas] Weeks house	1d
William Bartlett	1d
Occupier late Broms house	[blank]
Occupier late Harlins garden & Mr Bartlett tenements	2d
Occupier of Mr Burells tenements	2d
Occupier of Mrs Hellyers house	1d
John Culmes	[blank]
Occupier of Mr Palmers house	1d
Occupier of Mr Risdons house	2d
Occupier of Mrs Hesketts house	½d
Thomas Eustace or occupier	1d
John Cooke *a taylor*	½d
Richard Bedruggett	½d
Mathew Wyatt or occupier	6d
Occupier late Thomas Drakes house	2d
fo. 21v. col. ii	
James Drake	½d
Charles Gendall or occupier	2d
Occupier late Rewallins house	1d
Mr Sanford	5d
Occupier of Mrs Hesketts house	5d
Occupier of Mrs Hesketts house	2½d
Philip Hooper	½d
Occupier of *the White Lyon*[2]	3d
Occupier of *ye Dung platt*	1d
Mr Clarke	[blank]
Occupier of Watkins house	3d
John Searle	½d
Occupier of Mr Viles house	1d
William Pike	[blank]
Charles Bellman	1d
John Osmond	4d
Richard Armstrong	1d
Occupier of Mr Elises house	6d
John Sealey	½d
Stephen Holditch	½d
Occupier late Brocas house	3d
Richard Jermam	½d
James Markes	½d
John Yovatt or occupier	6d
Occupier of late Mrs Crosses house	4d
Occupier of Mr Dowdalls house	3½d
Mr Bartlett	1d
Bartholomew Poyton	½d
Mr Lobridge	6d
fo. 22r. col. i	
Mr Long for *the Vise plat* tenement & barn	1½d

[1] The *London Inn* stood at the top of Paris Street. It later became the *Bude Hotel* and will be remembered by many citizens as such. Many royal and noble guests were entertained here during the eighteenth century (Dymond, *The Old Inns and Taverns of Exeter*, p. 27).

[2] The *White Lion* used to stand on the North side of Sidwell Street, facing down Paris Street.

Occupier of Mr Longs, late Legers 2d
Occupier of Mr Longs, late Beckets 2½d
Occupier of Mr Longs, late Banfeild [blank]
Occupier of Mr Longs in *Chaple Park* ½d
Occupier of Mr Longs late Webbers 2½d
Occupier of Mr Longs near *the Chaple*[1] 2d
Occupier of Mr Longs against the Church 4d
Occupier of Mr Longs where Mr Bidgood liveth 3½d
Occupier of Mr Longs in *Parris Street*[2] 2d
Occupier of Mr Longs where Gill liveth 1½d
Occupier of Mr Longs where Robert Bennet liveth 2d
Occupier of Mr Longs late Wottons 2d
Occupier of Mr Longs where Sones liveth 4d
Occupier of Mr Longs barn & stable 1d
Occupier of Mr Longs in *Longbrook* 1d
Occupier of Mr Longs att *the Kings Arms* 3d
Occupier of Mr Longs late Moggridges ½d
Occupier of Mr Longs, Ann Browning 1d
Samuell Mathew or occupier of the late Risdons tenement 1d
Mr Staniford 1d
Occupier of William Chaples tenement & garden 1d
fo. 22r. col. ii
Occupier of the late Philmores, now Edward Dallys ½d
Occupier of the late John Mounstephens ½d
Thomas Collibeer ½d
Thomas Coram ½d
Otho Channon ½d
Lewis Lee 1d
John Dennis or occupier 1d

Total 33s 10½d

The poor Weekley

William Harte 2s
Elizabeth Putt 1s
James Darts wife 1s 6d
Edward Silvester 2s 6d
Flachers child [blank]
John Gardner [blank]
Widdow Jerman 6d
Widdow Henly 6d
Nathaniel Richards 1s 6d
Richard Ball 1s
Susanah Jenkins [blank]
Robert Radford [blank]
Jane Pim 1s 6d
Widdow Trobridge 1s 6d
Widdow Reed 2s
Elizabeth Wall [blank]
Nicholas Dun 2s
Joan Bond 3s
Mary Davy & sonn 1s
Roger Drews wife [blank]
fo. 22v. col. i
Joseph Baker 1s
Robert Jones 2s 6d
Radfords child [blank]
John Frost 2s
John Turner 9d
John Carter 1s 6d
Richard Cooke 2s 6d
Widdow Small 6d
Fishers child 1s 6d
Widdow Hellyer 9d
Mary Tozer [blank]
Widdow Gibbons 2s
Zachariah Sweetland 1s 9d
Roger Cann 2s
Widdow Fisher 2s
Thomas Raynolls 9d
Old Cooper 1s
Widdow Webber 1s 6d
Grace Carter 1s 6d
James Adder 2s 6d
Elizabeth Lee 2s
Widdow Whiteing 1s 6d
Widdow Norman 1s 6d
Widdow Mounstephen 1s
John Turners wife 2s
Elletts child 1s 6d
Tuckfeilds child 2s
Widdow Cane 1s 6d
James Norman jun. 6d
Alice Meare 3s
Richard Mays wife [blank]
fo. 22v. col. i
Richard Writes wife [blank]
Widdow Wotten [blank]
William Pasmore 1s
Mary Fishmore 6d
Popes child 1s
Folletts children 2s 6d
Jane Court 1s
Widdow Flood 6d
Widdow Painter 6d
Chouns child 2s
Samuell Nichols 2s 6d
Robert Smyths wife 6d
Thomas Barkwell 6d
James Norman 1s 6d
Judith Clapp 1s 6d
John Bedson 2s
Elizabeth Stephens 9d

[1] St. Ann's Chapel at the top of Sidwell Street.
[2] So called today; its original name was Shitbrook Street, as it ran down the hill to the stream of that name.

Samuell Giles wife	2s 6d
Widdow Jerman	1s 3d
Widow Clouter	1s 3d
Widdow Andrew	2s
Dorothy Hex	3s
Parkhouses child	1s 6d
Robert Parkhouse	1s 6d
George Raynalls	2s
Widdow Greene	1s 3d
Widdow Edwards	1s
Widdow Drew	2s 6d
Widdow Penrose	[blank]
Widdow Lake	1s 6d
Linnard Ireish	2s
fo. 23r. col. i	
Widdow Fishmore	[blank]
John Rolls	2s 6d
Robert Bunny	1s 3d
Widdow Luxen	1s 6d
Lewis Baker	1s 6d
Peter Hellyer	2s 6d
John Culmes	2s
John Coods wife	[blank]
Widdow Filmore	1s
Widdow Collings	[blank]
Widdow Clarke	9d
Martin Turner	1s 6d
Urith Southard	3s
William Savory	1s 6d
Widdow Manning	1s
John Wiles	1s 6d
Widdow Brodbeere	[blank]
Sarah Ares	[blank]
John Oliver	1s
Widdow Norton	2s 6d
Hayward boy	[blank]
Robert Staddon	1s
Josiah Treat	6d
Arch. Fishmores wife	[blank]
William Downing child	[blank]
Hester Swell	[blank]
Widdow Lisset	1s
Lucas children	4s
Pitfeilds wife	9d
Samuell Teakell	1s 6d
Widdow Squires children	2s 6d
Mary Verrian	6d
David Johnsons C (*sic*) [? child]	6d
John Whiden jun.	2s
fo. 23r. col. ii	
Goody Brock[1]	[blank]
Widdow Risdon	[blank]
Mary Newcome	1s
Commins children	4s
Griffens child	1s 6d
Greens wife	[blank]
Gon. Waterman	[blank]
Peter Shafes child	9d
Thomas Densham	1s
Alexander Norishes child	6d

Total £7 13s

The Land Rate

Occupier of the Sheafe & Barn behind the Church	4d
Occupier of Samuell Mathews Ground behind the Church	1d
Occupier of Edward Rices Ground	3d
Occupier of Mr Burells Ground	2d
Occupier of *Mr Burells Brickfeild*[2]	½d
Occupier of Mr Rhoods Ground	3½d
Occupier of St Stephens Parish Land	2½d
Occupier of Stephen Tollers Ground	[blank]
Occupier of Mr Isaacks Ground	6d
Occupier of John Ridlers Ground Late Hopwoods	1d
Occupier of Samuell Mathews Ground Late Pennyes	1½d
Occupier of Mrs Hills 3 peices of Ground	2d
Occupier of another feild of Mrs Hills	1d
fo. 23v. col. i	
Occupier of late Potburys Ground	1½d
Occupier of Mr Fords *Witheybed Meadow*	3d
Occupier of Mr Fords *Wisdoms Heyes*	3d
Occupier of Mr Fords Ground *Colver Lane*	2d
Occupier of Francis Lotts Ground	½d
Occupier of Esquire Mathews Ground	1d
Occupier of Mrs Cradits Ground	3d
Occupier of Doctor Osmonds Ground late Mrs Skinners	2d
Occupier of Mr Sanford Ground late Neebones	1½d
Occupier of Mr Dowdalls Ground	2d
Occupier of Esquire Mathews Ground	1d
Occupier of Person Nutt ground late Mr Bones	2d
Occupier of the little Gore	1½d
Occupier of William Baileys ground	1d
Occupier of Mrs Lythbridges Ground near *the Chaple*	½d
Occupier of *Chaple Closse*	1½d
Occupier of Arindall Ground	1d
Occupier of Wilcockes Ground	4d
Occupier of Mr Bants Ground	3d
Occupier of Mr Lythbridge Ground by *Hevetree*	10d
Occupier of Mr Anthonys Ground late Mrs Hynes	1½d
Occupier of John Tuckets Ground	½d

[1] 'Widdow' deleted.
[2] For the earliest brickfields in Exeter see Introduction, p. xiii.

Occupier of Mrs Hesketts Ground 1s 4d
Occupier of Mr Bants Ground late Pookes 3d
Occupier of Mr Roger Pines Ground 3½d
Occupier of St John Parish Land 1d
Occupier of Mr Longs Ground near *Spiller Lane* 1d
Occupier of Mr Longs late Mrs Webbers ½d
Occupier of Mr Nicholas Longs Ground near *the Cisteren* 2½d
fo. 23v. col. ii
Occupier of Mr Longs near the *Pest house* 1½d
Occupier of Mr Longs once Mr Carews 4½d
Occupier of Mr Longs once Duckes 4½d
Occupier of Mr Longs once Peter Paynes 7d
Occupier of Mr Longs once Mrs Webbers 3½d
Occupier of Mr Longs by *Southenhay* 1s
Occupier of Samuell Mathews late Mr Longs ½d
Occupier of Samuell Mathews now Mrs Bussell 2½d
Occupier of *Magdalene Feild* 3d
Occupier late Mr Battashall Ground ½d
Occupier of *Judge* Mallets Ground 1d
Occupier of John Shermans Feild & Stable 1d
Occupier of Mrs Tuckers Feild & Barn ½d

Total 12s ½d

ST. PANCRAS PARISH

Andrew Bagwill
John Dally *Churchwardens*

John Lethbridge
Thomas Wood *Overseeres*

Maddam Brodridge 3d
John Dally 1½d
For his house 3d
John Perriam 1½d
fo. 24r. col. i
Occupier of Mr Edward Cross houses 10d
Peter Battishill 1½d
For his houses 5½d
Binjamin Robins 1d
For his houses 3d
Thomas Ley 1d
Thomas Cole 1d
Occupiers of Athertons houses 5d
Moses Merle 1d
For his house 2d
Thomas Edwards 1d
Occupiers of *the Turkshead Inn*[1] 4d
John Pearse 1d
Occupiers of Mr Stephens house 4½d
Henry Traverse 1d
For his house 3d
Occupiers of *the Three Tuns* & Stable[2] 3½d
Andrew Bagwell 1d
For his houses 2d
Occupiers of Peter Risdon houses & Garden 2½d
Giles Bussey ½d
For his house 1½d
Edward Heamer 1d
For his houses 2½d
Thomas Wood 1d
For his houses 2½d
Occupier of George Toms house ½d
fo. 24r. col. ii
Occupier of the late Martyns estate 1½d
John Lethbridge 1d
For his house 4d
John Cholwill 1d
Occupiers of Kennicotts house 1d
Joseph Stevens ½d
Occupiers of the late Macombers house 2d

Total 7s

To the Poor Weekly

Ann Perriman Widdow 4s
John Evans children 3s

Total 7s

ST KERIANS PARISH

Richard While
Bartholomew Parr *Wardens*

John Rice &
Charles Loder *Overseeres*

Jasper Raclife *esq.* or occupiers 5d
Madam Elizabeth Hele or occupier 5d
Robert Glanvill or occupier 3½d
Zachary Mayne or occupier 7d
Occupier of Mr Lants Sellers 2½d
Mary Cross or occupier 4d
James Tucker or occupier 4d
Esquire Anthony or occupier for Crosses house 3½d
Esquire Anthony or occupier for his other houses 6½d
fo. 24v. col. i
The Elephant[3] or occupier 5½d

[1] The *Turk's Head* still stands next to the Guildhall on the South-west side.
[2] The *Three Tuns* formerly stood next to the Guildhall on the North-east side.
[3] This still stands on the East side of North Street.

Jonathan Ivie or occupier	4d
Edward Rowe or occupier	2d
Philip Wareman or occupier	1d
Thomas Northmore *esq.* or occupier	6½d
Richard Hacker or occupier	1½d
Mr Horwood or occupier	6d
Mrs Prideaux or occupier	3½d
John Pym or occupier	3½d
James White or occupier	3½d
For Mr Rices houses	1½d
Mrs Boyland or occupier	6d
Richard White or occupier	4½d
Peter West or occupier	1d
John Vickery or occupier	2½d
John Dewdney or occupier	1½d
Richard Lawerance for Tappers house	2½d
Peter Parr or occupier	6½d
Peter West for *the George Inn*[2]	4d
Daniell Ivie	6d
Madam Elizabeth Hele	5d
Joseph Conway	1d
Jerom Roch	2d
Richard Osmond	1d
Thomas Potter	1½d
Robert Glanevill	2d
William Bellew	2d
Emanuell Hole	2½d
Robert Eveleigh	1½d
fo. 24v. col. ii	
Peter Young	1d
Richard White	2d
Ikeiah Cheeke	1d
Mr Dolman	3d
Robert Lydstone	3d
Richard Bunt	1½d
Jonathan Ivie	4d
Philip Wareman	1d
Henry Gird	2d
John Drake	3d
Charles Loader	1d
Edward Edgcombe	2d
Dorcas Lovering	3d
John Philips	2d
Thomas Cowell	2d
James White	4d
John Rice	1d
Thomas Brooking	6d
Nicholas Brooking	3d
Elizabeth White	2d
John Vickary	3d
Ezekiel Cleake	1d
Richard Lauerance	1d
Peter Parr	3d
Bartholomew Parr	2d
George Mannaton	1d
Peter West	1d
Abraham Cornish	2d

Total 16s 2d

To the Poor Weekely

Hanah Palmer Rent 6d	2s 6d
Philip Robinson	2s 6d
Basterd child	2s 6d
Widdow Pafford Rent 6d	2s 9d
fo. 25r. col. i	
George Markes Rent 6d	2s 6d
Widdow Bowbear Rent 9d	2s 9d
Widdow Adams Rent 6d	2s 6d

Total 18s

ST. PETROX PARISH

Thomas Butler
Nicholas Browne *Wardens*

John Vowler &
Richard Byrdall *Overseeres*

Gilbert Yard *esq.* & house	1s
Occupier of *Alderman* Cokes houses	8d
William Sandford & house	10d
Widdow Quash & house	4d
William Newton	½d
Occupier of *the Fountaine Taverne*[2]	1s
Occupier of Mrs Knowlings house	3½d
Edward Edmonds	1½d
William Spiller	1d
William Ekins 3d the house 3½d	6½d
Nicholas Browne 1d the house 2d	3d
Hugh Knowlton 1d for house 4d	5d
William Arnold	2d
Occupier of Mr Arnolds house, Mr Nicholas Carwithen	4d
Mr Pitfeild	1½d
Mr Nicholas Carwithen for Mr Pitfeilds house	2d
John Slade	½d
Mr Starr for Mr Slades house	1½d
Samuell Stephens	1½d
fo. 25r. col. ii	
Occupier of Mr Tacks house that Mr Stephens lives in	3d
Occupier of Mrs Hornes house	½d
Joshua Pope 1½d the house 2½d	4d
Mrs Lauerance 1d the house 4½d	5½d

[1] This stood where No. 9 North Street now is (Southard & Sons, tailors). Behind the Victorian brick front much of the original inn still survives in a disguised form. As an inn it goes back at least to the sixteenth century.

[2] This stood on Fore Street (E. side), where Nos. 78–79 stood, which were two fine examples of Elizabethan domestic building. These were destroyed in the air raid of May 1942 (see frontispiece of this volume).

Richard Stretchly ½d the *Vintage Taverne*[1] 8d	8½d
Joseph Woolcombe 1d the house 6d	7d
Widdow Steed 1½d the house 3½d	5d
Thomas Butler & house	2d
Roger Prowse 2d the house 6d	8d
Jonathan Connett	½d
Robert Force	½d
Widdow Eveleigh 1d the house 3d	4d
Samuel Symmons 1d the house 3d	4d
Edmond Richards ½d the house 2d	2½d
George Cary 2d the house 2d	4d
Mr Crocam ½d for the house 1½d	2d
Richard Pounsford & house	7d
Anthony Vickary and house	7d
John Vowler 1½d the house 4d	5½d
Occupiers of Jasper Radcliffs houses	6d
John Dell and house	4½d
Robert Bussell	1d
John Southcombe and house	3d
John Woolcott ½d the house 1d	1½d
John Atkins	3½d
Occupiers of Sir William Davyes house	1½d
Peter Tucker ½d the house 2d	2½d
John Ash ½d the house 1½d	2d
Occupier of Henry Darts house	2½d
Occupier of Mr Jeves house	1½d
fo. 25v. col. i	
Mr Ridgeman	½d
Mr Birdall	1d
Occupier of Nicholas Woods house	1½d
John Mathews	½d
Occupier of Mr Lees house	2½d
Mr Cursons	½d
Occupier of the parish house	1d
Occupier of the house Barned Wood lately lived in	1d

Total 16s 6½d

To the Poor Weekely

Elizabeth Randell	4s 6½d
John Poole	3s 6d
Ann Parker	3s
Sarah Jordaine	3s
Mary Downing	2s 6d

Total 16s 6½d

[2nd column blank]
[f.26 blank]

fo. 27r. col. i

ST. STEPHENS to ST. MARY THE MOORE

Peter Skiner for his house	1½d
James Tradennick his house	1¾d
Jasper Jaine 1d house 5d	6d
Thomas Bennett 1d house 1d	2d
Samuel Jefferys	1d
Widow Triggs for her houses	5¼d
Charles Knowles 1½d houses 1s 1d	1s 2½d
Mr Jeves house	6½d
Mr Pirke 1d house 1s 9d	1s 10d
The City of Exon for the shopps and stables	8d
William Searle 1d house 4d	5d
Mr Hoopers house	3d
New Stables behind Mr Hoopers house	2d
Occupiers of Mr Sandfords house	3d
John Burell 2d house 4¼d	6¼d
Isarell Stafford 1d house 3¾d	4¾d
Peter Tooker 1d house 3d	4d
Joseph Trobridge 1d house 4¼d	5¼d
Anne Mills for her house	4d
Samuell Pope	1d
John Vickary 1d house 3¾d	4¾d
David Bingham ½d house 3¾d	4¼d
fo. 27r. col. ii	
John Withers ½d house 2¾d	3¼d
Nicholas Purchase	½d
Occupiers Mr Pims house	3½d
John Medland house	1½d
Thomas Wheadon 1d house 3¾d	4¾d
Widow Beake for her house	3¾d
Occupiers Mr Rundles house	1½d
William May and house	1d
Christopher Baker 1d house 7d	8d
Richard Attwill	2d
George Gold 2½d house 8d	10½d
John Lyford	2d
Widow Daveys 1d house 4½d	5½d
John Smyth	½d
John Pince ½d house 3¾d	4¼d
John Gandy 2d house 5½d	7½d
John Row ½d house 3¾d	4¼d
Deliverance Larkcombe 1d house 2d	3d
Charles Challice 2d house 4½d	6½d
Mr Richard King for his severall tenements 1s 5d	1s 5d
James Norrington	1d
William Mahoone ½d house 1d	1½d
Occupiers Mr Cudmores house	3d
Benjamin Hawkins 2d house 5d	7d
Thomas Ford	2d
Edward Collings	1½d
Occupiers of Mr Horswells house	2¾d
William Southmeades house	1s
Samuel Buttler or occupiers	3¼d

[Total] £1 0s 0d

ST. OLAVES to ST. MARY THE MOORE

Nicholas Brooking *esq.* for his estate	2d
fo. 27v. col. i	
William Battishill or his estate	1½d

[1] This stood in the High Street, exactly opposite St. Petrock's Church. The site (now Messrs. Moon & Son) is marked on a city map of 1818–19 as " West of England Bank anciently the Vintage Tavern "

John Salter for the house he lives in ½d
The occupiers of Mr John Pyles estate 1½d
The occupiers of Mr Jacob Rowe estate 1½d
The occupiers of Mr Nicholas Kennicotts estate ½d
Mr Nathaniel Dudney for Mr Francis Splatts estate 1d
Mr James Taylor for Mrs Alice Bampfeilds estate 1d
Mrs Mary Pease for her estate ½d
Mr Tristram Whitter for his estate 1½d
The occupiers of Mrs Glandvills estate 2d
Mr Benjamin Atwill for his estate ½d
The occupiers of Mrs Anthonys estate 1d
The occupiers of Sir Peter Culliton estate 1d
Mr Thomas Salter for his estate 1d
Mr Thomas Harris for his estate ½d
The occupiers of Mr Penes estate, late *ye Flower Deluce* ½d
The occupiers of Mr Pynes estate 1½d
The occupiers of Mr John Canns estate 2d
Mr Richard Dudney for his estate 2d
Mr Rallier & Mr Casirate 1½d
Mr Samuel Atkins for his estate ½d
The occupiers of Mr Robert Elicombe estate ½d
Mr Richard Baker for Mr John Salters estate ½d
Joshua Hickman *esq.* Mayor for his estate 2d
The occupiers of Mr George Macys estate 1d
fo. 27v. col. ii
Thomas Pilly for Mr Burdle estate ½d
Mrs Elizabeth Gibbs for her estate ½d
Mr William Sandford for his estate ½d
Mr Edmond Richards for his estate ½d
Mr William Smith for his estate ½d
Mr John Rowe for his estate ½d
Mr Anthony Westcott for his estate ½d

[Total] 2s 9d

ST. PETROCKS to ST. MARY THE MOORE

Gilbert Yard *esq.* and house 1s 2d
Occupiers *Alderman* Cokes houses 9d
William Sanford and house 1s
Occupiers of Mr Quash's house 4½d
William Newton ½d
Occupier of *the Fountain Taverne* 1s 2d
Edward Edmonds 1½d house 4d 5½d
William Spiller 1d
William Ekines 3½d & house 4d 7½d
Nicholas Browne and house 3½d
Hugh Knowlton 1d and house 4½d 5½d
William Arnold 2½d & house 4½d 7d
William Pitfeild 2d and house 2d 4d
John Slade ½d and house 2d 2½d
fo. 28r. col. i
Samuel Stephens 2d & house 3½d 5½d
Widow Homes house ½d
Joshua Pope & house 4½d
Ann Lawrence 1d and house 5d 6d
Richard Stretchly 1d, *Vintage Taverne* 9½d 10½d
Joseph Woolcombe & house 7d
Widow Steed 1½d house 4d 5½d
Thomas Butler & house 2½d
Roger Prowse & house 9d
Jonathan Connett ½d
Robert Forse 1d
Widow Eveleigh & house 4½d
Samuel Simonds 1½d
Samuel Simonds & house 3½d
Edmond Richard ½d house 2½d 3d
George Cary 2d house 2½d 4½d
John Crocomb & house 2½d
Richard Pounsford and house 8d
Anthony Vicary & house 8d
John Vowler 2d & house 4½d 6½d
Jasper Radcliff 2 houses or occupiers 7d
John Dell and house 5d
Robert Bussell 1d
John Southcombe & house 3½d
Joseph Woolcott ½d house 1d 1½d
John Atkins & house 4d
The occupiers of Sir William Davyes house 1½d
Peter Tucker ½d the house 2d 2½d
John Ash ½d the house 1½d 2d
fo. 28r. col. ii
Occupier of Mr Henry Darts houses 3d
Richard Birdall & house 3d
John Richmond ½d the house 1½d 2d
John Mathew ½d the house 3d [blank]
The Parish house 1½d [blank]
Barnard Woods house 1½d

[Total] 19s 0d

THE CLOSE to ST. SIDWILLS

The Dean and Chapter 13s
John Collings *Clerke* for his house 3d
William Burgoine *Merchant* and house 8d
Dennis Roll *esq.* or occupier 8d
Archdeacon of Barn[staple] or occupier 6d
Christopher Bale *esq.* 9d
George Crocker *gent.* 3d
Him for the house 3d
Doctor Osmond and house 1s
Elizabeth Courtenay and house 2d
Robert Burrington 1d
Sarah Davy widow or occupier 3d
William Martyn *esq.* & house 4d
Doctor Bidgoods Trustees 1s 6d
Robert Tristram *Merchant* 8d

Doctor Holwill & house 1s
Robert Pearse 1d
Philip Pethick 1d
John Mannington *gent.* 2d
John Vanengdon or occupier of his house 1d
Him for Mr Fords house or occupier 2d
fo. 28v. col. i
John Barons 2d
Benjamin Hawkins or occupier of his estate 1s
Thomas Downton 2d
Oliver Mustion & house 9d
Francis Oliver *gent.* and house 6d
Edward Yard *esq.* or occupier 2d
Philip Parsons or occupier 3d
John Reed 2d
Christopher Hunt 1d
Joseph Squib 1d
John Vanengdon 1d
Mr Subdean for his houses 8d
Occupier of the late Jonathan Gundryes house 1d
Occupier of late Dowdalls 2d
Elizabeth Cooke widow or occupier 6d
John Curson *esq.* 6d
Occupier of Mr Sainthills house 3d
Francis Pengelly or occupier 4d
Widow Bartlett or occupier 9d
Johan Sherum widow or occupier 4d
Nicholas Webber *gent.* and house 6d
Thomas Knott for his house 6d
Edward Martin 1d
Joseph Marshall or occupier 8d
Nathaniel Rowland *merchant* and house 8d
Elizabeth Webber widow 1½d
Charles Heron *gent.* or occupier 6d
Anthony Potter 2d
William Hull *gent.* 6d
Occupier of the late Richard Rossers 3d
Peter Purchas 2d
Abraham Horwood 1d
fo. 28v. col. ii
Robert Chafe & house 1d
Archdeacon of Exon. 6d
Doctor Walrond 3d

[Total] £1 13s 10½d

ST. PANCRAS to ST. SIDWILLS

Madam Brauderidge for Weeke 7d
John Dally his house 6d
John Perriam 3d
Mr Cross his houses or occupiers 2s
Peter Battishell 3d
His house 10d
Benjamin Robbins 3d
His houses 9d
Thomas Coles 2d
Occupiers of Athertons houses 10d
Moses Merrell 2d
Mr Starrs house 5d
Thomas Edwards 2d
Turkshead (or *Turks head*) 8d
Henry Travers 2d
The house he liveth in 6d
The *Three Tuns* and Stable 7d
Andrew Bagwill 1d
His house 4d
Occupiers of Peter Risdons house and gardens 5d
Giles Bursey 1d
Edward Heamer 1d
His houses 6d
Thomas Woods houses 6d
Occupier of George Thomes houses 1d
Occupier of the late Martyns estate 3d
fo. 29r. col. i
John Lethbridge his house 4d
John Cholwell 2d
Occupier of Kennicotts houses 3d
Joseph Stephens 1d
Occupier of Macumbers house 4d
Benjamin Hooper 1d
Occupier of Mr Stephens house 8d
John Pearse 2d
Madam Davis or occupier of stables and garden 2d
Robert Dogge 1d

[Total] 14s 0d

ST. MARTINS to THE HOLY TRINITY

Mrs Rouse or occupiers for her house 5d
Mrs Rouse for her house in *St Martins Lane* 2d
Mr Warren or occupiers his house 3½d
Mr Evans his house 3d
Mrs Knight or occupiers of her house 5¾d
Mr James Tucker or occupiers 2d
Mr Edmond Rennell or occupiers of 2 houses 2¾d
Mrs Isacke her house 4½d
Mr Alderman Smyth's house or occupier 9d
Mr Richard Smyths house or occupier 9d
Mr Francis Cooke for his house 3d
Mr Quash for the house or occupier 2½d
Mrs Cases shopps or occupier 2¾d
Mr Crossinge and shopps or occupier 3¾d
Mrs Spicer or occupier of her house 5d
Mr Christopher Spicer or occupier 4½d
Mr Benjamin Brimly[1] for the house 6d

[1] Altered from 'Bremly'.

fo. 29r. col. ii

Mr Jasper Radcliffe or occupier	8d
Mr Hugh Buttler or occupier	7d
Mr George Wiggington for the house or occupier	5¼d
Mr Mudge for the house or occupier	3½d
Mr Philip Pare for the house	5½d
Mr Avery for the house	4d
Mr Richard Crocker for the house or occupier	3½d
Mr Thomas Sampson for his house	8d
Mr Colliber for the house or occupier	3d
Mr Philip Bishopp for the house or occupier	2d
Mrs Hall or occupier	3½d
Mr Thomas Smyth or occupier	2½d
Mr Rosse or occupier	10d
Mrs Tripe for her house	4d
Mr Thomas Clarke for the house	2¼d
Mr Buttler for the house	2¾d
Mr Leigingham or occupier	3½d
Mr Charles Yeos house	1d
Mr Samuel Sampson for his house	4d
Mr Slade for the house	4d
Mr Longs or occupier	3¾d
Mr Thomas Richards and (*sic*) or occupier	1½d
Mr Dyte or occupier	3d
Mr Jerom Kings his houses or occupier	9d

Personall

Mr Jerom King	4d
Mr Henry Arthur	4d
Mr Humphry Evans	1d
Mr Colsworthy	2d
Mr Gabriel Maine	2d
Mr George Yard	4d
Mr Francis Cooke	4d
Mr Joseph Quash	4d
fo. 29v. col. i	
Mr Thomas Sommerton	? [1d]
Mr Francis Crossing	? [1d]
Mr Edward Spicer	4d
Mr Brimley	4d
Mr Thomas Saffin	3d
Mr Owen	2d
Mr George Wickington	2d
Mr Mudge	2d
Mr Philip Pare	2d
Mr Avery	2d
Mr Thomas Sampson	4d
Mr Collibeere	1d
Mr Philip Bishopp	1½d
Mr Thomas Tilly	1d
Mr Nicholas Wood	1d
Mr Ross	1d
Mr Cove	1½d
Mr John Hill	1d
Mrs Tripe	3d
Mr Thomas Clarke	2d
Mr Charles Yeo	2½d
Mr Samuell Sampson	4d
Mr Daniel Slade	4d
Mr Richard March	2d
Mr Joseph March	1d
Mr Nicholas Ellwill	4d
Mr Knight	1d
Mr Claxstone	2d

[Total] £1 2s 0d

ALLHALLOWES IN GOLDSMITH STREETE to ST. PAULS

Mr Richard Crockers house in *Gandys Lane*	½d
Mr William Moore & house	3d
Mrs Mary Pynes sellers or occupiers	2d
Mrs Elizabeth Reynolls or occupier	3d
fo. 29v. col. ii	
Mr Nicholas Wood	1½d
Mr William Bagwill	½d
Mr Wescombes house or occupier	1½d
Mr David Robertson	1½d
Mr Hutchings houses	6d
Mr John Stephens	2d
Mr William Pinckcomb	1½d
Mr John Bolt	1½d
Mrs Mary Heskett & houses	7d
Mr Trobridges houses or occupiers	7½d
Mr Richard Periam	4d
Mr Thomas Foxwill	1d
Mr Adam Pearces house or occupier	4d
Mr Nicholas Cheeke	1½d
Mr John Pym & houses	4½d
Mrs Mary Pearce	1d
Mr George Trosses house or occupier	2½d
Mrs Elizabeth Whites house or occupier	4d
Mrs Elizabeth Udall	1d
Mr William Moores house next to *the Swan*	1d
Mr John Palmer & house	2½d
Mr James Gould & house	4½d
Mr Symon Bayleys house or occupiers	4½d
Mr Thomas Tothill & house	2d
Mr William Browne house or occupier	2d
Mr Aaron Tozer & house	4d
Mrs Mountstephen & houses	3d
Mr Thomas Wood	½d
Mr George Stoning & house	2½d
Mr Gilbert Davies house	3d
Mr James Gould for *the Phenix*	2d
Mrs Hester Mapowders house or occupier	2½d
Archdeacon Drewes house or occupier	2½d
fo. 30r. col. i	
Mr Richard Buckland	1d
Mr William Jope & house	4½d
Mr Philip Jerman for himselfe and Tuckfeild house	1½d

Mrs Elizabeth Gandys house or occupier	3d
Mr John Mortimere	1d
Mrs Elizabeth Gandys house or occupier	1½d
Mr Henry Harris	1d
Mr Richard Stablie & house	1d
Mr Edward Hayman for Withicomb & Bests houses	1½d
Mr George Toms & house	½d
The Widow Edwards & house	1d
Mr John Bingham & houses	4d
Madam Tuckfeilds houses, Robert Foxwill & Richard Turner occupiers	2d

[Total] 10s 2½d

BRADNINCH to ST. PAULS

Sir Edward Seaward *Knight*	1s 6d
John Rooke or occupier	6d
The Widow Shuckburgh	4d
Mr Hooper or occupier	3d
James Jenkinson	6d
John Guswill or occupier	3d
John Tapley or occupier	4d

[Total] 3s 8d

ST. MARY ARCHES to ALLHALLOWES ON THE WALLS

Dame Mary Walkers house	¾d
Mr Richard Warren	¼d
Mr Thomas Whiteheares house	2d
fo. 30r. col. ii	
Mr William Staplehill	½d
Mr Jonathan Came	¼d
Mrs Elizabeth Walkers house	1d
Mr Thomas Copstone	½d
Sir William Davys house	1¼d
Madam Davys house	¾d
Mr Joshua Hickman *esq.* self & house	2½d
Madam Tuckers house	2¾d
Mr Charles Alden	½d
Thomas Mills house & self	¾d
Philip Andrews *esq.* house	4d
Mr Francis Bere	½d
John Banckes *esq.* houses	5½d
Mr Walter Ralph	¼d
Madam Cross self & houses	3¼d
Mr Benjamin Pearce, house	1¼d
Mr Benjamin Pearce, self	½d
Madam Wotton, house	1½d
Mr John Ridler	½d
Mrs Sarah Arrundle	1½d
Mr William Mawditts house	1¼d
Mr William Mawditt	¼d
Mr Hardys house	1½d
Mr Conways house	1d
Mr Conway himself	¼d
Mr Henry Harris	¼d
Mr Robert Newcombe	½d
Mr Isaac Gibbs	3d
Mr James Salters house	½d
Mr James Salter	¼d
Mr John Newcombes house	1¼d
Mr John Newcombe	½d
Mr Harris houses	3d
Mr Thomas Atkey	½d
fo. 30v. col. i	
Mr Richard Langman	½d
Mr James Tucker	1½d
Mr Peter Parrs house	½d
Mr Robert Newcombes house	¼d
Mr William Ekins stable	¼d
Mr John Dennis house	¼d
Sir John Elwills house	¼d
Widow Coumbes house	1d
Mr Herrons house	½d
Mr Chafes Lands	½d
Mrs Tuckers Garden	¼d
Samuell Fords houses	½d
Mr William Harris houses	½d
Mr Showers house	½d
Mr John Cross	¼d
Mr Luckhams house	¼d
Widow Tucker self & house	¾d
Mr Abraham Guswells houses	¾d
Mr Edward Crosses house	½d
Mr Northmores house	¼d
Mr Clarkes house	¾d
Mr Dudneys houses	¼d
Mr Joseph Miller	¼d
Mr Fowler	¼d

[Total] 4s 10d

BEDFORD to ALLHALLOWES UPON THE WALLS

Sir John Elwill *Knight*	2s
Eleanor Horne widow or occupier	6d
Adam Pearse or occupier	8d
Bernard Goddard	6d
Thomas Long *Clerke* or occupier	4d
fo. 30v. col. ii	
William Horswell or occupier	2d
Thomas Richardson	2d
Jonas Bampfeild or occupier	2d
Mr Stephens or occupier	2d
Mr Hoppin or occupier	2d
Arthur Jeffery	2d
[blank] Rodd widow [crossed through]	

[Total] 5s 0d

ST. KERRYANS to ALLHALLOWES UPON THE WALLS

Jasper Radcliffe *esq.* or occupier 5d
Mrs Elizabeth Hele widow or occupier 2d
Robert Glanvill or occupiers 1½d
Zachary Mayne or occupiers 2½d
Occupiers of Mr Lants Cellers 1d
Mrs Mary Cross or occupiers 1½d
Mr James Tucker or occupiers 1½d
Esquire Anthony or occupier 4d
The Elephant or occupier 2d
Mr Jonathan Ivie or occupiers 1½d
Edward Rowe ½d
Philip Wareman ½d
Thomas Northmore *esq.* 2½d
Horwood or occupier 2½d
Mrs Prideaux or occupier 1½d
Mr John Pym or occupier 1½d
Mr James White 1½d
Mr Richard White or occupier ½d
Him for Rices house or occupier ½d
Mrs Boyland or occupier 2½d
Mr Richard White or occupier 2d
fo. 31r. col. i
Mr John Vicary or occupier 1d
Mr John Dewdney or occupier ½d
Mr Lawrence for Tappers house or occupier 1d
Mr Peter Parr or occupier 2½d
The George Inn or occupier 1½d
Daniel Ivie 2d
Madam Hele 2d
Joseph Conway ½d
Jerom Roach 1d
Thomas Potter ½d
Robert Glanvill 1d
William Bellew 1d
Emanuell Hole 1d
Robert Eveleigh ½d
Richard White 1d
Kesiah Cheeke 1d
William Downman 1½d
Robert Lydstone 1½d
John Viccary 1½d
Peter Parr 1½d
Bartholomew Parr 1d
Abraham Cornish 1d
Richard Bunt ½d
Jonathan Ivie 1½d
John Drake 1½d
Edward Edgcombe 1d
Dorcas Lovering 1½d
John Philips 1d
Thomas Cowell 1d
James White 2d
Thomas Brooking 2½d
Elizabeth White 1d

[Total] 6s 6d

APPENDIX I. Acreages of Exeter parishes and precincts

(Taken from the Book of Reference to the Plan of Exeter, Ordnance Survey 1877)

1.	Allhallows (Goldsmith St.)	2·243	acres
2.	Allhallows-on-the-Walls	7·252	,,
3.	Bedford Circus (formerly B. Precinct)	3·149	,,
4.	Bradninch (formerly extra-parochial)	4·182	,,
5.	Cathedral Close (formerly extra-parochial)	16·241	,,
6.	Holy Trinity	49·565	,,
7.	St. Edmund	19·729	,,
8.	St. George	2·871	,,
9.	St. John	3·789	,,
10.	St. Kerrian	2·560	,,
11.	St. Lawrence	6·273	,,
12.	St. Martin	1·751	,,
13.	St. Mary Arches	3·240	,,
14.	St. Mary Major	12·940	,,
15.	St. Mary Steps	14·298	,,
16.	St. Olave	6·473	,,
17.	St. Pancras	1·744	,,
18.	St. Paul	8·601	,,
19.	St. Petrock	1·687	,,
20.	St. Stephen	3·350	,,
21.	Exeter Castle (Devon)	2·114	,,
22.	St. David	1148·773	,,
23.	St. Sidwell	387·813	,,

INDEX TO PLACES IN EXETER

INDEX TO FAMILY NAMES